MAY 2 2 2014

D0205880

Sink or Swim

Sink or Swim

How Lessons from the *Titanic* Can Save Your Family Business

Priscilla M. Cale and David C. Tate

 **PRAEGER**

AN IMPRINT OF ABC-CLIO, LLC
Santa Barbara, California • Denver, Colorado • Oxford, England

Library of Congress Cataloging-in-Publication Data

Cale, Priscilla M.
  Sink or swim : how lessons from the Titanic can save your family business / Priscilla M. Cale and David C. Tate.
    p. cm.
  Includes bibliographical references and index.
  ISBN 978–0–313–39834–6 (hard copy : alk. paper) — ISBN 978–0–313–39835–3 (ebook)
1. Family-owned business enterprises—United States—Management. 2. Small business—United States—Management. 3. Leadership—United States. 4. Strategic planning—United States. I. Tate, David C. II. Title.
HD62.25.C35   2011
658—dc23   2011023358

ISBN: 978–0–313–39834–6
EISBN: 978–0–313–39835–3

15 14 13 12 11   1 2 3 4 5

This book is also available on the World Wide Web as an eBook.
Visit www.abc-clio.com for details.

Praeger
An Imprint of ABC-CLIO, LLC

ABC-CLIO, LLC
130 Cremona Drive, P.O. Box 1911
Santa Barbara, California 93116-1911

This book is printed on acid-free paper ∞

Manufactured in the United States of America

This book is dedicated to the memory of Titanic, *her victims, and her survivors.*
May their legacy of hope live on.

Contents

An unnumbered photo essay follows page 108

Acknowledgments

We would like to extend our heartfelt thanks to friends, colleagues, readers, and contributors who have made this effort possible: Cindi Bigelow, Bill Bishop, Bonnie Brown Hartley, Michael Decata, Rich Dino, Don Dobbs, Gerry Donnellan, Stephanie Dunson, Mary Fitzgerald, Lucy Gilson, Barry Graff, Judy Green, Henry Hutcheson, Dennis Jaffe, Don Janezic, George Koether, Henry Krasnow, Alan Lovins, Bob Lyons, John Mathieu, Mary Frances McGuiness, Derek Mirabilio, Ron Norelli, Michael Pantalon, Rich Razza, Sue Roman, John Santa, Judi Spreda, Michael Stern, Alan Sturmer, Craig Sylvester, Mark Taub, Pat Terrion, Chris Ulbrich, Werner von Pein, John Wages, Luke Weinstein, Meghan West, and Lisa Wilson-Foley.

A very special thanks to our families for their belief in us, and their unending love and support: Jimmy Canton, Mena and Richie DeFrank, and David and Judith Tate.

Introduction

It is ironic that *Titanic*, a ship that sank on her maiden voyage approximately 100 years ago, leading to the untimely death of more than 1,500 souls, still survives so vividly in the minds of those who never knew her. In her sinking, her story truly began.

Titanic is commonly depicted as a sad story. Families were torn apart in the most gut wrenching of circumstances, and decisions were made on the spot as to the future value of a human being's life—who played a larger role in society, who was worth saving, and who was believed to be strong enough to fend for himself or herself. While the stories told by survivors reveal an evening of unimaginable terror, we reject the notion that the events of that awful night of April 14, 1912, stand as *Titanic*'s only legacy. We look beyond Reverend Charles Parkhurst's claim that those who perished essentially met their fate in "the glittering splendor of a $10,000,000 casket."[1] We believe that those who perished have stories of their own that still hold value today and that have not yet been told. While an icon of copious wealth—indeed, what many see *Titanic* as having represented in the short duration of her life—the ship fervidly renounces in her passing. Rooted in unforeseen tragedy, her legacy is one of hope and endurance. We write this book because while *Titanic* signifies loss to so many, to us she tells a different story. Here's how it began.

Several years ago, we were discussing a complex family business case. Two nonfamily managers phoned us and detailed their failed efforts at motivating the senior management team and family owners to develop a plan for succession. With the senior managers nearing retirement and at least half-dozen members of the succeeding generation involved in the business, not a single effort had begun toward planning for the continuity of the business. The nonfamily managers knew the business was headed for serious trouble.

In discussing this particular case, we explored other situations where danger was ahead, and those who had control failed to react in a timely manner. Then it hit us: What if you were the lookouts, Reginald Lee and Frederick Fleet, in *Titanic*'s crow's nest and you saw your ship on a collision course with an iceberg? What could you do to sound the alarm and bring about course correction?

Unbeknownst to many, *Titanic* received numerous warnings as the ship headed into an unusually congested ice field brought on by a mild winter. Similarly, family businesses receive many warnings about the precarious waters of succession—waters made more dangerous by inadequate resources and lack of forethought. Despite these repeated warnings, family business owners (more often than not) fail to adequately plan for succession, falling into the same destructive patterns. For *Titanic*, we know how her story ended. For businesses, owners have the opportunity to avoid a similar fate.

Like many, our initial thought was that *Titanic* had, indeed, experienced what *Titanic*'s Second Officer, Charles Lightoller, described as "a combination of circumstances that never occurred before and can never occur again."[2] Eventually, however, we came to reject this claim and find the merit of his statement to be implausible and wishful thinking at best. *Titanic*'s builders and operators knowingly took risks—risks that family business owners also take. In the end, it was the failure to address these risks that compromised the integrity of the ship and that similarly has the potential to undermine the vitality of any family firm.

Karl Marx observed that "history repeats itself, first as tragedy, second as farce."[3] Our goal in this book is to create a qualitative shift in how business owners notice and respond to risk, and to present a learning approach whereby family business owners can learn from the past and remedy nascent organizational flaws that surface, grow, and can threaten the survival of most family firms. As educators and practitioners to family firms, we found the parallels between *Titanic* and family business staggering. What initially seemed counterintuitive (*Titanic*, a massive, luxurious ocean liner, being compared to family firms, the majority of which are small and modest), turned out to be absolutely correlative. Our research led us to deduce that *Titanic* and family firms behave(d) similarly in five distinct ways: with regard to confidence, leadership, teams, architecture, and planning. We must remember that *Titanic*, too, was a business—a business with management, employees, a product, services, and customers—that was built and owned by two family firms, Harland and Wolff and White Star Line, respectively.

The definition of a family business can vary from narrow (e.g., multiple-generation involvement with full family control of daily activities) to broad (e.g., the family intends to keep the business family owned and maintains control over the strategy, but has little direct involvement in day-to-day operations).[4] For our purposes, we will use the broader, more inclusive definition.

Our focus on family business is intentional. As an area of research, family business is a niche field that is oftentimes seen as analogous to entrepreneurship research. Also, while the media often turn the public eye toward the affairs of large corporate giants, family firms remain the most predominant form of business organization in the United States. Consider the following statistics[5]:

- 92% of all U.S. firms are family owned
- 59% of the U.S. workforce is employed by family businesses
- 78% of all new jobs in the United States are created by family firms
- 50% of the U.S. gross domestic product is generated by family firms

Given family firms' contributions to society, the overall literature in the field is sparse at best. Yet their challenges are more complex and quicker to surface than those of non-family-owned firms. Not only must family businesses work through the economic conditions and the competitive environment of industry, but they also must carefully manage family dynamics, which under stressful conditions can range from subtle nonverbal communications to open hostilities and multigenerational family wars.

Family business owners must balance the "hard" issues and the "soft" issues, which are much more sensitive and personal in nature than in non-family-owned firms. If a family firm experiences an economic or business-related hardship, it is necessary to remedy the hardship without causing harm to the family unit. Similarly, if the family unit experiences a hardship in the form of family discord or situations in which trust or communication are compromised, it is necessary to work through those challenges without causing harm to the business. In both situations, a delicate balance must be achieved if both the family and the business are to prosper; however, the resources to strike this balance are few and far between. In fact, many of the challenges family businesses experience go largely unremedied because advisors and consultants are wary of getting involved in what they might consider "a family issue."

In the end, these "family issues" become everyone's concern when the business fails. And the numbers on this front are alarming: 70% of all family firms fail to transition from the first to the second generation and fewer than 15% make it from the second to the third generation of family ownership,[6] irrespective of revenue or number of employees. The percentages hold whether the family business is a small "mom and pop" operation or a large multinational firm. As it turns out, succession and all it entails represents the biggest threat to business survival.

In our work with family businesses, we have seen a remarkable need to address the challenges that family-owned firms face in a way that is meaningful, provocative and motivating. Our hope is to add to the literature by contributing a piece that is as original in its approach and analysis as it is compelling and enriching to the reader. In fact, in and of itself, one of the most unique and distinguishing features of this book is the use of *Titanic* as a metaphor/case study to convey both practical ideas and emotional urgency.

The benefits of case study analysis are broad and deep, affording readers the opportunity to approach real-time problems and solutions in their entirety while using their own decision-making processes. Our intent is that readers will be able to recognize, reflect upon, and apply key learning points from this case study—and from this endeavor, develop and execute informed decisions in their professional lives. In drawing parallels between family businesses and *Titanic*, we also offer risk management strategies that family business owners can begin implementing immediately to allow for the "safe passage" of the business and family through periods of growth and transition.

Sink or Swim: How Lessons from the Titanic *Can Save Your Family Business* provides advisors to family firms with a fresh new way to discuss problems, risks, and challenges with family business clients. Even more importantly, *Sink or Swim* can be successful in serving as a catalyst for generating meaningful conversation among family members and motivating family business owners to make positive changes in their firms.

PART I

●

Genesis of a Disaster

The first section of this book equips readers with the essential background information necessary to fully appreciate the context within which the *Titanic* disaster occurred. While the disaster itself resulted from a number of decisions and actions, some of those key decisions were influenced by the larger social, economic, and political forces of the times. Chapter 1 provides a description of the socioeconomic environment in the United States, the United Kingdom, and Ireland during the mid- to late nineteenth century. Particular attention is given to the innovations that emerged and the ways in which they contributed to the demand for transatlantic luxury travel in the early twentieth century. Further, contextual factors surrounding the design, construction, and management of *Titanic* are evaluated with regard to White Star Line and Harland and Wolff (*Titanic*'s owner and builder/designer, respectively)—both family firms.

Chapter 2 offers facts relative to the short life of *Titanic*, summarizing the events related to her conception, construction, sea trials, voyage, and sinking. Readers will also learn more about the captain and crewmembers responsible for ensuring that more than 1,300 passengers made it safely to their destination of New York City. These facts afford readers an opportunity to reflect upon the events that happen prior to a disaster occurring, and apply these reflections to their own circumstances (i.e., thinking about which forces propel important decisions and which risks are associated with these decisions in their own environments). Unless otherwise specified, facts relative to *Titanic* were drawn from five sources,[1] which were largely in agreement with another.

1

The Birth of a Dream: How *Titanic* Came to Be

Those who cannot remember the past are condemned to repeat it.
—George Santayana

The creation and sinking of *Titanic* were not isolated events. Rather, they were firmly embedded within particular social, political, economic, and historical contexts—contexts that are not unlike the social, political, and economic conditions found in current times. To understand *Titanic*'s story, it is important to consider these macro-level influences, as these influences affected the organizational inputs and resources that were relevant to *Titanic*'s short life. It is also important to explore the histories, values, and conditions of those individuals responsible for the ocean liner's ownership and operation. These forces were instrumental in shaping crucial decisions that, in the chain of events, ultimately led to the tragedy. They also provide a basis by which to recognize how organizations of today operate under similar circumstances.

In times such as the early twentieth century and the turn of the second millennium, change was rapid and widespread throughout the globe—forging more complex organizational models, leading to an aggressive increase in competition, and engendering a host of new values among consumers. Few times in history can capture this intensity as effectively as the "space race" among leading nations of the mid-twentieth century, wherein a young U.S. President, John F. Kennedy, summoned a nation's brawn and declared: "If this capsule history of our progress teaches us anything, it is that man, in his quest for knowledge and progress, is determined and cannot be deterred. The exploration of space will go ahead, whether we join in it or not, and it is one of the great adventures of all time, and no nation which expects to be the leader of other nations can expect to stay behind in this race for space."[1]

As history repeats itself, the same desire for progress, exploration, adventure, and dominance can be identified in the nineteenth century throughout Europe, the Americas, and Japan, all of which experienced a reformation in ideologies as they related to human progress and organizational evolution. It was during this complex time of the latter part of the 1800s that *Titanic's* story began and—whether knowingly or not—repeated itself throughout history.

INDUSTRIAL REVOLUTION

Titanic was the product of an era steeped in splendor and dizzying innovation. Its conception was largely influenced by the second Industrial Revolution (a period that lasted from the second half of the nineteenth century to the beginning of World War I) when social, economic, cultural, and corporate standards were transformed by major advancements in the manufacturing, transportation, and technology sectors. During this period, per capita income increased more than 10-fold, population increased more than six-fold, consumer consumption grew rapidly, and immigration to the "New World" was unstoppable.[2]

Many of the changes originated within the manufacturing, communications, and transportation sectors, as organizations became more concerned with production, distribution, and optimization of resources. A host of new industries and products emerged: the petroleum industry was founded; "electrification" allowed for mass production and improved working conditions; the telegraph, telephone, air brakes for trains, and various engines (steam, diesel, and internal combustion) were invented; and advancements in iron making by Henry Bessemer led to monumental innovations in steel making, allowing steel to be manufactured inexpensively and quickly. As a result, the ready supply of steel (which lasted longer than iron) paved the way for a more modern and accessible transportation infrastructure, replacing wood and iron in ships, allowing for automobile production, and updating the old iron railroad rails (which generally needed to be replaced each decade).

As a result of improved technologies and mass production, the price of goods decreased and general living and working conditions greatly improved. Although mass production also led to the closing of small businesses and periods of depression, the world economy, as a whole, grew despite these temporary setbacks.[3] Steam engines made transportation by ship more efficient, as ships could now carry more freight and passengers than ever before. These new engines also supported the mining industry, as demand for the coal needed to power the larger engines rose. The advent of the telegraph allowed for communications facilitating cross-border trade. A new stage in globalization emerged. Innovation would be the driver of the era's socioeconomic progress, with the United States having emerged as a leader in applied technology. In fact, the United States issued 500,000 patents from 1860 to 1890,—more than 10 times the number issued in the previous 70 years.[4]

The social impact of these innovations was immense—but included both benefits and drawbacks. The practice of child labor declined, labor unions wielded more clout, and the growth of the middle class changed consumption habits and increased demand for a broader range of consumer goods. In the United States, the expansion into the West beckoned immigrants seeking wealth and land, drawing hundreds of thousands of emigrants each year from Europe and growing the United States' consumer base. Yet, the challenges that the Industrial Revolution posed to smaller, closely held firms were felt deeply. Many of these firms did not have the capital necessary to invest in the new technologies of the day and, therefore, could not compete with the lower costs presented by companies embracing mass production. With intense competition on the rise and new industries rapidly unfolding, governments were forced to more actively manage the complex demands of this new globally competitive environment—and so their focus turned to the work associated with implementing tariffs, limiting corporate monopolies, managing immigration, building a central banking system, and developing social welfare systems. As the economy grew (and government's role in managing the growth and contraction of certain industries became more elaborate), the rise of the telegraph and more efficient transportation modes allowed for global trade and a resultant decrease in the cost of goods; thus a consumption-based culture emerged. It was the beginning of the Gilded Age.

THE GILDED AGE AND THE PROGRESSIVE ERA

The Gilded Age spawned new values in relation to class and wealth. With the Industrial Revolution came a need for education in engineering and professional management. Opportunities in white-collar jobs allowed for more complex management systems—systems whose evolution brought about an emphasis on reporting, career paths, middle management, and finance. The new opportunities that emerged based on better management systems and training led to the mass accumulation of wealth that defined the Gilded Age—wealth that was the result of industrial mergers, access to broader consumer markets, lower costs of manufacturing, and higher profit margins.

The Gilded Age was a period of tremendous opulence and an age marked by the rise of industrialists, entrepreneurs, financiers, and philanthropists such as J. P. Morgan, Andrew Carnegie, George Westinghouse, John D. Rockefeller, the Astor family, and Cornelius Vanderbilt. Many of these powerful figures were chiefly responsible for endowing academic institutions and libraries, financially supporting the arts, and redefining architecture.

In 1893, the United States was rattled by a depression that was due largely to Midwest drought and railroad speculation. The prosperity of the Gilded Age and the subsequent depression gave way to the Progressive Era in 1897—an era marked by an emphasis on technology, education, science, social activism, and government intervention in industry. It was within this richly complex environment—an environment of globalization, technological innovation, industrial competitiveness, and the celebration of wealth—that *Titanic* was born and White Star Line emerged as a major player in European shipping.

Interestingly enough, White Star Line (*Titanic*'s owner) was a family business whose managers faced the same challenges that family firms of any other era face: each era experiences similar economic conditions of growth and contraction. More interestingly, while the size and scope of White Star Line in relation to many family businesses may be dissimilar, the interpersonal challenges that *Titanic*'s owners experienced resonate with members of family businesses operating today. In fact, White Star Line *was* a family business that experienced its fair share of organizational challenges and family drama.

WHITE STAR LINE

With transatlantic travel on the rise during the latter part of the Industrial Revolution, a 30-year-old entrepreneur and son of a shipbuilder and timber merchant, Thomas H. Ismay, purchased White Star Line in 1867 after borrowing £1,000 to purchase whatever assets were left of the then bankrupt company. Having operated mostly for stewarding gold-seekers to Southeast Asia in worn-out wooden ships, White Star Line and its bankers declared bankruptcy earlier that year when the promise of gold and riches faltered in Australia and New Zealand. Given that financing for Ismay's purchase originated from Gustav Schwabe, Ismay agreed to have subsequent White Star Line ships outfitted and built exclusively by Gustav Wolff, Schwabe's nephew and part owner of a shipbuilding company named Harland and Wolff. In 1870, Ismay invited William Imrie (a second-generation family owner of Imrie & Tomlinson, another shipbuilding business) to merge his operation with White Star Line. Imrie agreed, partnering with Ismay and establishing Ismay, Imrie and Company—the parent company of White Star Line.

Similar to the principles of the "project triangle," in which firms can choose to compete on the basis of quality, cost, or time (generally, firms can be most competitive in one or two of these domains at most), White Star Line needed to determine how to best compete with its major competitors (Cunard, Inman, Hamburg-Amerika, and Norddeutscher-Lloyd, primarily). Ismay and his partners weighed the advantages of each attribute: quality (having the most luxurious ships), cost (having the lowest fares), or time (having the fastest service or best channels of delivery). Ismay decided that White Star Line's best chances for success would be competing on the basis of luxury and speed. Of course, with ships being built by Harland and Wolff—widely considered to be the best and most expensive shipbuilding company in Europe—competing on cost would not be feasible. If Ismay were to attract wealthy travelers, White Star Line would have to compete on luxury first and foremost, and give secondary emphasis to speed.

The future of shipbuilding would be in iron and steel, Ismay concluded, and in the transportation of wealthy passengers to and from England and the New World (where he could make a higher profit with quicker turnaround). With that aim in mind, Ismay renovated his ships, outfitting them with iron hulls, and began transporting cargo as well as passengers. With two young sons at home—Joseph (who preferred to be called by his middle name, Bruce), born in 1863, and James, born in 1867—Ismay had no alternative *except* to succeed.

Within one year of operation, Ismay launched the *Oceanic* and made enough of a profit to issue £1,000 shares in White Star Line. The following year, *Oceanic* would be joined by three identical sister ships: *Atlantic*, *Baltic*, and *Republic*. The year after that, it was joined by the larger ships *Adriatic* and *Celtic* (the names of all White Star Line ships ended in "*ic*"). In 1874, Ismay added *Britannic* and *Germanic* to the fleet, hoping to capture the legendary "Blue Riband"—an unofficial title given to the passenger ship crossing the Atlantic in regular service with the fastest speed.

While Ismay expanded his fleet, he also established a dream of growing his business into a family-owned enterprise. In 1880, 17-year-old Bruce Ismay went to work for this father as an apprentice. Having been molded throughout his childhood as the heir apparent, Bruce focused on filling the shoes of his larger-than-life father. While tolerating an unpleasant first day of work (his father publicly reprimanded the "new office boy" for "[leaving] his overcoat laying about in my office" and ordered him to leave his hat and coat elsewhere),[5] Bruce went about his work with silent resentment.

The tension in the acrimonious relationship between father and son was palpable, but like many family business owners, the dream of perpetuating a family business dynasty was central to Thomas Ismay. Having expanded and established a White Star Line office in New York City, he assigned Bruce to that office in 1886—a reprieve for both father and son.

It was a powerful experience for the socially awkward 23-year-old. From time to time, he was referred to as odd, reticent, aloof, brooding, socially clumsy, tightly wound, standoffish, arrogant, intrusive, and not quite capable. While he may have created a character brimming with self-assurance, he was never quite able to escape the shadow of his domineering father. Yet, in New York, Bruce Ismay could find room to grow on his own. In 1887, he met and married Julia Schieffelin after a whirlwind romance and made a vow to her father that he would never take Julia away from her family in Manhattan. The couple would remain in New York City.

Thomas Ismay had other plans for his eldest son, however. A year and a half after their wedding, Bruce and Julia visited the Ismay family, bringing with them their young daughter, Margaret. It was at dinner that Thomas made his announcement—and gave his ultimatum. He planned to retire, but stay on as Chairman of White Star Line, and the job of day-to-day management was Bruce's if he desired. Of course, that would mean he would have to move back to England and break the promise he made to Julia's father. If Bruce did not accept the job his father offered, his younger brother James would take it, and Bruce would remain in New York and report to James. Notwithstanding his reluctance to work in his father's shadow in England, Bruce's choice was clear. He would rather break a vow to his father-in-law than work for his brother. In 1891, Bruce returned to England and joined the family business as a partner in Ismay, Imrie and Company. As promised, in 1892, Thomas resigned his day-to-day management. Seven years later, after a series of heart attacks, the man revered throughout the industry as a shipbuilding prodigy died at age 62.

This story explains how the Ismay family found its way through a generational transition in leadership—and it is a familiar example of how many family businesses manage succession. For Bruce and other members of a succeeding generation, entering or working in the family's business gives rise to a number of personal and professional challenges with relation to perpetuating the founder's dream, establishing independence and a sense of "self," managing family dynamics, and assuming authority within the family enterprise—all challenges explored in Box 1.1.

Box 1.1
Safe Passage in the Family Business:
Four Challenges for Successors

Michael L. Stern, PhD—Michael Stern Consulting

The child coming into the family business, especially one founded by the father, is embarking on a journey that both offers bountiful rewards and is filled with unique emotional hazards. Hodding Carter noted that a parent gives two important gifts to a child: roots and wings. In the family-owned business, achieving this feat is an even more challenging task, engendering four key challenges in the journey of emotional development:

1. *Delayed emotional development.* During adolescence and early adulthood, the child experiences challenges related to separation, family loyalty, establishing his or her own identity, and finding new ways of dealing with parents. Within a family business, the child often experiences delays or derailment of development in these areas. As children straddle the often unclear boundary between "family" and "business," they lose the opportunity to experience clarity about their own role and identity. For example, coworkers may continue to relate to them as the young child of the owner, rather than as a maturing colleague.

2. *Low self-esteem and self-efficacy.* In some families, the more capable and independent children go off on their own, with the less capable children going into the family business. Yet even a capable child in the family business faces challenges to self-esteem. He or she must follow in the shadow of the founder, who may be threatened by the successor's challenge or success. Also, the child's success may be discounted by others, who cite the privileged position from which the child started. As was said about one second-generation member's accomplishment, "Just because you woke up on third base, it doesn't mean you hit a triple."

3. *Difficulties in peer roles and relationships.* The children of owners cannot escape their special circumstance. Their unique position tends to isolate them from coworkers, and as "the boss's kid" sons or daughters may have no true peers in the workplace. Often, such children have assets and privileges that are in excess of those enjoyed by their early career peers.

4. *Achieving independence ("the wings").* Sometimes the child is tightly bound into the family business; at times, extrication from the family business system is necessary. Evan Greenberg, the 45-year-old president of the $40 billion insurance company AIG, felt it necessary to resign his position in 2000. His robustly healthy father gave no indication of leaving as CEO. Greenberg explained his choice by saying, "Everyone leaves home sometime . . . this is my time." Sometimes burdened by issues of self-esteem and alienation, achieving independence is one of the most challenging difficulties faced by the founder's successors.

The first challenge a successor faces is whether becoming the next leader of a family business is in alignment with his or her personal vision or dream.[6] In many cases, the dream of the founder burdens successors, as they feel responsible to embrace the founder's dream as their own. In turn, this factor can cause anger and resentment, as successors may feel that the burden is too much to bear—particularly when the successor feels that he or she must forfeit his or her own personal dreams to perpetuate and manage the dream of another.

Of note are the unique difficulties associated with father-and-son teams working in business together[7]—difficulties that father/daughter and husband/wife relationships do not experience because they are usually less competitive than father/son relationships.[8] The elder Ismay appears to have believed that "tough love" was the best method by which to raise a son into a strong successful man, and Bruce tolerated his father's rebukes and lack of praise. The effect this could have on any child of a "self-made man" is vast, resulting in diminished self-efficacy, delayed emotional development, entitlement, and difficulties in peer relationships.

A second challenge successors may experience relates to establishing independence. Young adults striving to become autonomous need to develop a better understanding of their personal strengths, weaknesses, preferences, goals, and desires. This may be difficult for family business successors to do—particularly if they know only their family business's culture and work habits and have not had the opportunity to explore external opportunities.

Encouraging a family member to work outside the family business gives successors the opportunity to work in environments that provide the best lifestyle fit as their needs and values change over time. For example, early career successors may have a need to experience professional growth and advancement (and may be more risk tolerant in their careers), while mid-career successors may wish to strike a balance between work and other pursuits and, therefore, seek stability.[9] Gaining outside work experience also helps to build a culture of meritocracy (versus a culture of entitlement), whereby initiation and employment are realized on the basis of performance and merit rather than on the basis of privilege or tenure.

A third challenge involves managing family relationships and interpersonal dynamics as they relate to working with other family members—particularly siblings, cousins, and parents. Learning to work together successfully often requires that family members move beyond previously held family roles and establish new ways of viewing and interacting with one another. This process is aided by self-assurance, strong communication, advanced conflict management skills, and mutual respect. The fear of fracturing family relationships due to workplace conflict may endanger the tightest of family relationships and business success, and has been cited as one reason that potential successors may decide against pursuing a career in the family enterprise.

A final challenge for the would-be successor is whether the founder or incumbent leader is willing to relinquish enough authority and control in order to give the successor the opportunity to grow as a leader. Successions characterized by a strong presence of founder's "generational shadow"—or inappropriate and undue influence exerted by a supposedly retired founder—are usually more difficult. In businesses where founders remain present and involved after the next generation assumes control, conflict is significantly higher compared to businesses with retired founders who are not involved in day-to-day business operations or do not attempt to exert control over the business.[10] Conversely, a harmonious relationship between the owner-manager and the successor—characterized by cooperation, trust, and mutual respect—has been related to satisfaction with the succession process and to continued business success.[11]

These are some of the prominent challenges facing would-be successors in enterprising families, thereby rendering the decision to enter the business much more complicated. Indeed, the younger Ismay faced many of the same challenges as he struggled with gaining independence and credibility outside the shadow of his father—a shadow that extended to the United States and was about to draw the attention of the indomitable J. P. Morgan.

INTERNATIONAL MERCANTILE MARINE

To the bewilderment of the Ismay family, a new entrant in the market had been causing panic among ship owners on both sides of the Atlantic. The company was the International Navigation Company of New Jersey (founded in 1893 and later renamed the International Mercantile Marine in 1902), and its founder was J. Pierpont Morgan.

At first, J. P. Morgan was reluctant to invest in the shipping industry, instead devoting his time and efforts to managing United States Steel and his financial empire. Eventually, upon learning of the shipping profits that could be made, he purchased a majority interest in the only two U.S. shipping companies working the North Atlantic tracks. In 1898, Morgan acquired the British Inman line; he followed this move with the purchase of the Hamburg-Amerika and Norddeutscher-Lloyd German lines in 1899. In 1900, his shipping empire spread through ownership or control of the Red Star Line, the Dominion Line, and the Leyland Line (all British companies). Now able to control fares in transatlantic voyages, Morgan put the pressure on White Star Line and Cunard to follow suit and join the International Mercantile Marine.

Cunard's best offense against being acquired by the International Mercantile Marine was to develop an even better defense. Cunard's owners lobbied the British government so that the company would remain British owned. Ultimately, the company received tremendous subsidies and low-interest loans to build speedy ships with the caveat that these speedy ships would have fittings for guns and armor for potential use by the Royal Navy. With the Cunard offer off the table, J. P. Morgan turned his sights to White Star Line, and began searching for an internal corporate liaison to the company who could champion his vision. He found his liaison in William Pirrie, Harland and Wolff's chairman.

Morgan's identification of Pirrie as the one who could best influence Bruce Ismay was shrewd and intentional, seeing that Pirrie had more to lose than Ismay should the deal founder. Pirrie was a long-time friend of the Ismay family and had worked closely with Thomas Ismay. A third-generation shipbuilder, Pirrie adored shipbuilding, having joined Harland and Wolff in 1862 at 15 years old. In 1874, the company's owners offered Pirrie the opportunity to "buy in." With savings and borrowed cash, he purchased £13,000 of corporate stock. Sixteen years later in 1890, he had controlling interest in the company and was chairman at age 43.

As the exclusive shipbuilder for White Star Line, Pirrie understood that a fare war (third-class passengers were able to cross the Atlantic by paying as little as £2 per ticket, representing approximately a 50 percent decrease in revenue for White Star Line) would essentially leave Harland and Wolff in ruin. The depression of 1893, the U.S. drought and resultant poor prospects for emigration, low passenger fares (leaving little capital to build new ships), and competitors' ships formerly pressed into service with the Royal Navy reentering as civilian passenger ships all threatened prosperity for both White Star Line and Harland and Wolff. The industry, if continuing on this fatal fare war, would be in ruin.

Like his father before him, Bruce Ismay was opposed to the idea of selling White Star Line to J. P. Morgan, but Pirrie's argument was persuasive, and Ismay trusted the elder businessman immensely. In 1902, the stockholders of White Star Line approved the sale of the company to the International Mercantile Marine. Even though the International Mercantile Marine was an American company, ships owned by White Star Line subsidiary would continue to fly the Union Jack, remain docked in England, be staffed by British citizens, and be governed by the British Board of Trade. Both Ismay and Pirrie were invited to serve as directors at the International Mercantile Marine, with Ismay remaining as president of White Star Line. In 1904, Morgan offered Ismay the job of president and managing director of the International Mercantile Marine—an offer he accepted.

TITANIC

In 1906, prompted by the building of the *Mauritania* and *Lusitania* ocean liners by Cunard, Pirrie launched a comprehensive modernization effort at Harland and Wolff. It was aimed primarily at enabling the firm to compete with Cunard, which by then had the two largest, fastest and most opulent ships afloat. Investing in new building slips that accommodated even larger-sized ships, Pirrie began drawing up plans for ships that (while not breaking speed records) would still be fairly quick transports and carry thousands on "floating palaces." The question was whether Ismay was up to the challenge.

In 1907, Pirrie shared his plans with Bruce Ismay over dinner, sketching on napkins and notepads and dreaming aloud. If White Star Line were to build a ship of this grandeur, Ismay argued, then one would not be enough. If, in fact, the company was to achieve transatlantic dominance, it needed two ships to offer weekly service (sailing east- and west-bound tracks) and a third ship in reserve. Further, the ships had to be constructed at a level of luxury beyond the general public's wildest dreams. The third-class compartments would have more comforts than those of any other liner and its revenues, together with those from the second-class berths, would pay the ship's overhead costs. Fares paid by first-class passengers would generate profit.

The ships, which would be referred to as "Olympic-class" ships, were named *Olympic*, *Titanic*, and *Gigantic*. *Olympic* would be completed in four years, with *Titanic* completed nine months later, and *Gigantic* (later renamed *Britannic*) nine months after *Titanic*. Pirrie knew the ambitious goals could be met, and he knew just the team that could design the ships and execute the plan flawlessly.

Harland and Wolff, like White Star Line, was a family business. In fact, Pirrie married his first cousin, Margaret, and employed Margaret's brother, Alexander Carlisle, as managing director of Harland and Wolff (thus Alexander was not only Pirrie's cousin, but also his brother-in-law). Another family member, the young Thomas Andrews, would join Pirrie and Carlisle in 1888. Andrews was the son of Pirrie's sister, Eliza.

By all accounts, Andrews was a competent and well-respected member of the Harland and Wolff team, both within administration and among shipyard employees. He joined the company at only 15 years of age, first working as an apprentice on *Majestic* and shadowing within various departments to learn the intricacies of electricity, plumbing, metal working, assembly, architecture, and engineering. Andrews spent the final year and a half of his five-year apprenticeship in the drawing office. By the age of 28, he was principal manager overseeing construction.

By 1907, Andrews had proved himself to be an accomplished builder, working as principal constructor, designer, or superintendent on such grand ships as *Celtic, Gothic, Cedric, Baltic, Mystic, Germanic, Adriatic,* and *Oceanic.* Given the experience of Andrews and Carlisle, Pirrie felt confident that Harland and Wolff could execute on its promise to build *Olympic, Titanic,* and *Gigantic.* As he showed Carlisle and Andrews the renderings, the significance of such an undertaking was felt deeply by all.

Carlisle, Andrews, and Pirrie got to work right away planning and designing the new ships. The ships were to be enormous—50 percent larger than any Cunard vessel. The plans called for ships that would measure 882 feet 9 inches in length, 92.5 feet in width, and 175 feet in height from the bottom of the keel to the top of the funnels. The vessels would each weigh approximately 40,000 tons (and more than 45,000 tons when loaded with coal, passengers, food, and freight) and would require that piers in New York and Southampton be extended by several hundred feet just to accommodate their size. Each vessel had 10 decks and was designed to hold 735 passengers in first class, 674 passengers in second class, 1,026 passengers in third class, and more than 900 crewmembers.[12]

Beyond being the largest ships built to date, the Olympic-class ships afforded passengers in all classes the best in luxury to a degree unrivaled in the industry. Although *Titanic* and *Olympic* were constructed from the same set of architectural blueprints, *Titanic* was upgraded to include additional first-class staterooms and two Promenade Suites that included a private enclosed promenade, thereby making *Titanic* a slightly more attractive traveling option for the ultra-wealthy than *Olympic.*

First-class passengers enjoyed accommodations that were, according to *Shipbuilder* magazine, "unrivaled in extent and magnificence,"[13] and equal to or better than the finest hotels. Even the third-class accommodations were thought to be superior to the first-class accommodations of many other ships. *Titanic*'s passenger fares reflected the grandiose experience offered to those sailing aboard: one-way fares cost first-class passengers with a parlor suite £870 ($4,350 U.S. dollars in 1912, equaling $99,000 in 2010), £30 for a first-class berth ($150 U.S. dollars in 1912, equaling $3,400 in 2010), £12 for second class ($60 U.S. dollars in 1912, equaling $1,360 in 2010), and £3 to £8 for third class ($14 to $40 U.S. dollars in 1912, equaling $340 to $900 in 2010).[14]

While White Star Line emphasized luxury and service over speed, its owners also planned a design that would outshine their competitors in terms of safety. Using a number of newly available advancements in modern shipbuilding, *Titanic* and her sister ships were designed to incorporate three important features to emphasize safety: a powerful Marconi wireless system, a double bottom, and watertight compartments.

Titanic was equipped with advanced communication systems aboard, including a telephone switchboard for intra-ship calls, a call button system to contact stewards and stewardesses, and the Marconi wireless system. The Marconi wireless system, with a 5-kilowatt radio transmitter, was the strongest of any ship at that time and allowed passengers (for a fee) to send or receive telegrams, known as "Marconigrams." This feature was a novelty for people wishing to keep in touch with family or conduct business while traveling, and many took advantage of the new technology. No doubt this service was used mainly by the wealthier passengers: the fee was 12 shillings and sixpence ($3.12 U.S. dollars in 1912, equivalent to $70 in 2010) for the first 10 words, and 9 pence per word thereafter.

The Marconi wireless system was not just a novelty for passengers; it was a necessity for seafarers and a key component of a ship's safety features. With two sets of equipment (one for sending messages and the other for receiving them), any ship could call on *Titanic* for assistance. Likewise, *Titanic* could use the system to call other ships for help. Because most ships were outfitted with Marconi wireless systems, the Marconi Company trained its operators to employ a common call to indicate serious trouble. The CQD call—translating as "all stations: distress"—was a precursor to the more modern, but not yet widely adopted "SOS" call that had become an official worldwide standard in 1908. Although these transmitters had a minimum range of 400 miles, at night or under clear weather conditions, the range could extend to more than 2,000 miles.

With many serious or deadly shipping accidents occurring when ships were grounded or made contact with something that resulted in the bottom being opened up to the sea, the double bottom of the ship was, literally, a second bottom with about 7 feet of space between the outer bottom and the inner bottom. Throughout this area were a series of sealed compartments, and other compartments that could be used for storage. The idea was that if the outer hull plates were pierced, the inner plates would prevent water from entering the rest of the ship.

The most highly celebrated safety feature of *Titanic* was the watertight compartments. Previously, ships had one or two bulkheads in the bow, which would prevent flooding if the ship hit an object head on. *Titanic*'s hull was divided into 16 watertight compartments, created by 15 watertight bulkheads (or walls) that ran across the ship from the port (left) to starboard (right). The idea behind these carefully planned compartments was to further guard against flooding in the case of collision or damage to the hull. Based on analysis of prior shipping accidents, the ship was designed to float with any two compartments flooded, and designers ascertained that a collision with another ship would not flood more than two adjacent compartments. In fact, the ship could still float with as many as four compartments flooded. The compartments were separated by large watertight doors, which were normally left open for routine operation. In the case of flooding, they could be closed in a number of different ways: by officers on the bridge using electric switches; by other crewmembers manually; or by a device next to each door that automatically closed the bulkheads if it detected the presence of 6 or more inches of water.

On April 30, 1907, the order to proceed with *Titanic*'s construction was given and a purchase order was issued by White Star Line on July 31, 1908. Eight months later, on March 31, 1909, construction officially began. The ship would be built at Harland and Wolff's shipyard in Belfast, Ireland. It eventually took nearly 15,000 Belfast workers working in 12-hour shifts for six and a half days per week to complete the job.

While construction manager and head of Harland and Wolff's design department, Andrews had never had the opportunity to oversee the entirety of a construction project—from construction of the keel to the delivery of the final product—so the oversight of the project went to Carlisle as chief draughtsman. Because he had experience building the largest of White Star Line ships up to that time, Pirrie put Carlisle in charge of equipment, davit design, and overall architecture and style. The ship's design resembled a yacht, but was fancier than the grandest of hotels on the inside.

Early in the project, as issues of power and authority strained Pirrie and Carlisle's relationship, Carlisle had a change of heart. At 53 years of age, and with a series of health concerns, he tendered his resignation to Pirrie, giving him one to two years' notice. Carlisle left Harland and Wolff in 1910, well before completion of the project, and became shareholder in the Welin Davit & Engineering Company, a firm supplying davits to Harland and Wolff.

Andrews succeeded Carlisle in assuming oversight of the great project, managing each detail of the Olympic-class ships' construction. The hulls of the great ships were framed on adjoining slipways, with a huge wood and steel gantry towering over the slips that allowed workers (and Andrews himself) access to every inch of the ship. The skeletons of the ships were constructed with 10-inch steel beams spaced 3 feet apart amidships and reduced to 24 inches at the bow and 27 inches in the stern sections. The ships' shells were made of steel plates that were, on average, roughly 6 feet wide and 30 feet long and weighed between 2.5 and 3 tons each. The shell plates were painstakingly fastened using approximately 3 million rivets (weighing 1,200 tons) that were applied both by hand and hydraulic press.

Because no ships of this magnitude had ever been constructed and observed at sea, caution was taken in the design of and specifications for the Olympic-class ships' hulls and rivets. Andrews increased the required hull plating from 1 inch to 1¼ inch and the rivets from ⅞ inch to 1 inch. Multiplied by the size of each ship, the adjustment meant another 4 million pounds of iron and steel required for construction, plus an additional 25 tons of coal expended daily for extra power. The resurgence of coal strikes in the United States and England from 1868 to 1910 made the cost of coal extremely volatile, and this fuel represented the single largest cost aboard ships. Concerned about the project's cost, Ismay approved only the use of 1-inch steel and ⅞-inch rivets—all that was required by the British Board of Trade during that time. Welin davits would be drafted for use; these items employed an innovative new design that allowed 360-degree movement that could handle the stowing and dispatching of more than one lifeboat. Original plans for the ships called for one lifeboat to be assigned to each davit (16 davits total) and another 16 to 32 lifeboats stored elsewhere on the ship.

Exceeding existing Board of Trade legal requirements, yet eschewing Harland and Wolff's original plans and recommendations, *Titanic* was ultimately outfitted with a total of 20 lifeboats: 14 large wooden lifeboats with a capacity for 65 people each, 2 smaller wooden lifeboats with a capacity of 35 people each, and 4 Englehardt Collapsible lifeboats, each with a capacity of 49 people.

May 31, 1911, was a day of celebration for Harland and Wolff, White Star Line, and the city of Belfast. *Olympic* completed her sea trial and returned briefly to Belfast before leaving for Southampton, where her maiden voyage would begin in two weeks' time. But what drew more interest (and 100,000 spectators) was the launch of *Olympic*'s sister ship, *Titanic*. The launch was led by William and Margaret Pirrie (now Lord and Lady Pirrie after having been ennobled in 1906), and was attended by Bruce Ismay and J. P. Morgan. At the time of their launches, the only thing completed on each vessel was the skeleton and outer shell. Once in the water, the ships were "fitted out" over the next 10 months with everything else: the funnels, lifeboats, engines, boilers, electrical systems, interiors, furniture, and myriad of other fine details. In all, *Titanic* would cost $10 million to complete, a sum equivalent to approximately $230 million in 2010.

CHAPTER SUMMARY

- The social, political, and economic environment into which *Titanic* was born was a time that is similar to today's social, political, and economic conditions: vast changes in industry were taking place relative to innovation; consumer values, preferences, and expectations were changing; immigration was a central issue relative to leveraging the opportunities it brought about while minimizing the challenges it presented; and globalization brought about increased competition for low-cost, high-quality goods and services with rapid turnaround.

- White Star Line's assets were purchased by Thomas Ismay in 1867, who grew the company by focusing on the benefits of iron and steel and opportunities of transatlantic voyage. He had two sons—whom he hoped would succeed him in the family business: Bruce (born in 1863) and James (born in 1867).

- Bruce joined his father at the business and later faced many of the challenges that fathers and sons experience when working together, such as defining a personal vision and dream (and deducing whether it is in alignment with joining the family business), establishing independence, managing family relationships and interpersonal dynamics as they relate to working with family members, and getting out of a predecessor's "generational shadow" by building confidence in leaders so that those leaders are comfortable relinquishing authority and control.

- *Titanic* was conceived in 1907 after William Pirrie (chairman of Harland and Wolff, a shipbuilding design firm) met with Bruce Ismay, sharing with him the vision of partnering and building "floating palaces" so regal that they would achieve unmatched dominance in the marketplace. Harland and Wolff was also a family firm, with Pirrie's brother-in-law, Alexander Carlisle, serving as managing director, and nephew Thomas Andrews working as construction manager and head of the design department.

- Even though Ismay rejected Andrews's recommendations regarding rivet size, lifeboat numbers, and hull plating specifications to be used, *Titanic* was built incorporating a number of safety and "best in class" features, including a doubly reinforced steel bottom, watertight compartments, and a powerful Marconi wireless operating system. These safety features were believed to render *Titanic* virtually "unsinkable."

2

The Life and Death of *Titanic*

From the builders' hands she was plunged straightway to her fate and christening salvos acclaimed at once her birth and death.
—Senator William Alden Smith

The story of *Titanic*—a grand ship, built by the world's best designers that sank on her maiden voyage—offers a chilling reminder of the brevity of life and vulnerabilities that individuals possess. That which seemed safe, solid, and mighty suffered a single mortal blow and, within only a few hours, vanished completely. The same can be said of businesses which, despite a history of solid performance, can quickly collapse and cease to exist. It is in this context that it becomes essential to take a deeper look at the events leading up to *Titanic*'s striking of an iceberg on April 14, 1912, and sinking the following morning. How could this have happened? Who were those entrusted with her care? What could have been done to avoid the calamity? And why did so many people have to die? This chapter answers these questions by describing the key people and events involved in *Titanic*'s maiden voyage.

By the time Captain E. J. Smith joined *Titanic*'s crew, he was already a legend. Dubbed the "Millionaire's Captain" because many of England's elite would sail only on vessels commanded by Smith, his life had a more modest beginning than the lives of the privileged whom he shuttled around the world.

Born Edward John Smith in 1850 in Hanley, Stoke-on-Trent, England, young "Ted" grew up the son of a pottery presser, Edward, and grocer, Catherine. It was his older half-brother, Joseph (a sailor who joined the Merchant Navy the year Ted was born) who made the largest impression on the youngster. At 17 years of age, and having worked since the age of 14 at a metal foundry, Ted made his way to Liverpool, where he met up with his brother, who by then was the captain of an American sailing ship, *Senator Weber*. Ted asked his older brother for an opportunity to sail with him, and Joseph pointed him in the direction of Andrew Gibson & Co., which would bring Ted onboard *Senator Weber* as an apprentice.[1]

Smith's career flourished from those humble beginnings. He sailed around the world and gained more responsibility as he passed his certifications—from third mate to second mate, and ultimately earning his first mate certificate in 1873 at only 23 years of age. Just two years later, Smith earned his master's certificate of competency, allowing him to command his own ship, which he would do just one year later. However, the lure of joining White Star Line and piloting its luxurious vessels was so strong that he opted to take a junior position aboard White Star Line steamships rather than command a lesser sailing ship. In 1880, Smith left Andrew Gibson & Co. and joined White Star Line.

Throughout his tenure at White Star Line, and up until the construction of the Olympic-class ships, Smith would work on nearly a dozen vessels— *Adriatic, Baltic, Britannic, Celtic, Coptic, Cufic, Germanic, Majestic, Republic,* and *Runic*—working his way up through the ranks from Fourth Officer to Commander. With White Star Line building bigger and bolder steamships in its quest for transatlantic shipping dominance, Smith was assigned as Commander for the maiden voyages of *Baltic* and *Adriatic*—the last two of the "Big Four" ships being built (the "Big Four" initiative was the predecessor to the "Olympic-class" thrust). In 1911, Smith was given command of *Olympic* and just one year later, at age 62, he was given command of *Titanic*. At that time, he received a salary of £1,260[2] ($140,000 in 2010)—about double what most sea captains earned.

Arriving in Belfast on March 31, 1912, Smith boarded *Titanic* and immediately took command of the ship and crew members. Having just recently commanded *Olympic*, he was well aware of the superior capabilities of the Olympic-class ships, yet not willing to take undue risks. The following day, April 1, was to be the day of *Titanic*'s sea trials. Given the wind and adverse weather conditions, Smith was reluctant to maneuver *Titanic* down the narrow channels and shallow waters of the River Lagan into open waters. As a consequence, her sea trials would be postponed to April 2.

Meanwhile, *Titanic*'s crew went about settling in and learning their duties. Assigned to *Titanic* by White Star Line management, a crew of seasoned mariners would work together to see *Titanic* through her maiden voyage, familiarizing themselves with the decks and layout, understanding how she worked, and learning their respective duties.

The most senior officer (besides Captain Smith) was Chief Officer William McMaster Murdoch, who carried on his family's seafaring tradition when he graduated from school at 14 years of age and began his apprenticeship at William Joyce & Coy in Liverpool. A quick learner who earned a reputation for being highly proficient and dependable, Murdoch worked his way through the ranks, graduating to larger ships and ultimately earning a job (and senior officer status) at White Star Line in 1900. Having experience on nine White Star Line vessels—including serving as First Officer of *Olympic* in 1911—Murdoch, at age 39, was selected to serve as Chief Officer on *Titanic*'s maiden voyage.

Charles Herbert Lightoller was selected to serve as First Officer. Having begun his apprenticeship at age 13, Lightoller had a long and storied seafaring career prior to joining the crew of *Titanic*. By the time he sailed on *Titanic* at age 39, he had already been shipwrecked, survived malaria he contracted on voyages to West Africa, and left his seafaring career to join the Klondike gold rush in 1898 (only to abandon that prospect and become a cowboy and cattle wrangler). In 1900, Lightoller decided to return to the sea and joined White Star Line—serving on *Medic*, *Majestic*, and *Oceanic* prior to being called for service on *Titanic*.

The Second Officer to serve aboard *Titanic* was David Blair. While little is known of Blair, he was considered an experienced mariner. At 37 years of age, he had previously served on at least two White Star Line ships—*Oceanic* and *Teutonic*.

Among the ship's junior officers (serving as Third Officer, Fourth Officer, Fifth Officer, and Sixth Officer, respectively) were Herbert Pitman, Joseph Boxhall, Harold Lowe, and James Moody. Having joined White Star Line in 1906, and at 34 years of age, Pitman was the more experienced seafarer of the group. He joined the Merchant Navy at age 18 and completed further nautical training through the Merchant Venturers' Technical College. Boxhall, however, was considered a superior navigator. At 28 years of age, and having joined White Star Line in 1907, Boxhall had served on both *Oceanic* and *Arabic* prior to joining the crew of *Titanic*.

Serving as Fifth Officer, Lowe was a runaway who joined the Merchant Navy at age 14 and quickly moved up the ranks, earning his first and second mate's certificates by the time he joined White Star Line in 1911. Joining *Titanic*'s crew in Belfast at 29 years of age, this was to be his first transatlantic voyage. His colleague, who also joined him at White Star Line in 1911, was Sixth Officer Moody. The youngest of all officers at 24 years of age, Moody's education at sea began at age 14, when he underwent nautical training and ultimately earned his Master's Certificate from the King Edward VII Nautical School in London. His experience with White Star Line ships extended just to his work on *Oceanic*.

As Captain Smith met and evaluated the crew, he decided to contact Bruce Ismay and request a change in his senior leadership team. Initiating what would become known as the "officer reshuffle," Captain Smith suggested that having a Chief Officer who had never served in the Chief Officer capacity on *Titanic*'s sister ship, *Olympic*, was too much of a risk to take. Murdoch, though having served as First Officer on *Olympic*, had not served as *Olympic*'s Chief Officer—so Captain Smith did not see him as fit for the Chief Officer position on *Titanic*. The person who had that experience, however, was Henry Tingle Wilde.

Henry Wilde was just months shy of his fortieth birthday when the spring of 1912 rolled around. He had a long seafaring career by then. Beginning his apprenticeship at age 18, Wilde moved up through the ranks as third and second mates of various ships, and then joined White Star Line in 1897 at approximately age 25. His experience extended to *Covic*, *Cufic*, *Delphic*, and *Tauric*; in 1911, he added *Olympic* to his résumé, where he served as Chief Officer.

Wilde was not expecting to join *Titanic* on her maiden voyage; in fact, he had prepared to sail on *Olympic*—or perhaps have command of a smaller White Star Line ship, such as *Oceanic*—in early April. However, word came from White Star Line that he was to await further orders as to where he would be assigned. Just a day before *Titanic* was to set sail on April 10, Wilde got the word that Captain Smith requested him to serve aboard *Titanic*. In the early morning of April 10, Wilde joined *Titanic*'s crew in Southampton as Chief Officer, thereby causing the demotion of senior officers Murdoch and Lightoller by one rank (Murdoch was demoted to First Officer and Lightoller was demoted to Second Officer) and displacing David Blair, who left the ship entirely when it reached Southampton. All four junior officers' ranks remained unchanged.

Ultimately, *Titanic*'s crew would number 891, not including subcontractors (such as the 8-person orchestra, 5 postal workers, and 9 members from Harland and Wolff there to oversee the ship's maiden voyage). Most of the crew were natives of Southampton, and were hired just a few days prior to *Titanic*'s departure. Notwithstanding those few crew members who had previously worked aboard *Olympic*, most of the crew were completely unfamiliar with the Olympic-class ships' layout and operations. With more than 100 distinct roles allocated across 3 departments, it took quite some time for crewmembers to familiarize themselves with their colleagues and their respective functions and responsibilities.

SEA TRIALS

On April 2, Smith readied his crew for *Titanic*'s sea trials—the final element of a ship's construction that would test the ship's performance and seaworthiness. The sea trials included rudder, engine, turning, and stopping tests. They also included tests of all machinery and equipment.

Besides testing the ship itself, the trial afforded officers and crew a valuable opportunity to practice operating the vessel and working together.

Being that *Titanic* was virtually identical to her sister *Olympic*, only one day of sea trials was deemed sufficient. *Olympic* had undergone two days of sea trials prior to her maiden voyage and whatever necessary adjustments that were made following *Olympic*'s sea trials had already been incorporated into *Titanic*'s construction. Approximately 200 people were aboard *Titanic* for her sea trial—evaluating her performance, testing equipment, and generally enjoying the chance to be part of such a momentous occasion. The group included the ship's officers and crew, the Marconi operators (Jack Phillips and Harold Bride), Thomas Andrews, Harold Sanderson of the International Mercantile Marine (who stood in for an ill Bruce Ismay), and Francis Carruthers (a representative of the British Board of Trade who would evaluate *Titanic*'s performance).

By dusk, the sea trial was completed. Francis Carruthers signed off on paperwork indicating *Titanic* had met or exceeded the requisite Board of Trade standards, presenting her operators with a passenger certificate, "An Agreement and Account of Voyages and Crew," that was valid for one year. At that moment, *Titanic*'s ownership was transferred from Harland and Wolff to White Star Line.

On the evening of April 2, just after the sea trial was completed, *Titanic* left Belfast for Southampton. It took approximately 24 hours to make the journey to the port where she would take on her very first passengers.

SOUTHAMPTON

As sailing day dawned, additional crew boarded the ship, with passengers boarding shortly thereafter. Most of the 924 passengers who boarded in Southampton would arrive by boat trains, which left London's Waterloo Station at 7:30 A.M. and took two hours to reach the port. With each class boarding at different locations, the passengers' entry offered up a "who's who" of the day, as many prominent passengers and noted financiers, industrialists, and philanthropists crossed onto *Titanic*'s decks. Many of those wealthy passengers were leaders or successors of some of the most well-known family-owned firms of the day:

- John Jacob Astor IV: One of the wealthiest men in the world at the time, the 48-year-old Astor had managed his family real estate holdings since 1891, particularly a number of hotels in New York.
- Isidor Straus: Born in Germany, Straus was an entrepreneur who founded R. H. Macy & Company with his brother Nathan.

- Benjamin Guggenheim: The son of mining industrialist Meyer Guggenheim, Benjamin was a businessman on his way back to New York.
- George Widener: Son of wealthy streetcar magnate Peter Widener, George was heir to the largest fortune in Philadelphia.
- Henry S. Harper: Son of John Wesley Harper, Henry was a director at the family publishing business, Harper and Brothers.
- Washington A. Roebling II: Roebling was president of Roebling Steel Company and grandson of John A. Roebling, designer of the Brooklyn Bridge.

With officers having been assigned their schedules determining when they would be on watch, George Bowyer (the harbor pilot) boarded the ship and met with Captain Smith to ensure that all the officers were in the correct stations. Five tugboats were on hand to assist in towing *Titanic* off the dock and into the River Test, where she would then set off for Cherbourg, France. At noon on April 10, the whistles blew, the gang-planks were lowered, and the great ship pulled away from the dock with some 50,000 onlookers there to see her off.

Because the departure occurred soon after low tide, the waters of River Test were still shallow and the crew had to be very careful so as not to damage the enormous ship's hull. Yet, as *Titanic* slowly made her way down the River Test toward the English Channel, she displaced a large amount of water. Passing *Oceanic* and *New York*—both passenger ships that were unmanned and dormant due to the then-current coal strike—the wake from *Titanic* created a strong suction that caused *New York* to snap her mooring lines and drift toward *Titanic*. A collision was narrowly avoided, thanks to quick thinking by the tugboat *Vulcan*'s captain, who managed to get ropes attached to *New York*'s stern in time to slow the ship's movement. At the same time, Captain Smith gave power to the port engine, creating a wave that pushed *New York* away. It was a defensive action that would further delay *Titanic*'s voyage by more than an hour as Captain Smith stopped the engines and ordered an inspection. As luck would have it, no boats suffered any damage.

As *Titanic* steamed across the English Channel to its next stop in Cherbourg, Captain Smith used this leg of the trip as an opportunity to develop a better sense of how the ship handled by executing a number of S-turns and other maneuvers along the 70-mile route. Passengers enjoyed their first meal aboard and took note of how smoothly the ship steamed along, with no vibrations whatsoever.

Unlike the ports in Southampton and New York, Cherbourg did not have the docking facilities for a ship the size of *Titanic*, so the crew dropped an anchor a mile off shore to allow another 274 passengers to board the ship via two smaller shuttle boats called "tenders." The tenders also took 24 passengers ashore whose final destination was Cherbourg. The loading process was finished at approximately 8:00 P.M. Shortly thereafter, the ship turned and headed west into the night toward its final port of call, Queenstown, Ireland.

Late in the morning on April 11, *Titanic* pulled into Queenstown's harbor. As in Cherbourg, Queenstown did not have the dock space for *Titanic*. Three hours behind schedule, the ship arrived at low tide, making it unsafe to anchor just a mile out in shallow waters; thus, covering a distance two miles from shore, two tenders ferried out the 120 additional passengers and nearly 1,400 sacks of mail. Seven first-class passengers disembarked in Queenstown, along with one crew member who absconded among some cargo bags. Now four hours behind schedule, *Titanic* once again got underway, steaming along the Irish coastline and then out into the Atlantic toward New York. With final accounts of the number of passengers aboard *Titanic*'s maiden voyage unresolved, she began her trek across the Atlantic with anywhere from 1,316 to 1,324 passengers and 899 crewmembers.

ATLANTIC PASSAGE

The first three days on the ocean crossing were uneventful, with calm waters and fair weather. Passengers settled into a routine and crew attended to their various duties. Meanwhile, in the Marconi room, Jack Phillips and Harold Bride were very busy processing wireless messages. While most of the messages were for passengers, some were of a different nature—warnings about ice in the North Atlantic.

The winter of 1912 had been unseasonably mild; in fact, it was the warmest winter on record in more than three decades. Sections of Greenland's ice fields broke off and floated southward, into the east-west shipping lanes of the North Atlantic, stretching over a 70-mile range from north to south and extending to places farther south than had ever been seen by many experienced sailors. Navigating through these areas was extremely difficult and dangerous, forcing many ships to stop in their tracks. In fact, most captains chose not to operate their ships through ice fields, opting instead to take the longer routes around the ice and out of danger's way.

As *Titanic* steamed across the Atlantic, many other ships were sending messages to one another and to *Titanic*, reporting locations of ice fields and characterizing the nature of the ice as large bergs or smaller growlers. These ice reports started in Southampton and continued throughout the journey. Over the course of the day on Sunday, April 14, *Titanic* received a total of seven ice warnings - many of which referred to heavy ice in the area 42° to 44° N latitude (Table 2.1). Yet, only three of these messages reached the captain or another of the ship's officers. As *Titanic* traveled the westbound shipping track (approximately 60 miles south of the eastbound track), little attention was given to the ice warnings, shown in Figure 2.1, that were reported from ships encountering ice on the eastbound track (even as ice was reported to be in the vicinity between the tracks and floating into *Titanic*'s westbound path).[3]

At 10 minutes before 6 P.M., Captain Smith turned the ship from its southwesterly direction to one headed due west. The turn was a regular part of the transatlantic crossing—a maneuver known as "turning the corner." In an effort to steer clear of the ice reported on the ship's original route, Smith waited an additional 30 minutes before making the turn, so as to bring the ship several miles farther south and out of the ice field.

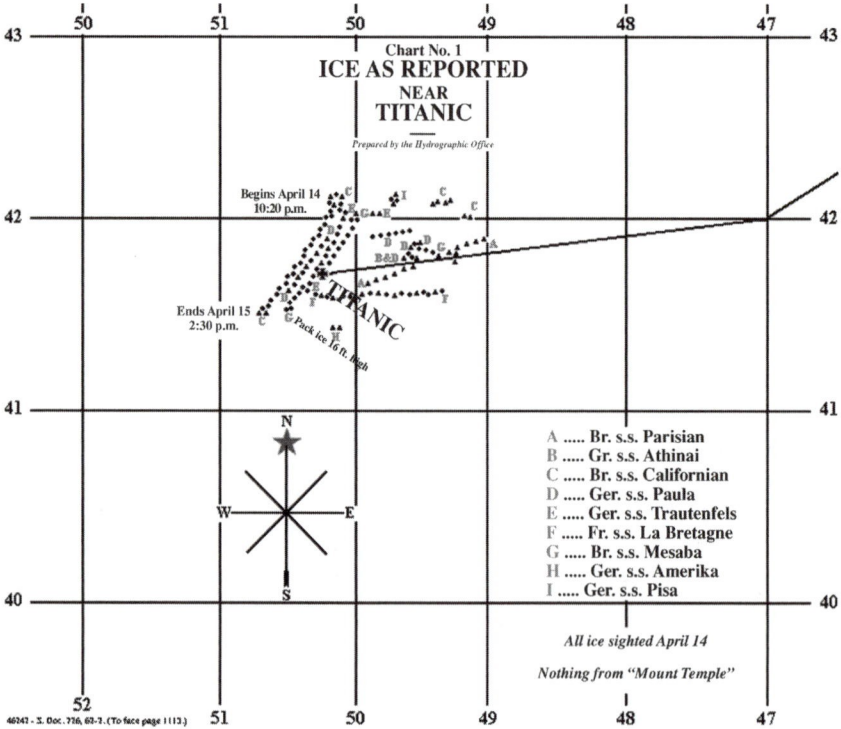

Figure 2.1
A map of reported ice sightings near *Titanic*—submitted as testimony to the U.S. inquiry by Captain John J. Knapp, a U.S. Navy hydrographer. (Source: http://www.titanicinquiry.org/images/charts/Chart1.gif)

Table 2.1

A Timeline of Ice Warnings Received by *Titanic* on Sunday, April 14, 1912

Time	Ship	Warning	Result
9:00 A.M.	*Caronia*	"Captain, *Titanic*, —Westbound steamers report bergs, growlers, and field ice in 42° N, from 4 9° to 51° W, April 12. Compliments, Barr."	Warning passed to Captain Smith, who posted it for officers to observe.
11:40 A.M.	*Noordam*	"Much ice" in same position as the *Caronia* earlier that morning (signaled to *Titanic*).	Message not received by any officer.
1:42 P.M.	*Baltic*	"Greek steamer *Athinai* reports passing icebergs and large quantities of field ice today in lat 41°51′ N, lon 49°51′ W. Last night we spoke German oiltanker steamer *Deutschland* ... not under control, short of coal, lat 40E42′ N Lon 55E11′ W. Wishes to be reported to New York and other steamers. Wish you and *Titanic* all success. Commander."	Message handed to Captain Smith, who showed it to Bruce Ismay. Ismay pocketed the message instead of giving it to the ship's officers. It was given to officers on the bridge hours later, at 7:15 P.M.
1:45 P.M.	*Amerika*	"*Amerika* passed two large icebergs in 41°27′ N, 50°8′ W on April 14." (A private message relayed through *Titanic*'s wireless to the U.S. Hydrographic office).	This message was not passed to the bridge or to commanding officers.
7:30 P.M.	*Californian*	"To Captain, *Antillian*: Six-thirty p.m .... latitude 42°3′ N, longitude 49°9′ W. Three large bergs, 5 miles to the southward of us. Regards, Lord." (message intercepted by *Titanic* from *Californian* to *Antillian*).	Message delivered by operator Bride to the bridge.
9:40 P.M.	*Mesaba*	"From *Mesaba* to *Titanic*. In latitude 42° N to 41° N25′, longitude 49° W to longitude 50°30′ W, saw much heavy pack ice and great number large icebergs, also field ice, weather good, clear."	Message was not delivered to the bridge.
10:55 P.M.	*Californian*	"Say, old man, we are stopped and surrounded by ice."	Message not relayed to the bridge.

Life on *Titanic* that Sunday, April 14, was fairly typical, as travelers and crew alike went about their day. The weather was relatively mild, allowing passengers to enjoy time on the open decks. The captain's inspection of the ship was conducted, with the officers and department heads checking the ship in its entirety. Normally, White Star Line ships also conducted a boat drill on Sundays after religious services were held, but for reasons left unclear, Captain Smith declined to hold them. Over the afternoon and into the evening, the outside air temperature steadily dropped and the ocean was eerily calm, set against a backdrop of a clear starry sky with no moon to be seen. It was an unusual setting for such a usual day.

The crew was engaging in their normal routines, rotating their watches and minding their checklists while Captain Smith enjoyed his dinner with guests. After "turning the corner," Chief Officer Wilde was relieved at 6 P.M. by Second Officer Lightoller and Sixth Officer Moody. Lightoller obtained an estimate of the ship's position and Fourth Officer Boxhall updated the plot. Upon learning of the ice warnings, Lightoller asked Moody to estimate when they would enter the region in which ice was reported. Moody calculated they would reach that area at approximately 11:00 P.M., but Lightoller figured that it would actually be closer to 9:30 P.M. After completing his dinner, and before turning in for the night, Captain Smith stopped by the bridge to speak with Lightoller, noting the weather conditions and the lack of wind, which created a "flat calm." With no moonlight, calm waters, and no wind, spotting icebergs would be inevitably more difficult, as waves breaking on the base of an iceberg created a visual cue alerting lookouts to its presence. Yet, the men felt comfortable enough that there would be at least some light reflected from the icebergs that would make them detectable. At 9:30 P.M., Captain Smith went to bed, advising Lightoller, "If it becomes at all doubtful, let me know at once. I shall be just inside." Lightoller instructed the lookouts to keep a sharp watch for icebergs.

At 10 P.M., Lightoller was relieved by First Officer Murdoch. After reviewing technical matters such as position and speed, the officers had some time together to talk during the change of shift. Lightoller later recalled their conversation:

> We both remarked on the ship's steadiness, absence of vibration, and how comfortably she was slipping along. Then we passed onto more serious subjects, such as the chances of sighting ice, reports of ice that had been sighted, and the positions. We also commented on the lack of definition between the horizon and the sky—which would make an iceberg all the more difficult to see—particularly if it had a black side, and that should be, by bad luck, turned our way.[4]

Black ice (also known as "blue ice") is caused when the underwater portion of an iceberg melts to the point where the exposed section becomes top heavy, causing the berg to turn over 180 degrees. The part of the newly overturned iceberg that has been underwater is very dark blue, nearly black, until it drains some of the water, at which point it returns to white. Set against the night sky, these black bergs are very difficult to see.

Earlier, during the 8 P.M. shift change, Quartermaster Hichens relieved Quartermaster Olliver at the helm, and (later at 10 P.M.) Frederick Fleet and Reginald Lee relieved the lookouts Archie Jewell and George Symons who passed on the instructions to keep a sharp watch for icebergs. The lookouts were stationed in the crow's nest, an open platform attached to the foremast 50 feet above the deck. At 11:35 P.M., Fleet and Lee saw a slight haze on the horizon, with Fleet remarking to Lee, "We'll be lucky if we can see through that."[5] For a few moments they tried to discern what they were looking toward. Fleet saw something approaching, reached up and rang the overhead bells three times, signaling an object ahead. He then picked up the telephone to the bridge and exclaimed into the receiver, "Iceberg right ahead!" The time was 11:40 P.M.—location 41.46N 50.14W.

DISASTER STRIKES

When Moody hung up the bridge phone, he immediately advised Murdoch of Fleet's alert. Taking control, Murdoch ordered "Hard-a-starboard!" to Hichens while simultaneously closing the watertight bulkheads. He also communicated with the engine room to stop and reverse the engines. Slowly, the bow of the boat turned to the left as the iceberg was coming up just on *Titanic*'s right (or starboard) side. One of the lookouts later described the berg as a "dark mass that came through that haze and there was no white appearing until it was just close alongside the ship, and that was just a fringe at the top."[6] As the bow of the ship neared the iceberg, Murdoch ordered Hichens to turn the wheel to the port side, in an effort to avoid a collision with *Titanic*'s stern. As the iceberg moved by the starboard side of the ship, it scraped the forward portion of the hull and chunks of ice from the berg were scattered on the decks, before the iceberg passed silently behind the ship into the darkness.

A number of different descriptions of the impact exist. Some people felt a vibration or a shudder that lasted a few seconds. Others felt a slight bump or jar. Still others noticed only a change in the engine activity. For many, if they felt anything at all, it did not seem cause for alarm. Many sleeping passengers did not even wake up.

Within a moment of the collision, Captain Smith arrived on the bridge and questioned Murdoch about what they had struck. Murdoch replied, "An iceberg, Sir. I hard-astarboarded and reversed the engines, and I was going to hard-a-port around it but she was too close. I could not do any more."[7] After going to the starboard rail in an effort to see the iceberg, the captain sent Boxhall to do a preliminary inspection of damage and see about the welfare of people in the area affected by the collision. Although an initial inspection showed no apparent damage, a short time later came reports from the ship's carpenter and mailroom workers, alerting the officers that the ship was very quickly taking on a great deal of water below deck.

Aside from the crew in the boiler room, who saw seawater pouring in immediately after the collision, it took some time for the officers, much of the crew, and the passengers to realize the extent of damage—and most never fully grasped the severity of the situation until the ship actually sank or they were far enough from the ship in lifeboats to see her tipping by her bow. Unbeknownst to crew and passengers, the first five watertight compartments were flooding. Eventually, as the weight of the water pulled the ship's head downward, the water would come up over the top of each watertight bulkhead, sequentially flooding the remaining compartments.

At 12:05 A.M., Jack Phillips—as per the captain's instructions—began sending out calls for assistance to other ships, indicating the most recent estimate of the ship's position. Phillips and Bride continued to work at their post, sending the CQD and SOS calls and receiving messages until minutes before *Titanic* sank. A number of ships, including *Frankfurt*, *Mount Temple*, and *Olympic*, received the messages. Some ships were too far away to provide assistance, but some accounts note that at least one ship might have been close enough to facilitate a quick rescue. Nonetheless, it was *Carpathia*, a Cunard liner, steaming east from New York toward ports in the Mediterranean that answered *Titanic*'s distress call and, being 58 miles away, took immediate action. Captain Arthur H. Rostron charted a course to *Titanic*'s coordinates, turned the ship around, and steamed full speed ahead to her aid. *Carpathia* would arrive at the scene in approximately four hours, sometime after 4:00 A.M.

EVACUATION

At 12:20 A.M., Captain Smith ordered Officer Wilde and others to uncover the lifeboats, and a short time later the loading process began. Once the boats were uncovered, they had to be attached to davits—or steel arms that swung out over the side of the ship, which allowed the boats to be lowered to the water. The noise of unused, escaping steam from the funnels was so loud that it was nearly impossible to hear any instructions whatsoever. Believing that they would be safer by remaining on *Titanic*, many passengers were reluctant to board the lifeboats—and, unfortunately, many of the lifeboats were lowered well below their full capacity. The crew kept order by attending to passengers and lifeboats on both the port and starboard sides of the ship and loading lifeboats with women and children first.

At 12:45 A.M., Boxhall shot off the first a series of eight distress rockets to signal any ships in the area about the trouble. In fact, as the ship was being evacuated, Lightoller and other officers noted the lights of a steamship off the port side of the ship, perhaps as close as five miles away. Boxhall attempted to signal the vessel with a Morse lamp. However, the mystery ship failed to respond and eventually its stern light was seen, indicating it was moving *away* from *Titanic*.

Over the course of the next hour, as the lifeboats were lowered and pushed off from the ship, awareness began gradually mounting that the ship was, in fact, sinking. The bow tipped lower as the ship developed a heavy list to the port side, and water could be seen in the stairwells rising rapidly. Many families were torn apart as wives said goodbye to their husbands, mothers tearfully parted with their sons, and children left their fathers—or in some cases both parents—behind. The likelihood, all understood, was that they might never see each other again. There were scenes of bravery and sacrifice, as some people relinquished their own seats in lifeboats for others, and women decided to remain onboard to await their fate with their husbands. There were also scenes of desperation and self-preservation, as some men tried to hide themselves in or leap into boats being loaded. A couple of men used shawls to disguise themselves as women. Some officers brandished or discharged firearms to keep crowds of increasingly desperate passengers under control.

At 2:05 A.M., all 14 wooden lifeboats, 2 emergency wooden cutters, and 2 of the 4 collapsible lifeboats were launched. Two of the collapsible boats remained unlaunched, but crew managed to get them untied such that, as waves began washing over the decks, the collapsible boats could float away. At about that time, Captain Smith advised the Marconi operators to abandon their post and save themselves, although Phillips desperately continued working for another 10 minutes. In *Titanic*'s fateful final minutes, the orchestra could be heard playing one final dirge and a priest heard confessions from a large group of people gathered around him.

People in the lifeboats watched helplessly as horrors unfolded before their eyes. The first of the four funnels toppled over, crushing people on deck before tumbling into the sea. As the ship's forward pitch became even more pronounced, the stern rose higher, pulling the huge propellers out of the water. Passengers on board attempted to scramble farther toward the stern (the back of the ship), holding onto whatever they could that might give them balance and a better chance of survival. The engineers, still working down in the bowels of the ship, managed to maintain sufficient power to keep the lights working until approximately 2:17 A.M., at which time the lights blinked, then went out. With no moon and in pitch-black darkness, those survivors on the lifeboats were forced to listen to the panic as the ship's machinery and much of its contents slid forward, crashing through the ship toward the bow. Hundreds of people began falling or jumping off the ship and into the frigid ocean. At approximately 2:20 A.M., nearly perpendicular out of the water, *Titanic* broke into two pieces, with the forward three-fourths sliding into the water. The stern section remained afloat for just several seconds before making its final dive into the depths—never to be seen again for nearly three-quarters of a century. The once-magnificent liner was gone.

Contrary to the fears of many in the lifeboats, there was no great suction that pulled people or boats down with it. But the anguish would continue as hundreds of souls floundered in the 28 °F water—screaming, moaning, and crying out for help. A few lucky passengers were plucked out of the water by those on lifeboats, or managed to climb onto one of the collapsible boats that acted as floats. Some of the people in boats wanted to return to rescue people struggling in the water; others feared that such an effort would lead to lifeboats being swamped, thereby increasing the loss of life. The desperation of the moment led to arguments, threats to throw survivors off lifeboats and into the frigid waters, and moments of tender humanity. Within 30 minutes, nearly all of the souls in the water perished either by drowning or by succumbing to hypothermia. Survivors prayed for a miracle that their loved ones in water would survive long enough to be rescued.

RESCUE

With the cries and moans having subsided, survivors were left in the deafening silence of the morning of April 15, 1912. Throughout the next two hours, passengers in the lifeboats sat in shock, coping as best they could with the events they had witnessed. Initially scattered for miles over the ocean, the boats were unable to see one another. Over time, however, some of the boats were able to join up and band together—trading passengers and crewmembers to even out the number of people per lifeboat and ensure that each boat had at least one able-bodied seaman onboard to help navigate, steer and row.

Shortly after 3:35 A.M., *Carpathia* arrived at the location given by *Titanic*. The coordinates given by Boxhall were off by several miles, and all

Carpathia's crew saw were a number of large icebergs—and no lifeboats. In the distance, Captain Rostron and his crew detected a green light low on the water, and headed toward it. Boxhall fired off some green flares, which assisted in further guiding *Carpathia* toward the survivors. Shortly thereafter, most of the people in the lifeboats could see that a steamer was making its way toward them. Given the ice field and large icebergs in the vicinity of where *Titanic* sank (and where the lifeboats were floating), *Carpathia* could not risk another tragedy. She would remain outside the ice field, requiring survivors to row to her location. All engines were stopped until daylight to better allow *Carpathia*'s crew to coordinate further rescue efforts safely (alleviating the risk of running into a lifeboat or ice in the dark).

At 4:10 A.M., and still in the dark, the first of the lifeboats reached *Carpathia*. As the dawn came, boat after boat came up alongside the ship and survivors climbed out onto a Jacob's ladder or were hoisted aboard. At 8:45 A.M., all of the lifeboats were accounted for and the last survivor, Lightoller, was brought onboard. By that time, *Mount Temple* and *Californian* had also arrived at the scene. With all lifeboats accounted for, both ships stayed in the area a bit longer to continue the search for survivors in the water while *Carpathia* headed for New York.

Through the use of wireless technology, news of the incident reached the media within hours of the collision. For various reasons, the messages sent and received were not always reliable, resulting in mass promulgation of false hopes. On Monday, April 15, a morning message received from the wireless offices at Cape Race, Newfoundland, indicated that "ALL TITANIC PASSENGERS SAFE, VIRGINIAN TOWING THE LINER TO HALIFAX." The vice president of White Star Line and manager of the International Mercantile Marine office in New York, Philip A. S. Franklin, sent word of this good news to many passengers' families. Another report in the afternoon indicated that all of *Titanic*'s passengers and crew were safe aboard *Carpathia*, and *Parisian* was towing *Titanic* back to New York. But the first accurate report of the massive loss of life came at 4:30 P.M. from the most powerful radio transmitter/receiver on the U.S. East Coast—the wireless station atop Wanamaker's Department Store in New York. It picked up a message from *Olympic* stating that *Titanic* had foundered at 12:47 A.M. New York time, and that 675 people— the only known survivors—were headed to New York aboard *Carpathia* and would arrive on the evening of Thursday, April 18. As shown in Table 2.2, there were 706 survivors in all, or 32 percent of the total number of people aboard—a percentage that is chillingly close to the 30 percent survival rates of first-generation family businesses transitioning to the second generation.

Table 2.2
Number and Classification of *Titanic*'s Survivors

Status	Number Aboard	Number of Dead (%)	Number of Survivors (%)
First-class passengers	329	130 (39.5%)	199 (60.5%)
Second-class passengers	285	166 (58.2%)	119 (41.8%)
Third-class passengers	710	536 (75.5%)	174 (24.5%)
Crew	899	685 (76.2%)	214 (23.8%)
Total	**2,223**	**1,517 (68.2%)**	**706 (31.8%)**

Source: U.S. Inquiry, Final Report.

CHAPTER SUMMARY

- Captain Edward John Smith, dubbed the "Millionaire's Captain," was chosen to take command of *Titanic*'s maiden voyage.
- *Titanic*'s senior officers consisted of Chief Officer William Murdoch, First Officer Charles Lightoller, and Second Officer David Blair. Her junior officers were Third Officer Herbert Pitman, Fourth Officer Joseph Boxhall, Fifth Officer Harold Lowe, and Sixth Officer James Moody. Only days after the crew was formed, Captain Smith appointed Henry Wilde to replace William Murdoch as Chief Officer, demoting Murdoch and Lightoller, and bumping David Blair from the ship altogether.
- *Titanic* left the shipyard in Belfast, Ireland, on April 2, 1912 after her sea trials. She steamed to Southampton to pick up passengers, leaving there on April 10 to make subsequent stops in Cherbourg, France, and Queenstown, Ireland. She left Queenstown to sail to New York City on April 11. Her passenger count, when sailing to New York, has been estimated at 1,316 to 1,324 passengers and an additional 899 crewmembers.
- Due to the abnormally warm winter of that year, icebergs had been reported farther south than normal in the Atlantic Ocean, right in the North Atlantic shipping lanes.
- *Titanic* received at least seven ice warnings from various ships in the vicinity. Only three warnings were sent to the bridge and delivered to Captain Smith or the ship's other officers.
- The weather conditions were extraordinary, with no moon and an extremely calm ocean that made spotting icebergs difficult.

- *Titanic* struck an iceberg at 11:40 P.M. on April 14. Lifeboats were uncovered and loaded at 12:20 A.M. The ship sank two hours later at 2:20 A.M. With too few lifeboats, only 706 passengers and crewmembers (32 percent of the people aboard) survived—a percentage remarkably similar to the percentage of family firms that survive from the first to the second generation.

PART II

●

The Five Fatal Flaws

In the weeks that followed *Titanic*'s sinking, U.S. Senator William Alden Smith lobbied U.S. President William Howard Taft to conduct an inquiry to determine why and how *Titanic* sank. Smith was motivated to uncover evidence of negligence on the part of J. P. Morgan and the International Mercantile Marine—*Titanic*'s owners.[1] As the magnitude of the disaster became clear, Smith's efforts paid off. The Committee on Commerce passed a resolution calling for a hearing and appointed Smith chairman of the subcommittee investigating the *Titanic* disaster. When the Navy intercepted messages sent by Bruce Ismay while aboard *Carpathia* indicating that he and *Titanic*'s crew planned to return to England on Friday, April 19 (the day after docking), Senator Smith and Francis Newlands (a member of the subcommittee) boarded *Carpathia* upon its arrival in New York and subpoenaed Ismay and various members of *Titanic*'s crew.

The first day of the inquiry was held on Friday, April 19, at the Waldorf-Astoria Hotel in New York City, with later sessions held in Washington, D.C. In all, 86 witnesses—ranging from passengers, to crewmembers from *Titanic* and other ships, to members of the press, to senior management representing the Marconi Wireless Company and the International Mercantile Marine—were called to give testimony over 18 days of hearings. In England, a formal British Wreck Commissioner's inquiry by the British Board of Trade was also commissioned. Many of the same witnesses, and members of the British Board of Trade itself, endured another two months of official hearings.

The facts gleaned from the hearings have allowed historians and other interested parties to develop an understanding of how and why this horrible event occurred. But as survivor Laurence Beesley described the senseless nature of the loss, he implored humankind to take a proactive approach to averting the perils of the world.

> Think of the shame of it, that a mass of ice of no use to anyone or anything should have the power to fatally injure the beautiful *Titanic*! That an insensible block should be able to threaten, even in the smallest degree, the lives of many good men and women who think and plan and hope and love— and not only to threaten, but to end their lives. It is unbearable! Are we never to educate ourselves to foresee such dangers and to prevent them before they happen?[2]

In this spirit of learning from the past to prevent tragedy in the future, Part II of this book presents an analysis of each of five flaws that, based on testimonial evidence and subsequent scrutiny, contributed to the catastrophe. Each flaw (overconfidence, ineffective leadership, lack of planning and preparation, frail architecture, and team fragmentation) is first evaluated with regard to how it was manifested in the case of *Titanic*. Then, using descriptive survey data,[3] scholarly articles, and case examples, we describe how each flaw surfaces in family firms.

3

Overconfidence

Pride goes before destruction and a haughty spirit before a fall.
—Proverbs 16: 18.

Confidence has been defined as assurance; freedom from doubt; a belief in yourself and your abilities; a feeling of trust in someone or something; and a state of hopefulness that events will be favorable.[1] Confidence is helpful for success in business and other life pursuits. Self-efficacy—or a person's belief in his or her ability to succeed in a particular situation—is a related concept that has been widely studied and linked to improved functioning in health, education, athletics, and organizations.[2] Simply put, having a strong belief in one's ability to achieve a goal facilitates the realization of that goal.

Confidence is also an attractive quality in others, especially in leaders. Successful leaders often project a sense of optimism to engender a feeling of security and confidence among their followers, including employees, customers, and investors. However, there can be a fine line between confidence and overconfidence.

Overconfidence is the first fatal flaw that led to *Titanic*'s demise and its associated horrific loss of life, and it can lead to serious trouble for family firms as well. In this chapter, aspects of overconfidence—including over-optimism, narcissism, and entitlement—are explored relative to family firms. But beginning with *Titanic*, overconfidence was manifested in a number of ways: in the press and in the public relations strategies set forth by White Star Line; in the attitudes, beliefs, statements, and actions of leaders Captain Smith and Bruce Ismay; and among White Star Line's employees and *Titanic*'s passengers.

OVERCONFIDENCE: *TITANIC*

Captain Smith had strong faith in the safety of shipping and in his own safety record and abilities. Five years before *Titanic*'s maiden voyage, Smith granted an interview to a newspaper reporter after arriving in New York on *Adriatic*'s maiden voyage, making statements that would later prove to be sadly ironic:

> When anyone asks me how I can best describe my experience of nearly forty years at sea, I merely say, uneventful. Of course there have been winter gales, and storms and fog and the like, but in all my experience I have never been in any accident of any sort worth speaking about. I have seen but one vessel in distress in all my years at sea . . . I never saw a wreck and never have been wrecked, nor was I ever in any predicament that threatened to end in disaster of any sort.[3]

Perhaps Smith was alluding to that fact that his long seafaring career showed no incidents that resulted in human casualties; yet, his performance record was by no means free from blemishes. He had been captain of three ships that ran aground and two ships that had serious fires aboard, and he was in command when *Olympic* collided with *Hawke*, a British warship.[4] In observing Smith's manner of maneuvering a ship, Second Officer Charles Lightoller wrote, "[I]t was an education to see him con his own ship up through the intricate channels entering New York at full speed. One particularly bad corner, known as the South-West Spit, used to make us fairly flush with pride as he swung her around, judging his distances to a nicety; she heeling over to the helm with only a matter of feet to spare between each end of the ship and the banks."[5] What might appear as confident behavior to some people may appear as cocky or even reckless to others. While he was skillful in handling ships much of the time, Smith was not impervious to error, faulty judgment, or miscalculation.

Described by some as the "Storm King" owing to his propensity in pushing ships to their limits through all sorts of weather conditions,[6] Smith believed that the advances in technology within the shipbuilding industry virtually eliminated the possibility of any major catastrophe at sea. When asked about the safety of the ships he sailed, Smith responded, "I cannot imagine any condition which could cause a ship to founder. I cannot conceive of any vital disaster happening to this vessel. Modern shipbuilding has gone beyond that."[7] In fact, loss of life at sea due to shipping accidents had been extremely rare over the previous three decades at the time Smith made those remarks. Prior to the *Titanic* disaster, the worst nonmilitary maritime disaster was the sinking of the ship *Atlantic* off the coast of Halifax, Nova Scotia, in 1873, in which 546 people perished;

since then, only 4 people had died in transatlantic crossings.[8] It seems the relative absence of serious problems within his own realm of experience lulled the captain into a false sense of security, leading him to minimize risks in his own mind. Indeed, Senator Smith, who led the U.S. inquiry into the *Titanic* disaster, said with regard to Captain Smith, "Overconfidence seems to have dulled the faculties usually so alert."[9]

The primary way in which overconfidence played out with regard to *Titanic* was the belief that the ship was unsinkable. This myth originated in writings about *Titanic* and *Olympic* before *Titanic* was even completed. It began with an article published in 1911 about the Olympic-class liners in *The Shipbuilder*, a periodical that described in great detail the building, launch, and outfitting of the latest ships. The article highlighted the use of the multiple watertight bulkheads and compartments, stating that their presence made these ships "practically unsinkable."[10] This sentiment was echoed in marketing materials distributed by White Star Line that stated, "As far as it is possible to do so, these two wonderful vessels are designed to be unsinkable." Even though many accounts suggest the unsinkability myth originated *after* the ship sank, the evidence indicates that many people believed no level of serious damage could sink *Titanic*-and this belief resulted in decisions that were critically related to the tragedy.

First, overconfidence may have affected the treatment of the ice warnings, minimizing the crew's perception of the danger they foretold. Not all of the ice warnings that the captain received were shared with the officers, and certainly not in a way that signaled any sense of urgency about them. The best example was the warning received at 1:42 P.M. from *Baltic*. For some unknown reason, Smith nonchalantly and without saying a word handed this message to Ismay, who read it and—"in a fit of absent-mindedness"[11]—put it in his pocket. At supper, Ismay took the note out of his pocket and read it to two female passengers with whom he was dining. Finally, more than five hours after having received the message, Smith asked Ismay to return the message so that he could bring it to the chart room where other officers might view it. It is striking that neither Smith nor Ismay appeared particularly concerned about the warning. While both were aware the ship was headed into a region where ice was reported, their reactions appeared to be dismissive of the threat.

Of critical significance was Captain Smith's decision to operate the ship at nearly maximum speed that evening as the ship moved through the area where ice had been reported. A popular myth about *Titanic* is that the ship's captain and owners were trying to break a speed record. While this supposition does not appear to have been the case, making a speedy crossing was something ship captains and shipping company managers strived for. With such esteemed passengers and business owners aboard *Titanic*, arriving behind schedule could be disastrous to White Star Line's reputation and probability of future patronage. The importance of staying on schedule created a pressure to arrive at or ahead of the appointed time, independent of weather conditions. Ismay later testified that he saw nothing wrong with the captain's decision.

Attorney-General:	What is the object of continuing at full speed through the night if you expect to meet ice? Why do you do it? . . .
Ismay:	I presume the man would be anxious to get through the ice region. He would not want to slow down upon the chance of a fog coming on . . .
Attorney General:	It seems to have been rather in accordance with your view, that the faster you could get out of the region the better?
Ismay:	Assuming the weather was perfectly fine, I should say the Captain was perfectly justified in going full speed . . . I do not see any reason why he should not, so long as he could see sufficiently far to clear the ice.[12]

The fact of the matter remains: had the ship been traveling at a slower rate of speed, the crew would have had more time to react to the iceberg once it was seen. Indeed, the British inquiry into the disaster cited "the excessive speed at which the ship was being navigated" as contributing to the loss of *Titanic*.[13]

Another crucial misjudgment made by Captain Smith was his assessment that the lookouts would be able to spot an iceberg in the unusual environmental conditions that prevailed that night. Even with no moonlight, no waves, and exceedingly cold temperatures, Smith and Lightoller agreed that the outline of an iceberg would be visible to the naked eye. They did not appreciating the handicap that these conditions imposed on the lookouts. In fact, with no moonlight, icebergs were difficult to spot. Moreover, with a calm sea, a trained lookout would not have the visual cue of waves breaking on the ice. Had they considered these challenging circumstances as serious risks, they might have doubled the lookouts or placed additional lookouts at the bow of the ship, as was customary in cases of poor visibility.

One of the most unfortunate consequences of overconfidence in the unsinkability of the Olympic-class liners was the decision to carry fewer lifeboats than the ship was designed to hold. Bruce Ismay was ultimately responsible for making this decision. At a conference in 1910, Ismay met with senior personnel at Harland and Wolff to finalize the design details for the three new Olympic-class ships. Designer Alexander Carlisle later recalled that decorations were discussed for 4 or 5 hours, while lifeboats were discussed for 5 or 10 minutes. When presented with a plan to equip the Olympic-class ships with up to 48 lifeboats each (carrying a capacity of 2,886 people), Ismay rejected this idea, stating that the lower number of boats required by the British Board of Trade would be sufficient. This unfortunate decision was a topic of keen interest, closely scrutinized by examiners at the British Board of Trade investigation. When questioned by W. D. Harbinson (a member of the Mersey Commission assembled by the British Board of Trade, who represented the interests of all third-class passengers aboard *Titanic*), Ismay offered the following assessment:

Mr. Harbinson: Did you give any special consideration to the question of providing additional lifeboat accommodation to cope with the additional number of passengers that you proposed to carry?

Ismay: I do not think any special attention was given to that.

Mr. Harbinson: Would not that have been a consideration that should have specially engaged you?

Ismay: I think the position was taken up that the ship was looked upon as practically unsinkable; she was looked upon as being a lifeboat in herself.[14]

The decision to equip *Titanic* with fewer lifeboats was also due to cost considerations. Coal was an extremely volatile expense, and the cost-saving measure was not lost on Charles Lightoller:

> [*Titanic*'s engineers] had all loyally stuck to their guns, long after they could be of any material assistance. Much earlier on, the engine-room telegraphs had been "rung off"—the last ring made on board ships at sea, and which conveys to the engine-room staff the final information that their services below can be of no further use, that the case (from whatever case) is hopeless. At the same time, it releases engineers and stokers from duty, leaving them free to make the best of their way up to the boats. Of course, in theory each had his appointed place in a given boat... But before that tragedy brought home to the world the utter fallacy of the "unsinkable ship" I'm afraid that many "appointed places"—as far as lifesaving equipment was concerned—were just so much theory, concocted ashore with a keen eye to dividends.[15]

Ismay acknowledged that lifeboats were not thought of as necessary, except for aiding other ships or going ashore. In hindsight, this was a grave mistake, largely attributable to his overconfidence in the ship's capacity to float following an accident. While financial considerations were likely a more prominent factor behind the decision not to have more lifeboats, the rationalization that lifeboats were not really needed for passenger safety must have made this cost-saving measure seem justifiable. However, even though the ship was thought to be unsinkable, she was not necessarily thought to be fireproof. Given that a coal fire in bunker number 6 had been smoldering for nearly two weeks since the sea trial (and was fully extinguished only on Saturday, the day before *Titanic* struck the iceberg), a fire reaching the passenger decks was not entirely out of the realm of possibility. In fact, Lightoller offered the following analysis: "Touching on fire, the modern ship's equipment is such that it is almost impossible, with fair play, for a fire to get a serious hold. I say this, despite the fact that quite recently no less than three modern liners have been burned out."[16]

The attitudes of the leaders in many organizations often trickle down and are adopted by other members of the organization. White Star Line was no different, as a number of employees made statements that demonstrated their belief that *Titanic* was unsinkable. A second-class purser's clerk said to Mrs. Ruth Becker, "You don't have to be afraid at all. If anything should happen to this ship the watertight compartments would keep it afloat until we get help."[17] As Mrs. Albert Caldwell was boarding, she asked a deck hand, "Is this ship really non-sinkable?" He replied, "Yes, lady, God himself could not sink this ship."[18] As word was reaching New York City about *Titanic*'s accident (and rumors were swirling about its sinking), White Star Line's Vice President, Phillip A. S. Franklin, issued the following public statement: "We place absolute confidence in the *Titanic*. We believe the boat is unsinkable."[19]

Not surprisingly, the press and advertising about the safety of the Olympic-class liners (as well as the beliefs promulgated by leadership and employees) took hold in the minds of the passengers. Perhaps the idea that *Titanic* was unsinkable gave some passengers a temporary and false sense of comfort. Survivor Lawrence Beesley described this experience, just hours before *Titanic* sank, at the second-class dining saloon evening hymn sing-along (which was conducted by Reverend Carter):

> Mr. Carter brought the evening to a close by a few words of thanks to the purser for the use of the saloon, a short sketch of the happiness and safety of the voyage hitherto, the great confidence all felt on board this great liner with her steadiness and her size, and the happy outlook of landing in a few hours in New York at the close of a delightful voyage; and all the time he spoke, a few miles ahead of us lay the "peril on the sea" that was to sink this same great liner with many of those on board who listened with gratitude to his simple, heartfelt words. So much for the frailty of human hopes and for the confidence imposed in material human designs.[20]

The idea of feeling safe and confident sounds innocuous enough, but it appears that passenger and crew overconfidence in *Titanic* may have discouraged some of these individuals from entering the lifeboats. When the order was issued for women and children to enter the lifeboats, some passengers refused, while passengers (and even crewmembers) ridiculed or made fun of the idea. John Jacob Astor stated, "We are safer here than in that little boat," and as Mrs. J. Stuart White entered Lifeboat 8, a friend chided her, "When you get back you'll need a pass. You can't get back on tomorrow morning without a pass!"[21] It seems that for some, confidence in *Titanic*'s unsinkability prevented them from taking potentially life-saving actions.

OVERCONFIDENCE IN FAMILY BUSINESS

In family firms, overconfidence is driven by three prominent factors: (1) over-optimism about business performance and prospects, (2) underestimation of or failure to appreciate risks, and (3) narcissism and entitlement.

Surveys show that family business leaders across the United States are confident and optimistic. In one national survey, more than 70 percent of family business owners reported that they expected increases in revenues over the next year and were very optimistic about the company's prospects.[22] More than one-third of the respondents expected the number of full-time employees to increase. In a survey of regional family businesses, slightly more than half of the respondents were optimistic about the firm's profitability over the next 12 months, with 48 percent expecting increases in net profits and 30 percent predicting the addition of more jobs over the next year.[23] In hindsight, these optimistic beliefs were misguided, as a major global financial crisis was unfolding at the time the latter regional survey was undertaken in 2008. Many of these hopeful business owners would soon learn that their projections were wrong, as very few could have predicted the full effect that the economic crisis would have. Nearly half a million U.S. businesses closed in the first half of 2009 alone, resulting in 1.6 million jobs lost.[24]

Over-optimism has been recognized by scholars and management consulting practitioners as a red flag signaling the potential for family business failure. Some leaders of companies that experience a decline in their profit margins and reduction in working capital focus on sales as a solution, believing: "We can sell our way out like we have in the past."[25] Other executives who experience "delusions of success" may have difficulty making accurate estimates for return on investment when taking on new projects.

> When forecasting the outcomes of projects, executives fall victim to what psychologists call the planning fallacy. In its grip, managers make decisions based on delusional optimism rather than on a rational weighting of gains, losses, and probabilities. They overestimate the benefits and underestimate

the costs. They spin scenarios of success while overlooking the potential for mistakes and miscalculations. As a result, managers pursue initiatives that are unlikely to come in on budget or on time—or to ever deliver the expected returns.[26]

Corporate leaders prone to over-optimism can lead their companies towards ruin in a number of ways: (1) by moving into poorly considered ventures; (2) by setting expectations so high that employees are either forced to avoid them by leaving the company or achieve them by resorting to fraudulent means (e.g., misrepresenting financial figures); or (3) by stifling the communication of bad news from subordinates or advisors.[27] Indeed, there are many examples of business leaders who eschew bad news or neglect to listen to others who raise concerns. As one family business owner remarked, "I really don't like dealing with our accountant because he's so negative—always trying to get us afraid of something."

Lovallo and Kahneman suggest that the cognitive biases and organizational pressures that lead to unrealistic optimism can be offset by using a more objective method of forecasting that takes an "outside view" of the likely outcomes:

> This outside view, also known as reference-class forecasting, completely ignores the details of the project at hand; instead it encourages managers to examine the experiences of a class of similar projects, to lay out a rough distribution of outcomes for this reference class, and then to position the current project in that distribution. The outside view is more likely than the inside view to produce accurate forecasts—and much less likely to deliver highly unrealistic ones.[28]

In summary, optimism can be a tremendous tool for family business leaders, but only when proper analyses of "best case/worst case/most likely" scenarios have been conducted and safety is accounted for—thereby ensuring both the safety of firm operations and the safety of key stakeholders' vested interests (e.g., employees' jobs, family well-being). More than just a catch phrase, maintaining safety standards and providing a safe work environment must be preeminent in the minds of all involved, with appropriate procedures and processes implemented to assure that security.

UNDERESTIMATION OF RISK

A second driver for overconfidence is the underestimation of risk. Failure to consider risks is manifested in a number of ways, but particularly through minimization of risks and all-out denial. A type of psychological defense against dealing with unpleasant, anxiety-provoking, or otherwise upsetting information, denial serves to dismiss these undesirable stimuli outright by refusing to consider them in the first place. Closely related to denial is minimization of risks, wherein unpleasant facts are not dismissed entirely, but their impact is deemphasized or downplayed. While both of these defenses can protect people from feeling discomfort, in certain contexts they can be harmful or deadly. For instance, use of denial to cope with fears about health problems can lead people to avoid seeking routine or even emergency medical care. In fact, denial is considered a classic symptom among heart attack victims, who may tell themselves things like "It is just indigestion and will probably go away with an antacid and a bit of rest"—and who frequently do not survive to know just how wrong they were. As explained in Box 3.1, denial can surface when family members demonstrate excessive dependency on the founder or the business.

Box 3.1
Denial, Dependency, and Disaster

Barry Graff, PhD—Family/Business Systems

Denial is a frequently used mechanism to deal with difficult emotions. It can be quite destructive, as when family members ignore clear signs of drug or alcohol addiction. It can also be seen as "normal," as a means for avoiding what seems like unnecessary conflict. Denial can be constructive when it comes to putting aside painful truths: we do not ponder the inevitability of our death every hour of every day.

When we relate to leaders or evaluate their leadership behaviors, it is easy to pretend—and perhaps to overvalue their strengths or ignore their shortcomings. This is true with a national leader, a ship's captain, or the founder/parent in a family business. Unfortunately, when such denial is excessive, it can lead to the sinking of a ship, the failure of a business, or the disintegration of a family. One factor that supports this excessive denial is dependency.

Businesses and families work best when they function interdependently, rather than when some members rigidly uphold the hierarchy by maintaining a child-like and dependent position. For example, in one family business, even though the father had been diagnosed with early-onset Alzheimer's disease by the Mayo Clinic, some family members kept insisting that he was fine. While those family members were not working in the business, they were dependent on it for their income. The sense of entitlement often seen in the second and third generations of wealthy families is another aspect of this dependency. "I am entitled to wealth and material goods" may mean "I am afraid to be independently responsible for my own life."

We are appropriately dependent on a ship's captain, the owner or CEO of the business, or our parents. In contrast, dependency can lead to disastrous results when it:

- Is excessive.
- Springs from unmet emotional needs rather than appropriate role proscriptions.

- Leads us to deny or not trust our perceptions.
- Allows us to abdicate individual responsibility.

Every person on a ship carries some responsibility. Who would wait for a crew-member or the captain to arrive instead of quickly yelling, "Person overboard"? One wonders whether any passengers on *Titanic* noticed the shortage of lifeboats, yet ignored their own survival instincts and said nothing.

Denial is also frequently seen among people (and families) who harbor extremely high levels of shame. In families where there has been a violation of sexual boundaries—such as incest, sexual abuse, or marital infidelity—denial of these events preserves an appearance of normalcy and allows everyone to carry on with "business as usual." Denial and minimization are also quite common among people with alcoholism and other addictions, allowing them to maintain their destructive behavior patterns, while family members often collude with and enable the addicted individual by overlooking or denying the addiction.

It is particularly difficult for business-owning families to deal with painful or even seemingly shameful family secrets, because family members may fear that the secret's revelation will be explosive, destroying both family and business. Thus, among business-owning families with a shame-invoking family secret, denial and minimization may be well-worn strategies to avoid dealing with painful family issues as well as any other problems related to the functioning or future of the business. Regardless of the "merit" of the shame (which is a personal perception), shame-invoking secrets fall along a continuum of minimally shameful to extremely shameful, with common examples relating to a family member's personal competencies and capabilities, learning challenges, criminal history, addictions, personal financial problems, marital challenges, sexual orientation or gender identity status, behavioral issues, and even past business transgressions.

An even more common cause of denial and minimization in family firms is death. Denial is a relatively common way for people deal with issues pertaining to death—but in the case of family business, where proper estate and succession planning is essential for business survival, being in denial about the eventual certainties of death and taxes is perilous. In fact, in one study 30.5 percent of family business owners reported that they would never retire.[29] In addition, when business owners were asked why they had not designated a successor, the most popular responses related to the current leadership's perception that they were "too young" to consider succession (46 percent), even though 35 percent of the respondents were aged 56 to 65.[30] With 74 percent of family business CEOs unsure of whether or how a well-defined succession plan contributes to business success, these responses suggest that some family business owners may underestimate the impact that an absent succession plan and unforeseen death may have on the business.[31]

Indeed, family business incumbent leaders may display the "It won't happen to me" mentality with regard to a number of issues, oftentimes appearing flippant and aloof. "I'm healthy; I'm not going anywhere" ... "We've got great products and services; we don't need to change" ... "Our customers are loyal and will stay with us" ... "A handshake is all it takes" ... "My kids have their differences, but they'll work it out in the end." These words may provide reassurance in the short term and delay anxiety, but they all speak to underlying risks that, if left unchecked, could lead to complex problems, and ultimately severe financial strain.

Consider the story of the Japanese firm Kongo Gumi—the oldest continuously operating family business in the world. Founded in 578, Kongo Gumi operated in what had formerly been considered one of the least volatile industries in the world: construction of Buddhist temples. With millions of followers and an ancient belief system, the company had been around for so long and had been so successful that it was considered somewhat untouchable and infallible. Yet, when the family became victims of the real estate bubble of the early 1990s, coupled with a decline in donations, even Kongo Gumi became a casualty in 2006 of excessive debt and a difficult economic climate.[32]

The risks that both large and small family-owned firms take start out small and grow exponentially—and no efforts at minimizing or discounting these risks ever worked when seeking long-term prosperity. Some risky activities associated with believing the worst will not happen include the following:

- Events that trigger a need for shareholder liquidity, including death, disability, divorce, embezzlement, misconduct, negligence, or illegal behavior that could result in a lawsuit against the family or the company
- Relying on past success, key relationships or accounts, and family reputation
- Neglecting to develop "bench strength" or possible talent replacement
- Failing to adapt, change strategy, or innovate
- Declining to deal with interpersonal or intergroup conflicts

Family business leaders may not recognize these issues as risks and, therefore, may not address them at all; or they may see them as low-probability or low-impact issues and, therefore, may not respond to them with any sense of urgency. In fact, while 70 percent of family firms cite a belief that innovation is important to the future success of the family firm:

- Most firms do not have an active board of external advisors[33] with members who can help bring about new ideas for products, services, and processes.
  - Forty-two percent note that "lack of outside influence" is a challenge in running a family business.[34]
  - Fifty-two percent offer that the need to innovate is a challenge in running a family business.
- Only 29.8 percent believe they have taken full advantage of advances in information technology.[35]

NARCISSISM AND ENTITLEMENT

A third driver for overconfidence within family firms is a constellation of behaviors and personality traits related to narcissism. Narcissism exists on a continuum, with healthy narcissism on one end and pathological, destructive narcissism on the other end. Healthy narcissism can be thought of as a love for oneself that undergirds healthy self-interest, self-esteem, self-respect, and self-preservation—all of which are important for adaptive functioning and are normal aspects of human development. On the other end of the spectrum is destructive narcissism, found among people with narcissistic personality disorder. It is characterized by: arrogance or haughtiness; a grandiose sense of self-importance; a strong sense of entitlement; a lack of empathy for others; a preoccupation with fantasies of unlimited beauty, brilliance, success or power; feeling extremely special and unique; needing excessive admiration from others; and being interpersonally exploitative.[36] Paradoxically, this kind of narcissism is believed to act as a protective shell—guarding the narcissist from feeling a deep-seated (and mainly unconscious) sense of shame, inadequacy, emptiness, insecurity, and poor self-regard.

Interestingly, narcissism is common among people who rise to leadership positions—with their need for achievement or importance being a particularly powerful driving force. For the organizations they govern, narcissistic leaders bring some very positive qualities to the table. They pursue goals aggressively, drive toward innovation, and are highly competitive. In addition, they have a strong vision, are charismatic orators, and can easily attract followers.[37] They make bold decisions and major organizational changes. More "constructive" narcissists can do all of these things in a way that allows them to maintain flexibility, listen to others, energize subordinates around a common cause, and retain a sense of humor.[38]

In contrast, more extreme narcissists bring the dark sides of this personality quality to the surface. They are very thin-skinned, are sensitive to perceived disrespect and criticism, and, therefore, prefer to keep others at a distance. Under stress, they can become highly suspicious of others, including people close to them. Instead of assembling teams that will challenge ideas and think "outside the box," they surround themselves with "yes-men" and people who agree with them. They can be very difficult to work with. Because they prefer to stay with their own vision, they often do not listen to the advice or ideas of others. They need to feel in control of everything and, as a consequence, can end up micromanaging team members. Their lack of empathy can be hurtful to those working closely with them, as they can be insensitive, dismissive, and abrasive. Not surprisingly, narcissists have little interest in mentoring—either providing it or receiving it. Instead, they may devote more time to polishing their public image.

Narcissistic CEOs are more likely to develop grandiose strategic initiatives leading to broad swings in organizational performance.[39] In doing so, they may fall prey to overestimating their own or their company's capabilities, increasing the odds of a disaster.

> As he becomes increasingly self-assured, the narcissist becomes more spontaneous. He feels free of constraints. Ideas flow. He thinks he's invincible. The energy and confidence further inspire his followers. But the very adulation that the narcissist demands can have a corrosive effect. As he expands, he listens even less to words of caution and advice. After all, he has been right before, when others have had their doubts. Rather than persuade those who disagree with him, he feels justified in ignoring them—creating further isolation. The result is sometimes flagrant risk-taking that can lead to catastrophe.[40]

Further, narcissists may be slow to recognize when an initiative is failing, and they may adhere to a misguided course because they are reluctant to acknowledge their own mistakes. When failures occur, they are unlikely to accept personal responsibility, instead choosing to blame others or forces beyond their control.

A classic example of the hugely successful, but highly narcissistic entrepreneur was the founder of the iconic Ford Motor Company, Henry Ford. His story is cited as a model of the dangerous effect of hubris in family businesses in Grant Gordon and Nigel Nicholson's book, *Family Wars*. Ford was passionate about engineering and worked tirelessly on his inventions. He was described as a "mad genius" with an obsessive personality, who insisted on taking full credit for his company's success without acknowledging anyone else's contributions. When his only son Edsel— the heir apparent—joined the firm, Henry never gave him the opportunity to have any real power. Always just "the boss's son," Edsel tried to carve out a niche for himself in the company, but was perpetually dominated by his father. Ultimately, Edsel died an untimely death at age 49 from cancer, with alcohol abuse contributing to his poor health. Meanwhile, Henry's stubborn persistence—an asset in starting the company—became a liability as new strategies were needed. Deaf to advice that certain business practices were outdated and a new direction was needed, Ford's intransigence stymied the firm's performance. Only when his daughter-in-law, Edsel's widow, presented him with an ultimatum (turn over control of the business to his grandson Henry II, or she would sell her 40 percent of the company stock inherited from Edsel's estate) did Henry Ford step down from his post as company leader. He died two years later.[41]

Another more current and particularly infamous example of narcissism taken to a dangerous extreme involves the former NASDAQ chairman and financier, Bernard Madoff. His sociopathic and destructive narcissism brought down his family business and wrought havoc on scores of individuals, families, organizations, and communities, as described in Box 3.2.

Box 3.2
The Case of Bernard Madoff

For someone with the dubious distinction of running the largest Ponzi scheme in history, Bernard Madoff's beginnings were rather ordinary. He founded his Wall Street firm—Bernard L. Madoff Investment Securities LLC—with $5,000 he earned working as a lifeguard and sprinkler installer and a $50,000 loan from his father-in-law. His father-in-law also helped the business grow by referring his circle of friends and their families to Bernard. Over time, Bernard had a number of family members working in the business, including his younger brother Peter, his niece Shana, his sons Mark and Andrew, and his nephew Charles.

On a personal level, Madoff was said to be superficially charismatic and affable, ambitious and driven, obsessed with order and control, fastidious about his personal and corporate image, distant, standoffish, aloof, interpersonally exploitative and manipulative, and very intelligent. His investment business turned fraudulent, possibly as early as the 1980s. Although his funds were said to be a low-risk investment that delivered steady returns, new investor funds were not used to purchase securities, but rather to pay off investors who were cashing out. In December 2008, when his clients requested redemptions amounting to $7 billion, Madoff was cornered. He reportedly told his sons that the investment and advisory business was "just one big lie."

Regulators had failed to detect Madoff's long-term fraud despite the presence of numerous "red flags" and attempted warnings (over a 10-year period!) from financial analyst Harry Markopolos, who believed it was mathematically impossible to achieve the financial results Madoff purported to produce. Part of the reason for regulators' refusal to uncover the fraud was that Madoff had made a point of developing friendly personal and professional connections with regulators, who came to see him as one of the "good guys" on Wall Street. In addition, there were six "botched" investigations of Madoff's firm since 1992, wherein regulators failed to ask the right questions or request the proper information.

In the end, the scam resulted in investor losses of $18 billion, which included the endowments of many charitable organizations and many people's life savings. Madoff pled guilty to 11 federal crimes and was given the maximum sentence of 150 years in prison. As of January 2011, many of his family members were still under investigation or facing lawsuits for tax fraud, negligence, and breach of fiduciary duty. His legacy of destruction was darkened further on December 11, 2010—two years after Bernard Madoff was arrested—when his 46-year-old son Mark took his own life.

Sources: Creswell and Thomas, "The Talented Mr. Madoff"; Gandel, "Wall Street's Latest Downfall"; http://en.wikipedia.org/wiki/Bernard_Madoff

As business systems often come to resemble their leaders (91 percent of family firms exhibit values shared by the business-owning family),[42] both families and businesses may be shaped culturally by narcissistic leadership. Several factors may promote the development of a narcissistic culture within organizations:[43]

- Leaders who model, tolerate, or reward narcissistic behavior. This trait may be exhibited in family firms in the form of tolerating poor behavior from successors that would not otherwise be acceptable in other organizations or would not be tolerated if demonstrated by nonfamily employees.
- Valuing and rewarding individual "star" performers over teams. This characteristic may be exhibited in family firms through the perpetuation of nepotism and giving family members preferred perquisites.
- Focusing on short-term profits while discounting how those profits were achieved or how people treat others around them. In family firms, this trait can be exhibited by demanding family members be "on call" or making family feel guilty when not giving around-the-clock dedication to the family business.

In *Beyond the Looking Glass*, Alan Downs described how a few powerful narcissists who control the agenda create narcissistic organizations. They do so by diluting or obliterating more inspiring corporate missions and replacing them with monetary success as the sole value; rewarding greed by paying disproportionately high executive salaries; creating a "totalitarian" organizational structure that focuses more on individual personalities rather than work functions or products; by resisting changes that threaten the leader's powerbase; seeking dependent, nonthreatening subordinates; and becoming a closed system over time that is less responsive to external inputs (e.g., from markets or customer needs).[44] Given these tendencies, narcissistic organizations are at risk for disasters and failure. In his book *Narcissistic Process and Corporate Decay*, Howard Schwartz describes how narcissistic organizations lose touch with reality, leading to poor performance and tragic accidents.[45]

Within family systems, children of narcissistic parents often end up developing narcissistic traits themselves, thereby perpetuating the cycle.[46] When family businesses begin to develop a culture of superiority and entitlement, it can spell trouble for the company's future. Ivan Lansberg describes the connections between narcissism in the company founder, its impact on the culture of the family enterprise, and increased likelihood of business failure:

> The danger is that once the narcissism of a founder becomes ingrained in the family's culture, the family's capacity to sustain the enterprise is often diminished. Narcissistic families often close themselves down to learning. They develop a sense of entitlement, a feeling that they alone know better, a belief that their situation is too complex for anyone else to understand. In doing so, they foster complaisance, and a "we've always done it this way" attitude that ultimately hinders their adaptability. Many of these families go out of business because of their refusal to abandon obsolete products and practices, to accept new ideas, or to change strategy.[47]

Indeed, entitlement can manifest itself in the culture of a family business in a number of ways. In the senior generation, founders or incumbents may feel entitled to do as they please: "It's *my* business; I can do what I want." Senior leaders may feel entitled to retain control and authority as long as they want, often at the expense of preparing the next generation for leadership or allowing them to lead (ultimately at the expense of the business itself and its employees). This attitude can cause conflicts among other stakeholders who disagree with the direction of the founder's leadership. In one business, the son-in-law—a key manager—staunchly opposed the strategic direction that the founder was taking, but felt that talking to him about the issue was ultimately useless because "in the end, he's just going to do what he wants anyhow."

In another business, a group of siblings were in charge of their own separate divisions when their father was alive. Upon his death, the various business entities were owned jointly by the four siblings, but they did not see eye-to-eye with regard to how the different businesses were being run. Each maintained the attitude that—in the area each managed—they did not need to answer to anyone.

One family business owner used the business as his personal bank, taking cash out to fund other side-business dealings and pay off debts without informing his other sibling owners. In fact, family corporations are more likely to intermingle business and family finances in the direction of financial resources flowing *from* the business *to* the family than sole proprietorships (which are more likely to intermingle business and family finances in the direction of family finances flowing *into* the business).[48]

Still other senior-generation members appear more focused on preserving their own lifestyles (e.g., expensive homes, boats, and luxurious vacations) or public image (e.g., buying a "luxury box" at the professional football stadium or a membership to the prestigious community golf club) than on reinvesting in the business or putting monies aside to fund insurance policies or otherwise help the next generation afford estate taxes. In fact, most family firms do not set aside funds in profitable years to purchase shares.[49] Entitlement in family-owned firms is further explored in Box 3.3.

Box 3.3
Entitlement: The Family Business Killer

Henry Hutcheson—Regeneration Partners

When I read the headline "P. Diddy Buys $360,000 Car for Son's 16th Birthday," I could not help but think, "What a way to mess up a kid, but I guess it's none of my business." But if applied in the world of family businesses, I would have thought, "Well, there goes *that* business." After all, a sense of entitlement in a child may be the number 1 killer of a family business.

I would define entitlement as an attitude or behavior that "you are deserving of respect and privilege beyond your skills, knowledge, and experience."

Believing you have the skills to run a business when you don't, or thinking you can run the business just because your dad did, are terrific ways to drive your family business into a brick wall. The marketplace does not care what your name is or how much money you have. The marketplace wants the best product and service for the best price. If you can do this profitably, then you win. If you don't, you lose.

Entitled family business members can fail to listen to those who do have the necessary skills and experience. One business owner's son decided to bring all production in-house over the vehement protests of both the seasoned production manager and the chief financial officer. This move resulted in higher quality, but there was not enough work to justify the people or the equipment. The son thought that because his father was such a natural at business, he was, too. He was wrong. Today the company is out of business.

Raising a child with the appropriate balance of confidence and humility is certainly a challenge. Next time you are faced with a decision on this, just ask yourself, "What would P. Diddy do?"

And then do the opposite.

Entitlement in the succeeding generation has been identified by a number of scholars and practitioners as a problem, especially in families of wealth.[50] Children who are born into money and are accustomed to having whatever they want, may come to hold unrealistic expectations about the value of money, their own talent, their "deserved" places in the business, their ability to ignore or bypass nonfamily supervisors, the perks or privileges they should receive as family members, or their "right" to continue to receive family financial support. Some businesses function as a kind of social welfare state for the family, ensuring that everyone can find employment. Such businesses that employ family members who are technically unqualified, interpersonally inappropriate, or otherwise a poor fit for the job set themselves up for internal strife and poor performance. All of these kinds of entitlement attitudes can lower morale significantly in the business and create a toxic effect on the organization's culture.

As a risk factor for family firms, overconfidence can be difficult to assess from inside the system. Where is the line between confidence and overconfidence; between realism, optimism, and over-optimism; between underestimating risk and being fearful to take a risk; and between healthy self-interest and narcissism? The first step to examining this risk factor is to take the time to ask these questions, in earnest. Only by seriously entertaining and acknowledging risks can there be any hope for creating a plan to avoid them.

CHAPTER SUMMARY

- Overconfidence is driven by over-optimism, minimization of risks (and even outright denial of risks), narcissism and entitlement.
- White Star Line management exuded overconfidence by perpetuating hype over humility. *Titanic*'s owners, builders, and officers created a false sense of security by minimizing the dangers that existed, failing to respond appropriately to information received, and choosing not to adapt to the changing environment.
- Family firms, like many other businesses, are prone to minimizing risk—that is, of believing that the value of the family brand will "carry the day" and that the worst-case scenarios will never happen. Some family business owners also exhibit denial, clinging to hope that the business will continue to be profitable and growth oriented even during hard economic times.
- Narcissism was another key factor related to overconfidence that was seen both aboard *Titanic* and in family firms. Captain Smith believed so much in his abilities that he sped through an ice-laden area that

other ships found too dangerous to navigate, without ever decreasing the ship's speed or posting additional lookouts.

- Like Captain Smith, family business owners oftentimes believe so much in their leadership abilities that they fail to fully embrace the fact that they are aging within an increasingly complex business environment. Very few of these business founders have created a succession plan, very few leverage outside resources to help them make decisions and overcome intellectual isolation, and many believe they are too young to retire (some stating that they will never retire), thereby perpetuating the idea that tragedy (much less the inevitable) will not befall them.
- Like *Titanic*'s leadership, some family business leaders display complacency—eschewing the need to become proactive when warned of peril—with similarly disastrous consequences.
- Failure can result from an unwillingness to adapt to situations (believing that "If it ain't broke, don't fix it") or to prepare for upcoming scenarios that can be fatal to family firms, as it was on *Titanic*. Within family firms, being overconfident can lead to a failure to act (e.g., failing to adapt to innovations within industry, failing to develop necessary "bench strength" to meet future challenges head on, failing to prepare for events that may trigger shareholder liquidity, or failing to deal with conflict as it arises) and the results can be catastrophic. The bravado that once proudly carried a family business can ultimately wreak havoc on its legacy.

Ineffective Leadership

If your actions inspire others to dream more, learn more, do more and become more, you are a leader.

—John Quincy Adams

The success or failure of any endeavor hinges on the quality of leadership. Ultimately, the failure of *Titanic*'s leadership to make the right decisions was responsible for the ship's collision with the iceberg and the tragic loss of life. When family businesses go under due to lack of foresight, the company's leaders must bear responsibility for their unwillingness or inability to plan and take appropriate action. Conversely, family businesses that succeed owe a debt of gratitude to effective leaders who prevail over the substantial number of leadership challenges inherent in family enterprise systems.

This chapter first considers the leadership problems relative to *Titanic*, examining the decisions and actions (or inactions) of Captain E. J. Smith, Bruce Ismay, and Captain Stanley Lord. Subsequently, 12 leadership challenges within family firms are described, and the issue of how leaders and governance structures must change as family businesses advance beyond the second generation is explored. The chapter concludes by addressing the concepts of emotional intelligence and transformational leadership, including how they are related to family business success.

INEFFECTIVE LEADERSHIP: *TITANIC*

Leadership as a concept is oftentimes confused with management. While some individuals make good leaders, they may not make good managers. Similarly, good managers do not always make good leaders, as was the case with those involved with *Titanic*, where lackluster leadership was exhibited by Captain Smith of *Titanic*, Bruce Ismay, and Captain Lord of *Californian*. Beginning with Smith, his effectiveness as a leader was compromised by his failure to listen to outside sources of information, his failure to communicate clearly with his team, his practice of making important decisions without having considered all of the relevant information, and his failure to provide decisive commands during the crisis.

When E. J. Smith took command of *Titanic* for her maiden voyage, he was 62 years old. Smith's biographer, Gary Cooper, notes that "White Star's retirement age was 60, but the line often fudged the issue in official documents or newspaper reports with a few judicious white lies, sometimes listing Smith's age as 59 rather than his actual age of 62."[1] Smith had a long and successful career, and was popular among passengers and seaman alike. Some passengers noted the captain's involvement in fulfilling social roles aboard the ship (leading the Sunday prayer and hymn service and dining and mingling with notable passengers) which may have shifted his focus away from communicating with or monitoring his officer team. There is evidence that, although Smith had received information about ice before leaving Southampton (and personally received at least two further warnings on the day of the accident from the wireless operators), some of the officers were not made fully aware (or were left completely ignorant) of the threat. For example, Fifth Officer Harold Lowe gave the following testimony at the British Board of Trade inquiry[2]:

Mr. Rowlatt: Did you hear anything about any messages about ice?

Officer Lowe: There was a chit on the chart room table with the word "ice" on.

Mr. Rowlatt: You mean a little piece of paper with "ice" written on it?

Officer Lowe: A square chit of paper about 3×3.

Mr. Rowlatt: On the chart room table?

Officer Lowe: On our chart room table.

Mr. Rowlatt: What is that—"our chart room table"?

Officer Lowe: The officers' chart room table, and the word "ice" was written on top and then a position underneath.

Mr. Rowlatt: Can you remember what the position was?

Officer Lowe: I cannot.

Mr. Rowlatt: Is that all that was brought to your attention about ice that day?

Officer Lowe: That is all.

For reasons unknown, Smith did not personally convey to all members of his team that the ship was imminently entering an ice field.

Captain Smith also made some critical decisions that could have changed the outcome of the disaster—decisions that were not given full consideration or were made without evaluating all of the relevant data. To his credit, Smith made some effort to avoid the ice region by altering *Titanic's* course several miles south of the planned track. Yet, because there was no system in place to efficiently process ice warnings (which, if all had been plotted, would have revealed the true extent of the ice-filled region), he underestimated how far south he would need to go to avoid it. While it is crucial for leaders to use all information available to them to make strategic decisions, Smith's failure to leverage the wireless messaging system aboard, and the subsequent information it produced, reflected a leader who not only failed to embrace the technological changes of the industry, but also failed to take the time to recognize the opportunities the new technologies offered:

> The technology of wireless was still relatively new to many of these men, and as a consequence most of them hadn't thought out the implications of the increased communication capabilities wireless offered: very few had realized that wireless gave them the opportunity to virtually look over the horizon and anticipate danger before it hove into view. Even fewer had worked out set procedures for the wireless operators to follow when they received messages affecting the navigation of the ship.[3]

Another critical decision occurred shortly after *Titanic* struck the iceberg. Although there were signs of a collision from the bridge (in the form of chunks of ice scattered on the forward starboard decks), there was no obvious indication of damage to the vessel. The captain sent word to the ship's carpenter to "sound the ship" for damage. After the ship had come to a complete stop, Smith signaled the engine room to proceed "half ahead," notwithstanding the fact that the carpenter had not yet returned with his damage report. This choice to press on was especially puzzling, given his decision earlier in the voyage at Southampton *not* to move the ship after a near-collision with *New York*. Little did he know that from the moment *Titanic* came in contact with the iceberg, nearly 7 tons of water began pouring into the starboard hull per second.[4] The result of moving the ship forward, even at half-speed, was to accelerate the rate at which the flooding occurred. The ship ran for an additional 10 to 15 minutes before the damage reports came back confirming the serious nature of *Titanic's* injuries. Although the damage was severe enough that the ship would eventually sink in any case, it is possible that the pumps in the flooding compartments could have kept the ship afloat for more time—perhaps long enough for another vessel to arrive and get everyone safely off the ship.

Finally, when it became apparent that the shipped was doomed, Smith's leadership faltered. His diminished capacity to command was demonstrated in his "isolating himself on the bridge, failing to pass on critical information to his officers and senior seaman, acting and reacting slowly to reports and rapidly changing circumstances, and giving half-hearted orders, some of which the crew would openly defy."[5] Smith never communicated to the officer team his knowledge that the ship was definitely going to sink. Passengers were told that putting on lifebelts and getting into boats was merely precautionary. On the one hand, this lack of communication may have prevented an all-out panic; on the other hand, it failed to convey the urgency of the situation. Many passengers and crewmembers remained unaware of how grave the situation actually was. Had the crew been clear about the truth, perhaps they would have made greater efforts to fill every lifeboat to capacity. Also, rather than issuing clear, decisive orders throughout the evacuation process, the captain became more passive. Officers repeatedly approached him asking for permission to swing out, load, and lower the boats, given that Smith was not forthcoming with orders.

In the end, Smith was overwhelmed and not prepared in any way for the calamity he faced, and his ability to lead effectively was compromised. Indeed, the mettle of a leader is tested not when things go well, but when they go terribly wrong. With only hours left before the ship would sink, a waffling and indecisive leader leads one to question whether a stronger leader managing in the heat of the crisis could have saved more lives.

A second figure whose leadership was problematic was Bruce Ismay. Subsequent to the disaster, Ismay maintained that he was a passenger on the ship, no different from any other. Some evidence, however, suggests that he overstepped his boundaries by exerting his influence in ways that were counterproductive. Ismay acknowledged having had a conversation with Chief Engineer Bell in Queenstown, giving Bell instructions as to the speeds at which he wanted the ship to run on particular days. Ismay expressed his expectation that ship would work up to running at full speed toward the end of the voyage. This meeting occurred in the absence of the captain. As an owner, Ismay had a vested interest in seeing how his new ship could perform, and he was no doubt interested in the positive press coverage that a strong performance could generate. Nevertheless, by issuing his expectations directly to Bell, Ismay circumvented the captain's authority, possibly putting Bell in the uncomfortable position of needing to satisfy two bosses: one (the captain) who had ultimate authority and decades of experience at sea and the other (Ismay) who paid his salary but was not a seaman.

Ismay's interest in maximizing *Titanic's* speed is likely to have had some influence on Smith, perhaps influencing Smith's decision not to slow down when approaching the reported ice fields. First-class passenger Elizabeth Lines, in a deposition for the British Board of Trade inquiry, reported that she observed Ismay and Smith speaking intently in the first-class reception room:

> For some time after noting their arrival she paid them scant attention until Ismay started talking in an animated fashion ... Smith said nothing, merely nodding as Ismay rattled on, enthusing about the ship's performance and affirming confidently that at the rate they were going the ship would arrive on Tuesday [April 16]. Mrs. Lines said the two of them were there for hours and that Mr. Ismay carried the conversation, his attitude towards the captain striking her as being somewhat "*dictatorial*."[6]

Ismay's insertion of himself into engineering and speed-related matters was not the only case in which he overstepped his boundaries and became over-involved in operations. In fact, as the lifeboats were being loaded, Ismay took it upon himself to oversee the loading of Lifeboat 5, ordering Officer Pitman to load the boat with women and children, but before the order to do so was given by Smith. Pitman responded by saying, "I await the *Captain's* orders."[7] As the lifeboat was being lowered slowly to the water, Ismay shouted repeatedly, "Lower away! Lower away!" Officer Lowe, who was busy orchestrating the launch retorted, "If you get the hell out of the way, I'll be able to do something! You want me to lower away quickly? You'll have me drowned the whole lot of them!"[8] With that rebuke, Ismay left the area.

Once safely aboard *Carpathia*, Ismay missed the opportunity to demonstrate his leadership role in attending to the other survivors. Instead, his first move was to request a "room where I can be quiet" where he remained in isolation for the rest of the trip to New York—notwithstanding the distress of other survivors who just lost family members and were huddling in common areas. Later Ismay sent wireless messages to Philip A. S. Franklin at the International Mercantile Marine office in New York, one of which requested that the White Star Line ship, *Cedric*, be held so that Ismay could get himself and the crew back to Britain as soon as possible. He signed the message YAMSI ("Ismay" spelled backwards). This missive raised suspicions on the part of members of the U.S. Senate, who wondered whether Ismay was attempting to abscond before giving testimony in the United States. Overall, Ismay's behavior made him appear self-serving and even duplicitous, all of which did little to help his own personal reputation or that of White Star Line.

A final example of poor leadership in the tragedy was exhibited by someone who never once set foot on *Titanic*, Captain Stanley Lord, commander of the ship *Californian*. At the time of the disaster, *Californian* was stopped (due to large quantities of ice) some distance to the north of *Titanic*'s position. Lord ordered Cyril Evans (*Californian*'s sole wireless operator) to warn *Titanic* (the only ship in the vicinity) of the heavy ice. Evans sent *Titanic*'s wireless operator, Jack Phillips, a message at 10:55 P.M.: "Say old man, we are stopped and surrounded by ice." In transmitting this crucial warning, Evans did not follow protocol in two important ways. First, he did not attempt to identify himself or ask permission to interrupt *Titanic*'s wireless traffic, irritating Phillips. Second, he did not address the message to Captain Smith. He instead used the informal title of "old man" that wireless operators used when addressing one another. A wireless message directed specifically to the ship's captain is clearly a message of importance, and (1) might have gotten Phillips's attention and (2) been delivered directly to Smith.

As Evans went to bed, Lord spotted a steamer at approximately 11:30 P.M., which he estimated to be about five miles due south. The ship was steaming westward toward the ice. At midnight, when he retired to his cabin for the night, Lord instructed his replacement, Second Officer Herbert Stone, to keep him apprised of any changes to this ship, particularly if it moved closer to their position. At 12:35 A.M., Lord contacted the bridge to see whether the ship had moved; Stone indicated that it had not, and that they were unable to make contact with the ship using Morse signal lamps. At 1:15 A.M., Stone notified Lord that he had seen what appeared to be five signal rockets over the steamer that was stopped to the south. The captain asked, "Are they company signals?" (wondering if the signals were signal rockets used by a private company to signal other boats from the same company—a common practice among whaling vessels). Stone stated he did not know, but noted they were white rockets. Lord ordered Stone to continue to try to contact the ship with the Morse lamp and "when you get an answer, let me know." Later, his crew observed three more rockets being fired, and officer Stone and apprentice James Gibson thought that the ship looked "queer" or unnatural, with Gibson observing that ship appeared to have a heavy list to the starboard side. Stone remarked to Gibson that "a ship does not fire up rockets for nothing." They continued to observe the ship until after 2:00 A.M., when it disappeared, apparently steaming away to the southwest. It was not until 5:20 A.M. when, after seeing a ship to the south, Lord summoned Evans to try to contact the ship. Evans then received a message from the ship *Virginian* that *Titanic* had sunk during the night.[9]

Although Lord and his crew were aware that something unusual was happening with regard to the nearby ship, they failed to be proactive. Their failure to act may very well have meant the difference between life and death.

LEADERSHIP IN FAMILY FIRMS

Effective leadership is crucial to the survival of family enterprises. While the type of leadership best suited for a family firm may vary according to the family culture and the developmental stage of the business, some aspects of leadership are relevant for most family firms at any point in their life cycle. This section describes 12 leadership challenges within family firms, and discusses leadership issues in the family, ownership, and business domains in later-generation firms. Finally, emotional intelligence is explored as an important quality that promotes transformational leadership.

Although it is of vital importance, effective leadership of family firms is not easily accomplished as owners seek to balance the needs of the family with the needs of the business. In addition to the challenges of being an effective leader in the business, family business leaders must contend with "family baggage"—that is, the dynamics, dysfunctions, and drama often inherent in families. To be truly effective, leaders must be aware of and attentive to the needs of all stakeholders. Table 4.1 summarizes 12 leadership challenges in family enterprises that can make or break the firm's long-term survival.

THE TWELVE LEADERSHIP CHALLENGES

Challenge #1: Clarity

For family enterprise systems to function well, it is important that there is clarity on a number of levels.

First, it should be clear who the leader actually is. Although a position or title might seem to identify the leader, in many instances who holds the *authority* may be unclear. This situation commonly arises in family businesses when the incumbent leader and the succeeding leader are working together, or even after the successor has "taken over." Owners or retiring leaders (who may or may not be active in the business) may attempt to become involved with management in ways that do not go through the proper channels or that bypass the designated leader's authority. One family business CEO (son of the founder) noted that nearly every time he was overseas visiting clients, his father (who stayed on in the company as chairman) would call all the company's managers together and attempt to change some decision that had been made. In another business, a retired shareholder who lived half of the year in another state would arrive on the premises and loudly criticize perceived problems, ordering employees to respond to his concerns immediately. These situations put employees in the awkward position of having to decide whose authority to follow.

Table 4.1
The Twelve Leadership Challenges in Family Enterprises

1. Clarity	Creating and maintaining proper boundaries, so that it is clear who the leader is and what role everyone is playing
2. Coordination	Attending to the ways different parts of the system must interact to complete the task successfully
3. Culture	Being intentional about building a climate that maximizes both employee well-being and organizational success
4. Communication	Conveying the mission, vision, strategy, plans, and decisions to all relevant stakeholders, and listening to them
5. Conflict optimization	Approaching conflict as an opportunity to consider multiple viewpoints and build a stronger team
6. Counsel	Being open to input from others, particularly those outside the system
7. Courage	Having the strength to take calculated risks, to face difficult issues or feelings, and to make tough decisions
8. Character	Possessing attributes of integrity, honesty, and strength to do what is right
9. Commitment	Selecting and supporting leaders who are passionate and motivated to lead
10. Competence	Selecting and developing leaders with the right skills for the future needs of the business, who can produce positive results
11. Continuity	Being responsible for creating plans to identify, prepare, and develop future leaders
12. Clearing out	Making sufficient room for the succeeding leaders to be able to assume full control

Establishing clarity is also important with regard to people's roles and responsibilities within the organization, so as to clarify "who is in charge of what." When role confusion exists, not only can there be inefficiency relative to duplication of efforts, but there can also be frustration, hurt feelings, and resentment ("Why did you give *her* that project? I thought that was *my* area.").

Challenge #2: Coordination

Most businesses require the efforts of many different people, or groups of people, performing different tasks to achieve a common purpose. Everyone being clear about his or her own and others' roles is essential.

Once this understanding has been established, leaders must ensure that the efforts of all parties are well coordinated. Figuring out how all of the tasks in a complex multistep process will be accomplished requires careful synchronizations of activities, resources, and schedules. Without proper coordination and oversight, involved parties risk turning into silos—that is, disconnected operating units that fail to become interdependent and communicate with one another for the coordination of their efforts. The different subsystems (whether different departments or family branches) may compete for resources rather than collaborate and, at worst, attempt to sabotage one another. It does not take long before the lack of coordination in the business becomes evident to customers.

Planning efforts of the family on behalf of the business also require coordination of activities and congruence of goals. The timing of solving one issue (e.g., how do we decide the requirements for long-term family employment?) may need to be adjusted if another issue is more pressing at the moment (e.g., do we have enough money set aside to pay estate taxes?). To coordinate *how* things should happen, a good leader must first prioritize those events *most* important to establish an order in which to proceed.

Challenge #3: Culture

Organizational culture comprises the collectively held attitudes, beliefs, values, traditions, expectations, and business practices that determine how the organization and its members behave. Every organization has its own unique culture, but family firms have measurable cultural differences from nonfamily firms. For example, compared to nonfamily firms, family businesses have been found to have cultures characterized by stronger commitment, greater harmony, higher cohesion, and a longer-term view.[10] Culture is thought to be related to a number of aspects of organizational functioning, including financial performance[11] and strategic success.[12]

Leaders (especially founders) can have a major impact on organizational culture, for better or for worse. The leader's behavior is seen by others as evidence of what really matters, apart from whatever is said. For example, if the CEO pulls up to the office in a new luxury vehicle after instituting layoffs, that behavior can undermine morale and engender negative feelings about working for the company. In turn, lower morale can lead to higher turnover and sluggish performance. Effective leaders are mindful of culture—and their own role in its development. They try to retain and strengthen the positive and productive aspects while remedying or changing the negative and problematic aspects of culture. They are also aware of which behaviors are rewarded or punished, and they are careful to ensure that their own behaviors are consistent with the stated values of the organization.

Challenge #4: Communication

How leaders clarify roles, coordinate responsibilities, and influence culture relies heavily on their ability to communicate effectively. Effective communication requires a number of components. In particular, leaders must communicate the following:

- Mission: core purpose of the family and business
- Vision: an inspiring ideal future state that aligns and motivates others
- Values: principles that everyone should strive to embody through their actions
- Strategy: how the organization will go about accomplishing its mission, including the roles that individuals or groups will play and the ways in which they will interact with one another
- Intentions and plans: what the leader is thinking about doing and which plans have been made to carry out the stated intentions
- Feedback: how the organization is performing as a whole, and how the actions of individuals or groups contribute to performance
- Credit and appreciation: acknowledgment of the ways in which others have done a good job, enabled success, behaved laudably, or added value

Ideally, these dimensions should be articulated and communicated with respect to both the family and the business. Effective leaders communicate frequently and directly. They emphasize consistent messages using multiple tactics, such as written and spoken words, actions, symbolic gestures, and use of other media.

Ultimately, leadership is about influencing others. This feat can be more easily accomplished by leaders who are articulate, persuasive, or charismatic. Nevertheless, influencing is also accomplished through listening, and allowing oneself to be influenced.[13] Employees or family members are more likely to follow a leader if they feel heard or understood by the leader and trust that the leader has considered their ideas. Effective family business leaders create ways to get feedback from all of their constituents: shareholders, family members, employees, customers, and suppliers (among others). Conversely, when others do not believe that the leader is listening to their concerns, the result can be mistrust, resentment, and increased resistance.

Challenge #5: Conflict Optimization

A factor related to managing communication is managing conflict. Conflicts in organizations come in several varieties: task or cognitive conflict (conflict about business matters, such as goals and strategies); process conflict (disagreements about methods for doing things); and relationship conflict (negative, interpersonal conflict).[14] Indeed, conflicts also surface due to the many roles inherent within the family business system—roles that are oftentimes at odds with one another as participants juggle the different values and priorities associated with ownership, family membership, and business management. As Figure 4.1 demonstrates, the overlapping domains of ownership, management, and family create as many as seven different stakeholder groups within the system, each of which may possess different perspectives and needs.[15]

The complexity inherent in family enterprise systems makes family businesses particularly susceptible to conflict. At the same time, factors unique to family businesses (e.g., long histories, deeper underlying issues, concerns about straining family ties) may make the resolution of conflict

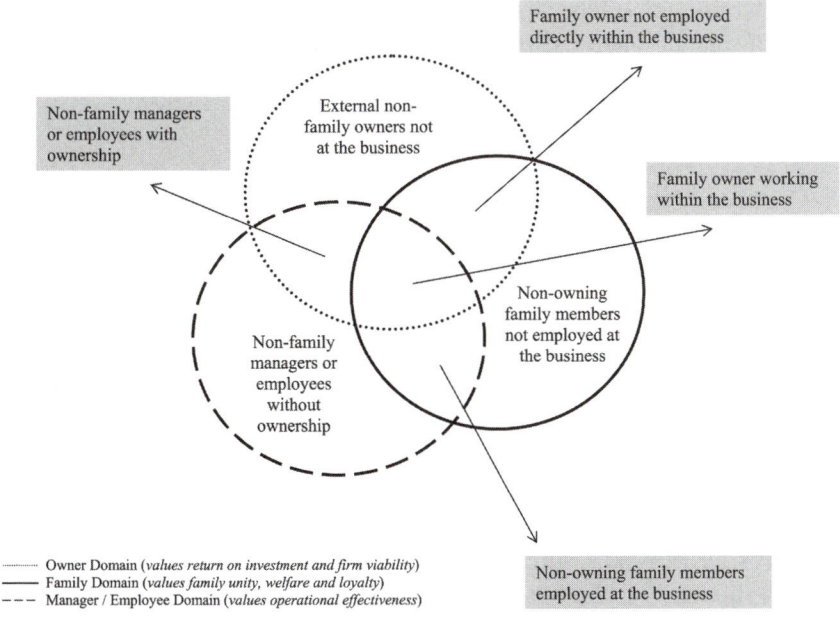

Figure 4.1
The Three Circles Model of the Family Business System. (Adapted from R. Tagiuri and J. A. Davis. "Bivalent Attitudes of the Family Firm." Working paper. Cambridge, MA: Harvard University Press, 1982. [Reprinted in *Family Business Review* 9 (1996): 199–208].)

more difficult.[16] While conflict may be inevitable in family businesses, it need not be destructive. In fact, disagreements can lead to improved decision making and collaboration, and can even have a beneficial effect on firm performance.[17] Exemplary family firm leadership entails dealing with conflict proactively by "thinking ahead" in a number of ways:

- Becoming knowledgeable about general categories of conflict and the underlying drivers of conflict
- Anticipating the specific kinds of conflicts that could occur
- Establishing methods of working through conflicts
- Detecting conflicts early by asking others for feedback about their presence
- Promoting the development of conflict resolution skills among team members
- Using external facilitators to moderate conflicts when necessary

Unfortunately, many leaders in family firms do not embrace a proactive approach to conflict. Leaders who ignore or avoid conflicts allow them to fester and evolve into toxic disputes. As a result, conflicts may go unaddressed until they reach the point where they threaten to destroy the family or business. When consultants get called in to "fix" the problem, the damage incurred may be so great that the situation is already beyond reconciliation.

Challenge #6: Counsel

Listening to others is not just important for effective communication, but it also supports the development of sound strategy. Forward-thinking family business leaders are cognizant of the fact that they do not have all of the answers, and they regularly seek out information and advice. Asking for input from others allows them to determine whether they have considered all of the options or solutions. External perspectives can come from advisors, customers, suppliers, or business owners (from similar or dissimilar industries).

One of the best ways family businesses can leverage the experience of others is by forming a board of advisors and/or a board of directors. Ideally, boards will include individuals with specialized knowledge or expertise in areas that are germane to the business; in addition, board members should be independent, and able to give very candid opinions, particularly those that challenge the ideas of the leader. Top management concerns, including the need to innovate and overcoming insular thinking, could be surmounted by an outside board. Boards can also help the family firm manage risks, plan for succession, mentor junior leaders, and determine the best path toward long-term continuity.

Unfortunately, the majority of family firms do not have an active board of advisors. Data from regional surveys indicate that only 30 percent of family firms have an active board of directors[18] and 16 percent or fewer have a board of advisors.[19] Among those firms with active advisory boards, the majority (more than 60 percent) report that the board's contribution is good, outstanding, or integral to the firm's success.[20] In Box 4.1, one family business president describes her experience in working with a board of outside advisors.

Box 4.1
Establishing a Board of Advisors: The Headache Remedy

Mary Planeta Fitzgerald—Acme Wire Products Company, Inc.

Acme Wire Products implemented a board of advisors in 1999, and our advisors are still actively engaged in guiding us through business challenges to achieve optimal results. It took a year of conversation and a year of planning before we actually had the board in place. The appointment of a "project leader" in the implementation of the advisory board was a key component in ensuring the project would be successful. We also set time frames for key objectives so that the project did not get off track.

We found that putting a board of advisors in place and keeping it going takes work but can bring incredible benefits to a family business. A board of advisors can perform the following functions:

- Advise on family and business issues
- Help professionalize the business
- Provide advice on what a larger, more established organization has done and outline the pros and cons of different paths
- Be objective when personal feelings take over
- Allow an owner to honestly discuss business issues that he or she may not feel free to divulge to banker, customers, suppliers, or friends
- Tell the business owner things that he or she may already know—but confirm that the company is traveling down the right (or wrong) path

At our company, we meet three times annually, and our advisors complained when we canceled a meeting because we felt there was not enough "stuff" to talk about! The advisory board grows and evolves every year as we address new topics and become better managers and leaders. Some topics our advisors have assisted us with include the following:

- Establishing how the company looks to outsiders
- Questioning an equipment purchase and determining its payback

- Determining management succession
- Selecting pricing strategies
- Ensuring alignment of goals—corporate, strategic, personal, and family

The membership of the board will vary based on the needs of the company. As one advisor counseled, however, "We are here to discuss your biggest headaches—you determine the agenda and priority."

Challenge #7: Courage

If leaders in many organizations require courage to shoulder great responsibilities, then family business leaders require a double dose. To face the challenges and conflicts that arise in conducting business with family members, family business leaders need courage to do the following:

- Take measured risks
- Ask hard questions, face volatile issues, and make difficult decisions
- Receive criticism and honest feedback
- Entrust others with power and ultimately transition from the leadership role

Family business leaders must take some risks and embrace change to be successful. To do so, however, requires confidence and courage, whether in launching a new product or location, acquiring a new division, or making a significant capital expenditure. Family enterprise systems are rife with challenging, emotionally charged issues, such as the compensation of family members, selection of a successor, or termination of a poorly performing family member. When leaders lack courage to make difficult calls or manage tough issues directly, the system can stay stuck in a state of confusion or dysfunction. There are always hard questions in family firms—questions relating to the competence or commitment of family members, the plans of the leading or succeeding generation, and the desire to remain family owned or sell the company. One family business founder avoided asking his children about their intentions of joining the business, tearfully justifying his position by positing, "Suppose they say no?" Lack of courage in asking difficult questions leads to a lack of clarity and organizational inertia.

It also takes courage to be able to seek and receive honest feedback from others about one's own behavior or decisions. Incumbent leaders, especially founders, need courage to step away from a business that represents their passions in life and to learn diversify their sources of meaning and happiness.

Challenge #8: Character

Character entails the constellation of attributes that determines a person's moral and ethical behavior. It includes features such as honesty, integrity, and the strength to "do the right thing." Leaders who display moral character inspire the trust of family members and employees alike, because they need not worry that they will be the recipients of unfair treatment or deceit. Leaders who are lacking moral character can wreak havoc on their families, businesses, shareholders, and others.

Consider what happened to the Adelphia Communications Corporation. Adelphia was founded in 1952 by John Rigas in Cloudersport, Pennsylvania. It was a family firm from the beginning: John partnered with his brother Gus to start the business, with John's sons Timothy and Michael later entering the firm. At its peak, Adelphia was one of the top five cable companies in the United States. In 2002, John was forced to resign as chief executive officer (CEO) after being indicted for multiple counts of fraud. His sons were also charged in participating in these crimes. The executives essentially looted the corporation by concealing $2.3 billion in liabilities from investors and by using corporate funds as their personal funds. John Rigas was convicted of the charges and sentenced to 15 years in federal prison. His son Tim received a 20-year sentence. Adelphia was forced to file for bankruptcy after it acknowledged that the Rigas executives had taken $3.1 billion in loans that were not recorded on the books.[21]

In a study of desirable characteristics in successors, respondents from 485 Canadian family firms were asked to rate the importance of 30 different attributes related to competence, relationships with family members, personality traits, and current involvement with the business. The attribute that was ranked highest in importance was integrity.[22] This finding appears robust, as integrity's first-place ranking was replicated in a sample of Indian family-owned businesses.[23]

Challenge #9: Commitment

The successor attribute ranked second in importance, just behind integrity, was commitment.[24] Being sufficiently motivated to lead is a key concern for family firm leaders, particularly beyond the founding generation. Vallejo described the importance of commitment, particularly in second generation family leaders:

> This commitment to the firm can and should be manifested in the achievement of high levels of loyalty and identification with the project of the first generation, as well as a constant and continuous improvement in the running of the business. In short, it is important for the second generation to be committed to the present and future of the business, as well as proud of its past and the legacy they have inherited. Only in this way can their enthusiasm and pride in the business be such that it infects the nonfamily member employees, consequently benefiting firm performance.[25]

Thus commitment becomes an important issue in the selection of leaders. The relative commitment of the second generation compared to the first generation is often a cause for doubt in potential successors and a source of conflict between the generations. Lack of committed leaders has been cited as a barrier to succession. Sometimes, however, different management or leadership styles are misinterpreted as a lack of commitment. For example, a founder who typically devoted 80 hours per week to the business had a more micro-managing style than his son, who was more comfortable delegating responsibilities. The fact that his son was able to do his work in 55 hours per week was a source of concern for his father, who questioned whether his son possessed sufficient drive. Ultimately, there needs to be a fit between the dreams of the previous generation and the dreams of the next generation if the business is to remain family led.

Challenge #10: Competence

In addition to commitment, competence is an essential quality for leaders and leadership selection. However, it may be difficult to define or measure what competence means as it relates to each family firm. Indicators of competence might include education, experience inside or outside the business, and past performance.[26] Financial performance and the ability to grow the company have been considered important markers for successor effectiveness.[27] Competence involves possessing the requisite knowledge, skills, and abilities for the technical aspects of the business (e.g., finance, marketing) as well as the needed interpersonal skills. In a study of important successor qualities, two aspects of competence—decision-making abilities/experience and interpersonal skills—were ranked fourth and fifth, respectively.[28]

Lack of competence among potential successors has been cited as a barrier to succession.[29] In one business, there were vast differences of opinion about the competence of the successor, a woman in her late forties who was running the business. This issue was very difficult for the family to discuss openly, as her supporters would become incensed at the suggestion that she was underperforming. The fact that several family members did not have faith in her ability to grow the business (coupled with members of the senior generation's refusal to relinquish control and decisional authority) was one of the reasons why the succession process stalled.

Challenge #11: Continuity

Planning for leadership continuity represents another leadership challenge for family firms. For the business to be sustained over generations, a system for identifying, preparing, and actively developing new leaders must be implemented. Successor and leader development is an ongoing process that entails a number of stages. A number of scholars have advanced a four-stage model[30]:

- Stage 1: The incumbent leader is a sole proprietor; the next generation may have no formal role in the business, but may be considered students or followers of the business.
- Stage 2: The incumbent leader is a monarch; successors have entered the business and are helpers.
- Stage 3: Incumbents move into the role of supervisor, delegating more responsibility to successors who assume a managerial role.
- Stage 4: The incumbents retire or remain as consultants, but leadership authority is passed to the successors.

At each stage, the incumbent leader can take a number of actions to facilitate the acquisition of developmentally appropriate knowledge and skills. However, successors should be responsible for the process as well; they can create personal development plans that describe their existing strengths, areas in need of development, and programs for acquiring the necessary educational opportunities and experiences.[31] Also, having a good relationship with the incumbent leader is extremely helpful for the process.[32] In addition, developing leaders can benefit from relationships with mentors, coaches, independent directors, or other people who can provide the developing leader with support and feedback. Planning for leadership continuity should align with the strategic vision of the firm's future, as this parallelism enables the firm to be more specific about the kind of leadership necessary to fulfill the vision. Box 4.2 discusses the importance of an executive coach in leadership development for enterprise continuity.

Box 4.2
Executive Coaching

Gerard J. Donnellan, PhD—Brandeis University

What is executive coaching?

- It is an individual activity that occurs between the executive and his or her coach.
- It is designed to improve the effectiveness of the leader in producing business results.
- It is informed by feedback and data from the coach and the executive's organization.
- It is a process that invites the executive to reflect on and learn from his or her own experience, and to practice new ways of thinking and behaving that produce more effective outcomes.
- It teaches the executive tools to continue learning after formal coaching has ended.

Coaching is a leadership development activity. It is not counseling or psychotherapy—and it is not a substitute for therapeutic work. It is a process of learning, with an emphasis on helping the client understand and "own" his or her individual style of learning.

What sets executive coaching apart from many other approaches is the emphasis on business outcomes and the use of a comprehensive development plan that includes an assessment at the beginning of the process. The client and the coach agree to a formal contract that outlines ground rules, time frames, goals, and specific measures of success. It is not an open-ended process. In a family business context, it is important that the coaching is *developmental* (i.e., focused on growth and change), as opposed to *remedial* (i.e., repairing something, or someone, that is broken).

Sometimes, however, the hiring of a coach is not appropriate. Some limitations of coaching in family business include using a coach for the following purposes:

- To deal with a spoiled, entitled relative who has no motivation to change
- To deal with significant mental health or substance abuse issues
- To repair a broken marriage
- To address what is primarily a business issue
- As a substitute for directly working on family issues

The decision to use a coach should rest on whether it makes good business sense, whether it will help the business in the long run, and whether the executive is someone in whom the business should invest.

Working with a coach is one part of an individual's development plan, and can be a tremendously helpful practice when sorting out what the next steps in a career might be, learning how to develop as a leader within the business, and identifying what one needs to do *right now* to be successful.

Source: Adapted from "Who Will Drive the Bus? Guidance for Developing Leaders in the Family Enterprise."

Challenge #12: Clearing Out

The final leadership challenge for family firms is "clearing out," or making sufficient space for the next generation of family leaders to assume full authority. Transitioning out of the central leadership role is a process that can be facilitated by forethought and preparation on the part of the leader. While nearly one-third of family business owners do not plan to retire completely,[33] a transition is not tantamount to leaving the business entirely. Nevertheless, it may mean adopting new roles and different behaviors that allow next-generation leaders to be unencumbered to lead as they see fit.

There are strong individual differences in an incumbent leader's ability to clear out—differences that are often rooted in the leader's personality. This diversity is best illustrated by Sonnenfeld's typology of retirement styles. Based on interviews with 50 retired CEOs, he described retiring leaders in terms of the following four types[34]:

- Monarchs: Do not leave office until they are forced out by death or revolt.
- Generals: Do not leave office unless pressured; they may leave willingly, but wait on the sidelines, plotting a return to power to rescue the firm from perceived incompetence of the successor.
- Ambassadors: Leave the firm willingly but retain ties to the firm and serve the new leader as a consultant or advisor.
- Governors: Leave the firm willingly, and do so by making a clean break, cutting ties, and moving onto other projects.

Among family firms, all four of these exit styles exist, but monarchs and generals are most prevalent—particularly among business founders.[35] However, there also exist examples of business leaders who executed the clearing-out process more smoothly and successfully, creating new roles and relationships that support the new leader after the transition.[36] Cadieux identified several different productive roles that the predecessor occupied after the new leader was instated. During the working together or "joint reign" phase of the succession process, predecessors acted as supervisors, teachers, protectors, introducers, and collaborators; in the withdrawal phase, they acted as administrators, consultants, and observers. Toward their successors, they acted as confidants, facilitators, advisors, and models.[37]

Nonetheless, the most critical factor is the extent to which the leader can view himself or herself as a distinct and separate entity from the business.[38]

FAMILY BUSINESS LEADERSHIP ACROSS
TIME AND GENERATIONS

For those family firms that meet the challenges of leadership in the first generation or two (and survive the transition to the third generation and beyond), new leadership challenges emerge. Changes in the family enterprise system, a larger number of shareholders, or a more loosely connected family may necessitate other forms of leadership and more formalized systems for governance. In this section, aspects of governance and leadership often seen in generationally advanced family firms are considered, including the use of nonfamily CEOs, family councils, and professional boards of directors.

The Nonfamily CEO

Family firms might decide to hire a nonfamily CEO for a number of reasons: (1) to provide an interim leader who can help mentor the next generation of family leadership; (2) to bring in outside experience needed to lead the business through a restructuring or major strategic change; or (3) to reduce tensions or conflicts in the family by taking family out of management roles.[39] Nonfamily CEOs (and other nonfamily executives) can help family firms avoid insular thinking by bringing in new ideas and different perspectives. Having a nonfamily CEO can inspire and motivate nonfamily employees by demonstrating that just because the firm is family owned, it does not mean that nonfamily members cannot ascend to the highest levels.

Leading a family firm can be a challenge for nonfamily CEOs—even those nonfamily shorter-term "bridge managers" or "bridge CEOs" who serve as stewards mentoring the succeeding generation (who would not have to report to family) while the senior generation transitions out of the business. "Nonfamily CEOs are responsible for generating superior business performance like their peers at other businesses but in an environment that daily resembles a large family reunion."[40] Adjusting to the reality of having to balance family, shareholder, and business considerations in decision making can be difficult, as the standard rules for business do not always apply. In Box 4.3, a former nonfamily executive describes his experience in navigating different aspects of family dynamics and family culture.

A number of factors have been identified as creating an environment that promotes success of nonfamily CEOs[41]:

- Selecting a leader who possesses both business acumen and strong interpersonal skills

Box 4.3
Observations of a Nonfamily Leader

Anonymous: Former Nonfamily CEO

In nonfamily companies, there is a common expression that directs most human relations actions and supplier relationships: "It's not personal; it's just business." My experience with family companies—especially those employing a significant number of family members and led by family executives—is just the opposite. In several instances, family values, dynamics, and politics took precedence in determining business practices over what might be considered "good business sense" in a nonfamily firm. My observations lead me to conclude that for nonfamily CEOs to be effective, they must first develop an understanding of the following issues:

- The stated aspirations of key family members versus the actions of those family members
- The informal family organization
- The balance between family member well-being and nonfamily employee well-being
- The amount of trust family executives place in employees and junior family members
- The ability to make decisions that reflect the best interests of shareholders, employees, and other critical stakeholders versus reflecting the values, needs, and dynamics of the family

At one company in which I served as president, it was discovered that a nephew had been stealing from the company consistently over several years. In a nonfamily company, the employee would have been fired with no delay. In our case (despite irrefutable accounting and video evidence), months of hand wringing, triple-checking evidence, and planning went into the timing of the termination (which was delayed to avoid unpleasantness at an upcoming family party). After the termination, the business's management team was criticized for moving too quickly.

In another case, several family members were deeply loyal to (and financially dependent on) the founders. They lacked job descriptions and were grossly overpaid for the "positions" they occupied. On pressing one of the founders to establish a job description for one family member, the founder commented that his job description is to "do whatever is necessary." He was paid more than $200,000 plus perks annually. On rare occasions, the founder questioned the cost versus the actual work accomplished; however, the founder never questioned loyalty—a value clearly prioritized above productivity or competence.

Occasionally, family founders and executives believe that absolute confidentiality is critical. One family member told me, "We don't ever give our employees good [financial] news because if we did, they would ask for pay increases." The result of this approach for management is that operating and financial processes are often not documented and knowledge is confined to a few "trusted" people, leading other managers to operate in a vacuum.

- A family council to air family concerns outside of the firm's business activities
- A strong board of directors that serve as a buffer between the CEO and family and provide support for the difficult decisions a CEO must make

The Board of Directors

When family firms grow to have a large number of shareholders, or the shareholders have fewer or more distant family connections to management, the board of directors becomes an important governance structure and leadership force. Ideally, board members are strong, independent individuals who demonstrate qualities of good leaders themselves (e.g., courage, commitment, character, communication, competence, etc.). The major responsibilities of the board of directors include the following:

- Representing the interests of the shareholders
- Reviewing the firm's financial status
- Asking critical questions that help refine the strategy
- Assisting in developing plans for succession and continuity
- Holding management accountable and ensuring ethical behavior is maintained
- Providing advice and fresh perspectives to the CEO on different topics[42]

In essence, the board provides monitoring and oversight to ensure that the CEO and the management team are capable of implementing a well-devised long-term strategy. Because the majority of shareholders are usually family members, the board also attempts to ensure that the business is operated in a way that meets the family's goals (in terms of both how the business is run and how its profits are managed). Yet, for the family's wishes to be communicated clearly and with one voice, it is very helpful to have a family council.

The Family Council

A family council is a governance structure for the family wherein family members (whether or not they are owners or employees) can discuss matters pertaining to the interface between the family and the business. Family councils are instrumental for family enterprise systems, because they meet the following needs:

- Create an opportunity for the family to discuss business issues so that the discussion does not interfere with other family events

- Provide a setting for educating family members about the rights and responsibilities associated with ownership and management
- Offer family members an outlet to voice their ideas or concerns about the business, such that they do not get expressed in unconstructive ways
- Allow families to develop family plans, policies, constitutions, or other agreements that help the family clarify its values and sharpen its vision[43]

As families grow more geographically and emotionally distant from the founder, the family council can help sustain the energy to preserve the founder's legacy. As Jack Moore, former fourth-generation director of the Benjamin Moore paint company put it, "Achieving continuity of family ownership is the family council's ultimate responsibility. An effective family council is the means by which family identity and values are maintained (and renewed)."[44]

EMOTIONAL INTELLIGENCE AND TRANSFORMATIONAL LEADERSHIP

Two concepts that can promote and enable effective leadership in family firms are emotional intelligence and transformational leadership.

Emotional intelligence (EI) has been defined in a number of ways. Mayer and Salovey define it as the ability to (1) accurately perceive and identify emotions, (2) integrate emotions to facilitate thought, (3) understand emotions and their causes, and (4) regulate or manage the emotions of self and others to promote personal growth.[45] Goleman, whose books on EI popularized the term, defines it as a set of emotional competencies: self-awareness, self-regulation, motivation, empathy, and social skills.[46] Still others view EI as a group of self-perceptions about their emotional abilities.[47] While these different definitions represent disagreements among authors about the nature of EI, they converge on the general idea that EI has to do with people's capacity and skill to assess, modify, and utilize the emotions of themselves, others, or groups.

Transformational leadership was first described by Burns as a process in which "leaders and followers help each other to advance to a higher level of morale and motivation."[48] He distinguished this practice from *transactional* leadership—which is based on a series of exchanges or transactions between leaders and followers, each giving something to get something they need in return. Bass extended the concept of transformational leadership by articulating four elements that describe how transformational leaders motivate their followers to work harder[49]:

- Individual consideration: attending to each follower's needs, acting as a mentor or coach to the follower, and listening to the follower's concerns.
- Intellectual stimulation: encouraging the follower's creativity, challenging followers to think and learn, and soliciting the follower's ideas.
- Inspirational motivation: articulating a compelling vision, communicating optimism about future goals, and challenging followers to achieve high standards.
- Idealized influence: being a charismatic role model for ethical behavior, and instilling pride, respect, and trust.

The result of these behaviors is that employees become intrinsically motivated because their identity becomes connected to the mission and collective identity of the organization. They are also inspired to perform based on their trust in and appreciation for the leader.

Studies examining transformational leadership in family businesses have found higher levels of transformational leadership in family firms than in nonfamily businesses.[50] Transformational leadership is also predictive of employee cohesion (e.g., employees liking and supporting one another).[51] Another study of leadership in family firms found that participative leadership (in which the head of an organization involves members in making important decisions,[52] a concept closely related to transformational leadership) was associated with a number of positive results, including greater employee satisfaction and commitment, and favorable family and financial outcomes.[53]

Perhaps it is not surprising that leaders with higher levels of emotional intelligence display greater levels of transformational leadership and leadership effectiveness.[54] The ability to lead effectively is related to one's ability to harness emotions as a powerful resource that, when skillfully deployed, can help realize the greater good for everyone associated with the family enterprise system. In conclusion, most of the important leadership practices in family firms (those practices associated with transformational leadership) are best accomplished by people with higher levels of emotional intelligence.

CHAPTER SUMMARY

- With regard to *Titanic*, several leadership problems occurred, such as lack of role clarity, poor communication and coordination, acting too quickly before receiving all of the relevant information, overstepping boundaries, and complacency.

- Like *Titanic*, family firms face a variety of leadership challenges, including clarity, coordination, culture, communication, conflict, counsel, courage, character, commitment, competence, continuity, and clearing out.
- As family businesses advance beyond the second generation, changes in the family, ownership, and business systems necessitate new kinds of leadership and governance structures, including nonfamily CEOs, boards of advisors, boards of directors, and family councils.
- Emotional intelligence is related to transformational leadership, and transformational leadership has been linked to positive outcomes for family firms. Both concepts are useful in understanding how family business leaders can achieve success.

Lack of Planning and Preparation

> Plan: A method of doing something that is worked out in advance.
> Preparation: The work or planning involved in making something or somebody ready or in putting something together in advance.[1]

It stands to reason that having a plan before acting increases the likelihood that the action will bring about the desired results and avoid unwanted and undesirable outcomes. This "common sense" notion is confirmed by empirical evidence showing that planning and preparation are related to success in organizations. A meta-analysis of 14 studies confirmed the positive association between planning and performance in small firms.[2] While most people would endorse the idea that planning is important for success, there exist wide differences in ideas about what planning means and what the scope should be. Which kinds of plans need to be created? What level of detail is necessary? Who should be involved in the planning process? What constitutes adequate preparation? How far into the future should a plan extend?

As "hindsight is 20/20" and history reveals what now seems obvious, the case of *Titanic* and those of unsuccessful family firms demonstrate poor planning and preparation for both expected and unexpected aspects of their journeys. This chapter explores the ways in which *Titanic*'s planning and preparation fell short, and how—if they had planned differently—its owners and crew could have saved more lives or made different navigational decisions that would have avoided the accident entirely. This chapter also explores the role of advanced preparation in family firms in terms of planning for expected and unexpected events, along with the various reasons why family businesses resist planning.

LACK OF PLANNING AND PREPARATION: *TITANIC*

Without question, a huge amount of planning and preparation went into *Titanic*'s maiden voyage. The coordination of the myriad details (from construction of the ship itself, to planning for sufficient coal, proper equipment, personnel, navigation, furnishings, food and beverages, and coordination of passenger loading and unloading) required intense fore-thought and organization. Unfortunately, those aspects of the voyage—both expected and unexpected—for which its leaders were unprepared resulted in additional loss of life. In particular, serious shortcomings were noted in the following areas: (1) communication about the presence and location of icebergs; (2) the number, size, and equipping of lifeboats; (3) the plan for communicating with passengers and crew in an emergency; and (4) the plan for executing a full evacuation of the ship at sea.

The fact that *Titanic* would encounter ice was not altogether unexpected. *Titanic*'s leadership and even some of the passengers were aware that their route would most likely take them near an area where ice was reported, and most of the ice reports transmitted to *Titanic* indicated the location of where ice was observed. Even so, it appeared there was no protocol in place for altering navigational decisions based on this information. The ship included two chart rooms (one for the officers' use and one for the captain's personal use), and it remains unclear whether the location of ice from dif-ferent reports was charted on one, both, or neither of these charts. Had the ice reports been charted appropriately, some sources suggest that the navigational team would have known that the ship's course would take them not just near but *directly through* the ice region. Consider the testi-mony of Fourth Officer Boxhall:

Senator Smith:	Did you know you were in the vicinity of icebergs that night?
Mr. Boxhall:	No; I did not know we were in the vicinity of icebergs.
Senator Smith:	Did not the second or first officer apprise you of the fact that they had information that you were in the vicinity of icebergs?
Mr. Boxhall:	I knew we had had information. They [first and second officers] did not apprise me that evening of it.
Senator Smith:	When did they [the first and second officers] apprise you?
Mr. Boxhall:	As a matter of fact, they [the first and second officers] did not mention it to me.
Senator Smith:	Had it never been mentioned to you?
Mr. Boxhall:	Oh, yes; the captain mentioned it.
Senator Smith:	The captain mentioned it to you?

Mr. Boxhall:	Yes.
Senator Smith:	When?
Mr. Boxhall:	I do not know whether it was the day before or two days before he gave me some positions of icebergs, which I put on the chart.
Senator Smith:	Which you put on the chart?
Mr. Boxhall:	On his chart.
Senator Smith:	Did the captain tell you that the *Californian* had wired the *Titanic* that they were in the vicinity of icebergs?
Mr. Boxhall:	No. The captain gave me some wireless messages from Southampton, I think, that we had had before we had sailed, and asked me to put these positions on the chart.
Senator Smith:	Did you know whether a wireless had been received from the *Amerika* that the *Titanic* was in the vicinity of icebergs?
Mr. Boxhall:	No; I could not say.
Senator Smith:	Do you want us to understand that you had no knowledge of the proximity of this ship to icebergs immediately preceding the—
Mr. Boxhall:	I had no knowledge.
Senator Smith:	One moment. [*continuing*] Immediately preceding the collision, or during the hours of your watch from 8 o'clock until the collision occurred?
Mr. Boxhall:	I did not realize the ship was so near the ice field.

The preceding exchange indicates that the ice warnings received *during the voyage* were not appropriately charted, and that there was poor communication about the threat of ice among the ship's officers. Had there been a protocol in place that dictated how to handle and communicate the warnings, perhaps the crew would have reacted differently to the presence of risk, and made operational decisions (e.g., reducing speed, taking a different course) that could have enabled *Titanic* to avoid the accident altogether.

The fact that *Titanic* would be faced with an emergency requiring full evacuation of the ship was highly unexpected. The ship's lifeboats were unable to carry all of the people aboard; and while *Titanic* carried approximately 2,223 people on her maiden voyage, the capacity of the 20 boats was approximately 1,176 people (or 52 percent of the passengers onboard). Had *Titanic* been completely sold out, only 34 percent of the 3,500 people aboard could have been accommodated in the lifeboats.

Clearly, Ismay and others (blinded by overconfidence) failed to plan and prepare for events that might necessitate a full evacuation of the ship. Subsequent to the sinking, management at White Star Line saw the error in judgment and planned differently—outfitting *Olympic* and *Britannic* with more lifeboats to ensure that all passengers and crew members would have a seat if an evacuation became necessary.

Beyond the fact that the number and size of *Titanic*'s lifeboats were insufficient to hold everyone, the lifeboats themselves were ill equipped, underscoring the idea that no one believed they would ever be used. Survivors described a number of different problems—mainly lack of equipment and provisions:

> There were absolutely no lights in the lifeboats, and they did not even know whether the plug was in the bottom of the boat to prevent the boat from sinking; there were no lanterns, no provisions, no lights, nothing at all in these boats but the oars. One of the officers asked one of the passengers for a watch with which to light up the bottom of the boat to see if the plug was in place ... [3]
>
> That as to equipment of the lifeboats there was none in her boat except four oars and a mast, which latter was useless; there was no water nor any food; that there was neither compass nor binnacle light nor any kind of lantern; that on questioning occupants of other lifeboats they told ... the same story—lack of food, water, compass, and lights, and that several boats had no oars or only two or three. [4]

Fortunately for those in lifeboats, the seas were calm, the night was clear, and rescue came in only a few hours. Had the conditions been worse or the time in the boats longer, the poor preparation of the lifeboats could have resulted in further casualties.

Another problem that demonstrated a lack of planning was the lack of an efficient, consistent, and reliable method for issuing emergency communications to the passengers or crew. *Titanic* did not have a public address system, nor were warning bells or alarms of any kind available with which to alert passengers of danger or to notify the crew of a problematic situation. Shortly after midnight, Captain Smith had instructed the crew to uncover lifeboats and muster the passengers. Officer Murdoch organized the assembly of passengers, but this operation was accomplished somewhat haphazardly: some crewmembers downplayed any sense of danger, while others were more curt and serious. For example, second-class steward John Hardy roused passengers by throwing cabin doors wide and shouting, "Everybody on deck with life belts on, at once!" His behavior stood in contrast to the experience of Elizabeth Shutes, who asked a passing officer whether there was an accident or danger of any kind. "None, so far as I know," was his calm, courteous reply. But moments later Miss Shutes overheard the officer whisper, "We can keep the water out for a while."[5] It did not seem clear whether the order to put on life belts and come up on deck was a precautionary measure or a signal of real danger.

In addition, the notification procedure and instructions differed according to class of service:

> In the First Class areas, the order was to put on warm clothing and a life belt and report to the Boat Deck. Second Class passengers were told to report to the dining saloon. Third Class passengers faired [sic] poorly in the warning process. Mostly the stewards just used their pass keys and threw open the cabin doors, pulled the life belts off the top shelf where they were stored, dumped them on the floor, and told everyone to get up and put them on. Those who did not speak English were left to their own devices to figure out what the stewards were telling them to do.[6]

Indeed, third-class passengers were farthest from and least familiar with the decks from which the lifeboats were being loaded. Steward John Hart took it upon himself to lead groups of third-class passengers through the circuitous route to the boat deck, as many of these passengers did not know where they were going or whether they were allowed to pass through certain areas.

Crewmembers were alerted using the organizational chain of command, but this practice was not completely effective. Fifth Officer Lowe was not roused by another crewmember, but instead awakened to the sound of passengers walking around with their life belts on. Another crewmember, Quartermaster George Rowe, who was stationed at the stern of the ship, did not know there was anything wrong until (to his surprise) he saw a lifeboat floating in the water. He called the bridge, and it was only then that officers realized he had been overlooked.[7]

Finally, there were several ways in which *Titanic*'s crew had not adequately planned or prepared for how to organize the ship's evacuation. While the crew had boat stations (assigned boats that they were to help load and lower), these assignments were not posted until that Saturday—11 days after the ship departed Belfast for Southampton—so people did not necessarily know where to go. Further, contrary to typical White Star Line procedures, there was no lifeboat drill conducted on that Sunday. However, the boat drill, as specified by the British Board of Trade, "only required a ship's officers to supervise a picked crew, mustered beforehand, to uncover a designated lifeboat on each side of the ship, swing it out over the ship's side, and climb aboard. Some officers would require the crewman to examine the oars, mast sail and rigging that were stowed in each boat; others weren't so demanding."[8] This drill did not require the crew to practice loading people into the boats or lowering the boats—two of the most important activities in an evacuation. Although a drill was conducted on the day of departure from Southampton in which two boats were lowered all the way to the water, this exercise was done at the dock, during the day, without a full load of people in the boat and in entirely auspicious conditions (with no listing or tipping). Even this training did not fully prepare crewmembers for the far more stressful conditions of a real evacuation.

Given the lack of practice, it is not surprising that the understanding of how the boats should be loaded differed among crewmembers. On the port side of the ship, Officer Lightoller oversaw the effort. His interpretation of the "women and children first" policy was that men were allowed in boats only to the extent that they were needed to operate the lifeboats. On the starboard side, Office Murdoch had a looser interpretation of the policy: men were allowed to board lifeboats if no additional women or children were present at the time the boat was launched. Further, it appeared that the crew lacked guidelines as to how full the lifeboats should be, resulting in broad discrepancies related to how many people could board each boat and concerns about the added weight of passengers in boats hanging from davits. Thus Officer Lightoller attempted a different strategy: instructing boats, once afloat, to row up to the gangway, where theoretically they would take on more passengers and fill the lifeboat to its full capacity. Unfortunately, this idea did not work:

> A plan to fill some of the boats from the lower gangways went completely haywire. The doors that were to be used were never opened. The boats that were to stand by rowed off. The people who were to go were left stranded. When the Caldwells and several others went all the way down to a closed gangway on C deck, somebody who didn't know about the plan locked the door behind them. Later some men on the deck discovered the group and lowered a ladder for them to crawl back up.[9]

Moreover, once the lifeboats were in the water, there was not a consistent or clearly understood set of instructions as to what to do next. Some lifeboats were told to stand by for the possible addition of further passengers. Others were commanded to row toward lights believed to be coming from another ship. As survivor Emily Ryerson recalled, "The order was given to pull away, then they rowed off—the sailors, the women, anyone—but made little progress; there was a confusion of orders; we rowed toward the stern, someone shouted something about a gangway, and no one seemed to know what to do."[10]

It was soon clear to those on lifeboats that many of the crew who were charged with operating the lifeboats were not sailors and did not have the experience needed to perform the job competently. Mrs. J. Stuart White described her experience in Lifeboat 8:

> All of those men escaped under the pretense of being oarsmen. The man who rowed me took his oar and rowed all over the boat, in every direction. I said to him, "Why don't you put the oar in the oarlock?" He said, "Do you put it in that hole?" I said, "Certainly." He said, "I never had an oar in my hand before." I spoke to the other man and he said; "I have never had an oar in my hand before, but I think I can row." Those were the men that we were put to sea with at night—with all the magnificent fellows left on board, who would have been such a protection to us. Those were the kind of men with whom we were put out to sea that night.[11]

Unfortunately, time ran out on the lifeboat loading operation. Two of the collapsible lifeboats were never properly launched, but rather were washed into the sea, with the few people who managed to get into or onto them. In the end, the lifeboats were operating at 39 percent below capacity, resulting in approximately 400 lives lost that, in theory, could have been saved. While the crew did their best (indeed, many survivors commended the crew for their thoughtfulness, dedication, sacrifice, and success in preserving order), failure to anticipate that such a disaster was possible led to minimal planning and preparation for the calamity that occurred. That lack of forethought and preparation in developing plans and related contingencies translated directly into the untimely deaths of hundreds of souls.

LACK OF PLANNING AND PREPARATION IN FAMILY FIRMS

Given the 30 percent survival rate of family firms transitioning from the first to second generation, scholars and practitioners have emphasized the need for planning ahead for generational transitions and long-term survival. Results from a number of studies suggest that family firms that engage in planning outperform those that do not.[12] Preparation for business success and continuity encompasses several different dimensions. Table 5.1 describes nine kinds of planning processes in family enterprise systems. Broadly, they can be grouped into planning for *expected* events (business planning, strategic planning, estate planning, retirement planning, succession planning, and wealth planning) and planning for *unexpected* or lower-probability events (contingency planning, business continuity planning, and risk management planning). The following subsections describe the different types of planning, outline the benefits of each, and explain why this planning is often avoided.

Table 5.1
Nine Kinds of Planning Processes in Family Enterprise Systems

	Planning Type	Description
Expected	Business planning	A planning process for start-up businesses, describing the purpose of the business; plans for marketing, operations, human resources and capital needs, along with correlating timetables
	Strategic planning	An organization's process of defining its strategy, or direction, and making decisions on allocating its resources to pursue this strategy, including its capital and people
	Estate planning	Planning for the transfer of property at death, including the will, trusts, beneficiary designations, powers of appointment, property ownership, gifts, and powers of attorney
	Retirement planning	Envisioning life after being the reigning business leader; includes financial, emotional, and logistical aspects of transition to post-retirement life
	Succession planning	A process for identifying and developing personnel with the potential to fill key or critical organizational positions; planning for transitions in leadership (among owners or managers)
	Wealth planning	Process for preserving family wealth, including aspects of planning for finances/ assets and the family
Unexpected	Contingency planning	Planning for specific situations when things could go wrong, such that people are prepared for anything that could happen
	Business continuity planning	Creating the processes, policies, and procedures related to preparing for recovery or continuation of infrastructure critical to an organization after a disaster
	Risk management planning	Identification, analysis, monitoring/ controlling, mitigation, and reviewing of risks (or events that have some probability of occurring and have an impact on the organization)

Planning for the Expected

In family enterprises, some aspects of being a family and running a business are certain. Knowledge of the needs of the business and the family, as well as how these needs will inevitably change over time, provides an opportunity to plan and prepare for these known elements. These issues include matters such as the operational needs of the business, the desire for the business to grow and prosper, the transitions of family members into and out of the business, the deaths of senior-generation members, the tax consequences of wealth transfers, and the desire to sustain family assets and core values over time. Several planning activities are geared toward these expected dimensions of the family business.

Business Planning

Business planning involves defining the purpose of the business; describing plans for finances, marketing, operations, and human resources' and articulating capital needs and correlating timetables. Creating a business plan is considered by many to be essential at the start-up phase of a business. Many factors important for success depend on this kind of planning, including obtaining outside funding or credit from suppliers, operational and financial management, business promotion and marketing, and achievement of goals and objectives. Even if outside financing is not needed, writing a business plan is useful as a roadmap that can help determine the answers to key business questions:

- Which resources (e.g., time, money) will be needed to get started?
- How long will it take for the business to become profitable?
- What information from potential customers, vendors, and investors is needed to market the business effectively?[13]

The business planning process also requires entrepreneurs to think more objectively about their businesses, in terms of both the big picture and the small details, necessitating hard research about markets, products, and competition. The result of this process can be a plan that creates direction for the company while helping to unify management, employees, family members, and investors behind the plan. In addition, the planning effort yields checkpoints that can subsequently be used to measure and evaluate progress toward goals.[14]

When entrepreneurs avoid this kind of planning, several different beliefs may be at play: (1) entrepreneurs may not see the necessity of committing their plan to paper being that they do not need start-up capital or because they prefer to remain reactive and "see where it goes"; (2) entrepreneurs do not feel they have the time or resources to invest in creating a plan; or (3) they lack the awareness of how to construct one. It comes as little surprise that without a proper business plan, entrepreneurs cannot adequately plan for the financial resources necessary to power the enterprise through its formative years—an omission that may lead to business failure as the organization runs out of cash due to undercapitalization and unrealistic financial expectations.[15]

Strategic Planning

Strategic planning is a form of business planning wherein more mature organizations define their strategy or direction, which in turn facilitates decision making about how best to leverage strengths, use resources, and capitalize on opportunities. This type of planning is usually perceived as a way to position the business for growth and enhanced profitability.

Strategic planning in family firms helps them to better leverage the available resources to gain a competitive advantage and improve performance, and has been found to be especially important in firms with a lower capacity for innovation.[16] This process encourages managers to look more carefully at the competitive landscape and assess the threats and opportunities that exist in their environment.

Another benefit of strategic planning to family firms is that it creates an excellent development opportunity for next-generation leaders. Mazzola and colleagues conducted a qualitative analysis of 18 Italian family businesses, and found that strategic planning yielded both educational benefits and relational benefits for the succeeding generation.[17] Exposure to the *contents* of strategic plans led next-generation members to gain the educational benefits in the following areas:

- Deeper knowledge of the environmental context, and tacit knowledge about the company's history and culture
- Understanding of the company's need for renewal
- Learning decision-making processes with regard to change and innovation, and building capability to make strategic decisions
- Learning how to create action plans, and being well versed in the necessary elements (e.g., corporate framework, resources, and obligations, people to involve, time horizons)
- Increased understanding of key value drivers, financial indicators, and ways to monitor them

Relational benefits were also evident in a number of respects, as the planning process itself created opportunities for successors to engage in the following activities: (1) collaborate and build relationships with incumbent leaders and internal and external stakeholders; (2) earn legitimacy and credibility with these stakeholders; (3) increase alignment with the senior generation; (4) strengthen their buy-in for plans created; and (5) promote their overall positive sense of belonging. Mazzola et al. concluded that the educational and relational benefits to the next generation are enhanced when there is a formal planning process, an ownership or business purpose behind the planning, and real involvement of the next generation in the process.

Nonetheless, Ward has identified some reasons why some family business leaders might be hesitant to engage in strategic planning.[18] Some have concerns that the process might reveal confidential information, expose poor management behaviors, or surface past embarrassments or current family conflicts. Others may see planning as boxing them into a set plan, thereby limiting flexibility. Still others see this activity as a waste of time, given how unpredictable the environment can be. Further, many see changes in strategy as threatening or risky, especially if they associate the old strategies with the reasons for their success.

Estate Planning

Estate planning is defined by the American Bar Association as a plan that "[covers] the transfer of property at death as well as a variety of other personal matters and [that] may or may not involve tax planning. The core document most often associated with this process is the will."[19] However, for family business owners who have significant assets and family involvement, a will is just one of perhaps many documents and plans that should be incorporated into an estate plan. Estate planning entails planning for the transfer of property at death, so it may include elements such as wills, trusts, beneficiary designations, powers of appointment, property ownership, gifts, and powers of attorney. This type of planning is often associated with the transfer of ownership interests in a business.

In a study of heirs from failed family businesses, most heirs believed that the root cause of the failure was inadequate estate planning, including inadequate planning to transfer the business, insufficient funds to pay estate taxes and operate the business, poor performance of the founder's financial advisors, and problems raising capital.[20] While estate planning is crucial for business continuity, some problems are frequently associated with this type of planning: (1) procrastination leading to insufficient time to prepare adequately, (2) pursuing tax minimization to the detriment of other goals, and (3) failing to communicate sufficiently with heirs to determine their needs and desires.[21]

In 2002, 69.8 percent of CEOs surveyed nationally indicated that their estate plan was complete (and an additional 19 percent indicated that only a will was complete).[22] Five years later, data showed similar trends, with 31.4 percent of respondents indicating that their estate plan was *in*complete and only a will was done.[23] By contrast, regional data showed that only 29 percent of CEOs had developed a comprehensive estate plan, with 44 percent having only done a will, 17 percent not having completed any facet of the estate plan (and with no will), and 10 percent who were unsure.[24] The inconsistent data from such national and regional surveys may lead advisors to question whether clients have a clear idea of what an estate plan truly is and what it entails.

When business leaders put off estate planning, they typically cite reasons such as these: "I don't have time"; "I'm too young for an estate plan"; ... "There's still lots of time." In reality, these excuses belie more deep-seated concerns about the process. When allocating assets, parents may become confounded with the attempt to treat all children with fairness, while allocating the organization's assets in an unequal manner (i.e., more to those who have been more engaged in the growth of the business). If an unequal distribution of the organization's ownership is chosen, parents may fear that children will become disappointed and embittered. If one or both members of a couple are uncertain about the stability of their marriage, it may lead to a delay in planning until they have resolved whether they will stay together. Finally, avoidance or denial of the eventuality of death can interfere with the motivation to conduct thoughtful estate planning.

Retirement Planning

Retirement planning involves envisioning life after being the reigning business leader and planning for the financial, social, emotional, and logistical aspects of this transition. The financial considerations include determining how much income is needed to fund the incumbent's retirement, how that money will be supplied, by whom, and over what time period. Investment planning is often an important component of the process.

Ideally, retirement planning includes some reflection upon how the transition from the business will affect the retiree's social world and emotional life. The social and emotional aspects of retirement planning center on building a fulfilling, meaningful life, in terms of both relationships and activities. For the individual making the decision to retire, this raises a number of important questions:

- What is most important to me in the next stage of life?
- Which activities or commitments will I find most rewarding?
- What will the change mean for my friendships and business relationships?
- Which relationships do I want to develop?
- What will the change mean for my marriage?
- Do my spouse and I share retirement goals?

Moreover, the period of reflection can help the incumbent examine how his or her identity will change after leaving the business, and figure out what it will take to smooth the transition. It sometimes takes a prolonged period of time to build sources of positive identity outside of the business; therefore, retirement planning should begin as early as possible.

Resistance to retirement planning stems from a number of concerns about what retirement means. This type of planning is especially difficult for leaders who are over-identified with the business or their leadership role. Many fear loss of power and status, or worry about feeling irrelevant and forgotten—going from a "who's who" to a "who's (s)he?" Concerns about loss of status may bleed over to the family domain, with fears about no longer being the family leader, and perhaps even feeling detached from the family itself (particularly in family firms with a lot of family involvement). Others associate retirement with being old, failing in health, or being one step away from death. Indeed, many of the myths and stereotypes about retirement are negative and serve to discourage leaders from thinking about it.

Succession Planning

Succession planning has to do with planning for leadership changes in the ownership or management of the business. Like retirement, succession is not a single event, but rather a multistep process that consists of a number of phases that require planning (outlined in Figure 5.1).

- Post-transition planning for the business and incumbent
- Assessment of leadership capabilities as well as successor selection and development
- Management transfer
- Ownership transfer

It is little wonder why "succession" arouses anxiety in business owners and their closest circles: the process itself can be complex and difficult to conceptualize. In fact, among business owners who have worked since

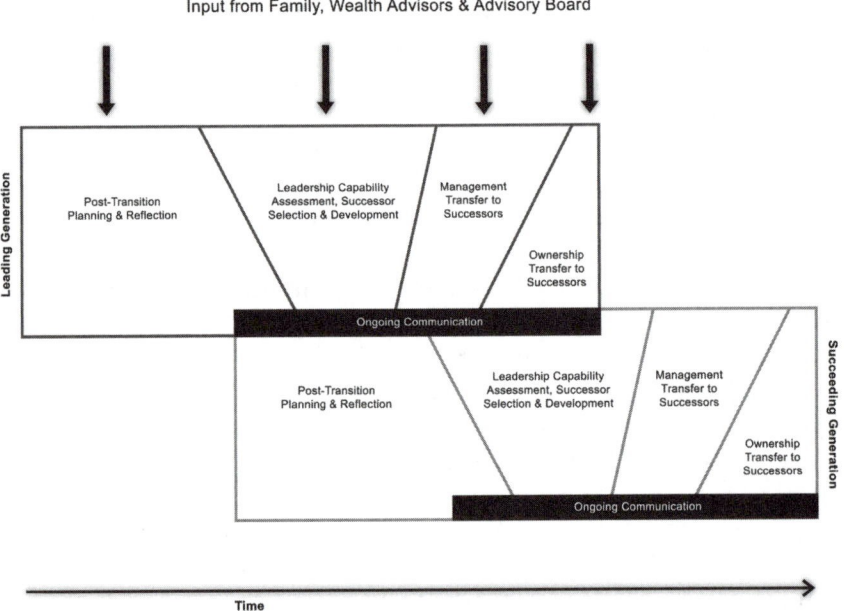

Figure 5.1
Conceptual model for succession

the age of 16, very few can truly conjure up a healthy view of retirement or a life without the everyday stress and demands of business ownership. With such a conceptual hurdle to overcome, the succession process can stop dead in its tracks before even gaining any momentum.

For many advisors, helping clients to engage in post-transition planning and reflection can be the largest obstacle to succession, requiring time and energy at the beginning of the process. Many of the reservations related to this phase include concerns about wealth (whether the incumbent will have enough money to preserve a satisfying lifestyle in retirement), fulfillment (whether the incumbent will feel that he or she still has "value" to the family and society, and whether the incumbent can find happiness in new adventures or hobbies), and relationships (whether the incumbent's marriage, for example, can withstand the increased time spent together and whether the spouse shares similar later-life goals). If the client answers "no" to any of these questions, then the succession process can be compromised. The challenges that retiring owners face as they adjust to spending less time in the business are captured in Sara Yogev's book, *For Better or for Worse . . . But Not for Lunch.*[25]

Once the vision for the post-transition period becomes clear, leaders must then engage in the task of assessing what the organization needs to be successful in the future. This endeavor includes determining which skills are required for future leaders, which potential successors best embody these skills, and how the chosen successors must be groomed for future leadership roles. Of course, not all successors arrive "ready" with the skills to manage and lead a growing or renewed organization; for this reason, successors and bench strength must be developed over time. Leaders must ask themselves the following questions:

- Which capabilities does this business need to thrive over the next decade?
- What talent is available in-house, and what talent needs to be brought in?
- How can talent be best nurtured, and which incentives are in place to keep potential leaders engaged?
- Who best embodies the values of the family and organization?
- Who can best work with customers, suppliers, industry peers, outside advisors, and employees?
- Who is passionate about the business and its continuity?

As the succession process moves into the assessment of leadership capabilities and the selection and development of successors, business owners should increase their involvement in external initiatives and hobbies. This might mean taking a day off per week from the firm, engaging in activities that are rewarding and fulfilling outside the business, and/or building shared interests with spouses or close family and friends. In addition, an important step during this period is that the members of the succeeding generation must (simultaneously) consider *their* post-transition planning, reflecting on what they want their lives to look like in later years. For some succeeding generation family members, an early retirement is most desired, such that their planned departure from the business coincides with the transition time frame of the leading generation. For others, a transition may be provoked when a certain financial goal is reached. For others, the decisions related to transition are weighted most heavily by the opinions of a spouse and the needs of the children. Therefore, to determine who the most suitable successor for the business may be, it is important to establish a strong dialogue focusing on the desires of the individuals (leaders and successors) and needs of the organization.

Progressing through the "post-transition planning and reflection" and "leadership capability assessment and successor selection/development" phases, can take up tremendous time and effort, occurring simultaneously among the generations and accounting for roughly 70 percent of the time and efforts related to the succession process. The latter stages of the process (the remaining 30 percent) are equally divided between the phases of "management transfer" and "ownership transfer" to successors.

Before ownership transfer can be fully achieved, and during the period in which the developing successor is gaining the confidence of advisors and stakeholders, leaders must begin the process of gradually transferring management responsibilities to the successor. For the successor, it is important to assume increased control and decision-making authority; likewise, for the leader, it is important to ensure that he or she is not casting an excessively large "generational shadow" over the successor. Some of the practices associated with this phase include communicating externally to customers, suppliers, trade associations, and other stakeholders (gradually) about the leadership vision and talent within the organization, and continuing an internal dialogue with employees about the transition in leadership. Successors who now assume management control should begin thinking about how to develop others—others who may one day be their own successors.

Lastly, ownership transfer is initiated as the transfer of management responsibilities tapers off. The transfer of ownership is generally the least visible phase, capitalizing on the resourcefulness of advisors and family communication. Even though the leading generation may have transferred management control, the ownership transfer can still take years to complete depending on the ownership structure of the business. During this time, the succeeding generation (who now has full management control and is assuming increased—if not total—ownership) must develop contingency plans in the event of an unplanned departure from the business. This challenge also entails developing future leaders who are committed to the business. Given that the complexity of these elements varies according to family and/or business size, generation, and culture, the extent of planning needed may be very different across businesses.

Research on succession planning in family firms suggests that planning is more prevalent among second- and third-generation businesses compared to first-generation businesses.[26] In addition, this kind of planning is more likely to occur within businesses that have an advisory board.[27] Sharma and colleagues found that the main driver of succession planning was the presence of a motivated successor who inspired trust and confidence in others; however, succession planning was not linked to the family's commitment to the business or the incumbent's desire to keep the business family controlled.[28]

A number of scholar-practitioners have explored the forces that can potentially interfere with succession planning. Lansberg observed that family business stakeholders experience much ambivalence about succession[29] and noted that founders may resist planning for many of the same reasons they resist the idea of retirement: concerns about loss of power, status, control, and changes in central aspects of their identity. They may also experience anger and jealousy toward potential successors, which may lower their trust in successors' capabilities. Spouses may worry about how succession will affect the family harmony and their own social and economic status. Children may avoid discussions about succession because they elicit fears of parental death, or they do not want to appear power-hungry, disloyal, ungrateful, or eager to displace their parent from a valued position. Senior managers may have developed unique working and personal relationships with the founder that make them feel comfortable, such that changes in this important relationship bring about uncertainty, worry, and anxiety. The same is true for clients and suppliers, who may have come to rely heavily on their relationship with the incumbent leader.[30]

Handler and Kram further described factors that promote and reduce resistance to succession planning.[31] Resistance to planning emerges at four different levels within family firms:

- The individual level. Resistance is higher among leaders who are in good health, lack other interests, identify with the business, retain control, fear retirement, and avoid self-learning and consultation.
- The interpersonal or group level. Resistance is higher in groups who are low in trust and open communication, have heirs who appear disinterested or incompetent, have multiple potential heirs, are high in family conflict that permeate the business, and are low in training.
- The organizational level. Resistance is higher in organizations with stable growth, a culture that stymies organizational development, or systems supporting unilateral control.
- The environmental level. Resistance is higher in environments that have many industry requirements, specialized professional prerequisites, and are generally nonproblematic.

Wealth Planning

Wealth planning involves a family's efforts to preserve its wealth over time. This multifaceted, interdisciplinary endeavor incorporates both financial and asset-related planning as well as family planning. Some of the central practices associated with the financial/asset preservation of wealth are tax planning, asset protection, investment planning, retirement planning, insurance planning, estate planning, and business planning.[32] Successful completion of these tasks requires consultation with advisors who have legal, financial, and regulatory expertise. On the family side of wealth planning are elements such as the articulation of family mission and vision, preparation of heirs, creation of structures for family governance, family philanthropy, and development of strategies for preserving family cohesion and transferring of family values. One unique aspect of family wealth planning is the expansion of the definition of wealth beyond material or financial wealth (e.g. human capital, intellectual capital, social/societal capital, spiritual capital, family capital, and structural capital).[33]

As with other types of planning, conversations about wealth can open up old wounds, intensify rivalries, or draw attention to other emotionally-fraught topics. Some families would prefer to avoid potential conflicts, rather than talk through them. Other families find the concepts involved in wealth planning to be overly abstract or impractical; they may prefer to focus strictly on tactics for preserving financial capital, as opposed to social or spiritual capital. Other families may not see themselves as having enough financial wealth to conduct such comprehensive planning.

Planning for the Unexpected

Not all changes, problems, or events that affect family businesses are expected or predictable. Planning for the unexpected is challenging because it is difficult to determine the nature of the issues that might emerge and it is logistically impossible to prepare for every conceivable low-probability event. Nevertheless, family businesses that take the time to plan and prepare for unexpected events have a better chance of minimizing the damages and surviving.

Contingency Planning

Contingency planning entails planning for specific situations in which things could go wrong, so that people are prepared for anything that could happen. These situations are sometimes referred to as "what if" scenarios: "What if a key employee or family member died suddenly?" "What if a new competitor moved into our space?" "What if our three biggest customers or suppliers folded?" "What if our bank folded?" "What if our workers walked off the job or contracted the same debilitating virus?" Having a plan in place so that people know what to do or what will happen can help to ensure that thoughtful decision making occurs, thereby stabilizing the system in the face of an unforeseen problem.

A type of contingency planning particularly relevant to family-owned firms is emergency succession planning. Emergency succession is necessary when the leader suddenly becomes unable to lead due to death, illness, injury, scandal, major life change (e.g., an ailing spouse or spiritual renewal), or some other reason or crisis. Emergency succession plans designate the key functions of the leader, outline a sequence of events that will occur in the short- or long-term absence of the leader, provide a process for the selection of an interim leader, and delineate how communication of the leadership transition will be managed among all relevant stakeholders. Michael Hartley and Bonnie Brown Hartley have developed a unique system for preparing for the sudden death of a leader and other unexpected events that might potentially affect family businesses. Their "Think Ahead" series features CDs with customizable Fire Drills for the individual, the family, and the business, as well as other tools for strategic contingency planning (Box 5.1).

Box 5.1
Why Do Fire Drills?

Bonnie B. Hartley—Transition Dynamics

Fire Drills help business families grow stronger, improve communications, and become more resilient in the face of "sink or swim" situations. They embody contingency planning that nurtures a vision and sense of purpose that can be understood and supported by all generations of the family and its firm's management team, board, and owners. For example, Fire Drills incorporate team building, strategic planning, and the opportunity to test assumptions about what will happen if a major stakeholder dies or is disabled suddenly, if aging members of the senior generation can no longer care for themselves, or if the business is sold. Fire Drills do not provide any guarantees, but they do offer the opportunity to establish models for managing unexpected change that will provide a point of departure, a confidence in the team's ability to manage change, and the "muscle memory" that comes from practice to respond quickly, thoughtfully, and effectively when sudden changes occur in the family's life.

Consider the following questions that provide a point of departure for a Sudden Death Fire Drill:

- If you died tomorrow, what would your survivors need to do first? During the first six months? During the first two years after your death?
- What would they need to know about your personal and professional life so that they could handle the issues that would arise around money, power, and love?
- How would your death affect their financial security, their place in the community, and their emotional security?
- What would your legacy to them be?
- How would they remember you?

Business Continuity Planning

Business continuity planning is a type of contingency planning that focuses on creating the processes, policies, and procedures related to an organization's recovery in the wake of an unplanned, disruptive event. This event could be either a natural disaster or a human-related disaster (e.g., a medical emergency or hostile attack). An excellent resource for business continuity planning is the "Ready Business" campaign. Launched by the U.S. Department of Homeland Security and the Advertising Council in 2004, Ready Business helps owners and managers of small- and medium-sized businesses prepare their employees, operations, and assets in the event of an emergency.[34]

From a psychological perspective, there are good reasons to engage in planning for emergencies. Research on the psychology of survival shows that, in the event of a life-threatening emergency, many people have impairments in their thinking that can hamper their ability to survive. In family business emergencies, the emotions of family members may be intense, making it very difficult to think clearly and strategically during times of crisis. Contingency and continuity planning allow for the relevant stakeholders to do the thinking ahead of time so that there is a roadmap in place guiding people in how to proceed. Box 5.2 evaluates the cognitive impairments of those involved in emergency situations.

Box 5.2
Research Notes: Survival Psychology

John Leach, a psychologist at Lancaster University in the United Kingdom, has studied the reactions of people in emergency situations ranging from shipwrecks to airplane crashes, parachute failures, oil rig emergencies, and natural disasters. Witnesses to such catastrophic situations have reported that some people who could have survived did not because their behavior was inappropriate to the situation. Common responses to an emergency are "fight or flight" behaviors—both of which are action oriented and usually adaptive. Other people respond to danger by "freezing"—that is, by becoming unable to respond productively.

The freezing response results from impairments in cognitive functioning, including difficulty accessing long-term memory,[1] deficiencies in attention,[2] and overloaded capacity of working memory.[3] Such cognitive impairment can "make flexible interaction with the survival environment difficult and the victim's behaviour becomes dominated by environmental cues at the expense of willful, goal-directed survival behavior. The often witnessed result is a victim who is unable to aid his own survival."[4] What may be surprising is that the vast majority of people in an emergency are likely to experience at least some degree of cognitive impairment. Leach estimates that 10 to 15 percent of people remain calm, able to think quickly, with intact reasoning and judgment; 75 percent are stunned, with some impaired reasoning and sluggish thinking; and 10 to 15 percent enter into a state of extreme shock or panic, demonstrating unproductive behaviors such as screaming or paralysis.[5] One implication of this research is the importance of training in survival procedures, which help people create schemas for what to do in an emergency, thereby increasing the speed at which they could perform potentially life-saving actions.

[1]Leach and Griffith, "Restrictions in Working Memory."
[2]Leach and Ansell, "Impaired Attentional Processing."
[3]Leach, "Cognitive Paralysis."
[4]Leach and Ansell, "Impaired Attentional Processing," 651.
[5]Leach, "Why People 'Freeze.'"

Financial preparation to withstand a disaster or period of acute distress should also be part of the business continuity planning process. Given that it is impossible to be insured against every possible threat, having a reserve of funds set aside for an emergency is sound practice. This idea is well illustrated by the story of the family-owned Sir Speedy Printing in Waterbury, Connecticut, in Box 5.3. This family's prudent financial practices made all the difference following a devastating fire that turned all of the business's equipment and inventory into ashes, but not the family's dream of revival.

Box 5.3
A Family Business That Was Prepared

Sir Speedy Printing of Waterbury, Connecticut

John and Heather Wages worked in the Sir Speedy Printing franchise owned by Heather's parents. This franchise, through years of hard work and humility on the part of the owners, became one of the top 25 Sir Speedy franchises in the United States.

In February 2006, John and Heather were awakened by a phone call bearing terrible news: a fire near their business location had spread to surrounding buildings. In the end, their 10,000-square-foot facility, all of its equipment, and 20 years of their hard work literally went up in smoke overnight—a traumatic experience for the family. Fortunately, John and Heather had prepared for times of trouble. Having lost his own father at a very young age, John was all too aware of the fact that that bad things can happen to good people. Above all else, he wanted to be able to take care of his family no matter what might happen. Ten years earlier, the couple had embarked on a quest to pay off their debt and build their personal financial security. They decided to follow the advice of author and financial guru Dave Ramsey, who emphasized the practice of slowly but steadily putting money aside for unexpected capital needs. Amazingly, just 30 days before the fire, the couple had reached their goal of accruing a financial cushion that fully covered six months of living expenses.

Heather's parents, who were nearing retirement age, made the painful but practical decision not to reopen the business—a decision that was made easier by the knowledge that John and Heather would be financially stable for a while. John found a new job and Heather stayed at home to care for their two sons and newborn daughter. But the dream of the family business never left them.

In the fall of 2007, a year and a half after the fire, John and Heather opened a new Sir Speedy franchise on the same piece of land as the old location. In February 2011, John happily reported that the business was—pardoning the pun—"on fire." Over the past 20 months, while other businesses had foundered, the couple's new venture had experienced steady growth.

John noted that it is difficult to convey how devastating the experience of the fire was. Nevertheless, the fact that he and Heather were prepared financially brought a level of peace to the family that made it possible to survive and rebuild. Taking nothing for granted, when asked about what advice he would have for other business owners, John had the following suggestions:

- Keep family finances and business finances separate. If the business goes down, the family can still remain afloat financially.
- Focus on becoming financially secure. Save six months' worth of emergency cash for the family, and establish additional financial reserves for the business.
- Be cautious and plan for the worst-case scenarios, while recognizing that problems rarely end up being the worst case.
- Strong, healthy finances *and* culture drive business success. Build a potent "A-team" culture that is competent and professional, and positive results will follow.

Risk Management Planning

Business continuity planning creates plans to deal with emergencies *after* they have occurred, but does not include more normative risks associated with doing business. Risk management planning is a preemptive approach to successfully managing unforeseen events, by working to minimize risk or avoid crises entirely. In addition, this type of planning focuses on assessing the known risks associated with "the cost of doing business" to determine which risks are worth taking. Risk management planning involves the following activities:

1. Identifying the universe of possible risks.
2. Assessing the probability of occurrence and severity of impact for each potential risk.

3. Prioritizing the risks by quantifying them in terms of a composite risk index (Composite Risk Index = Probability of Occurrence × Impact of Risk).
4. Managing each risk using one of four strategies:[35]
    a. Risk avoidance: Not participating in any activity that carries risk, thereby eliminating the risk entirely.
    b. Risk reduction: Reducing the probability that a risk will occur and/or reducing the negative impact the risk could have on the organization.
    c. Risk sharing: Sharing with a third party the costs (or benefits) associated with risk, and sharing the measures taken to reduce the risk.
    d. Risk retention: Accepting the risk and being prepared to deal with the consequences should the risk occur.
5. Tracking, reporting, and reviewing risks.

Risk oversight has received increasing attention since the 2008–2009 financial crisis, with many people holding corporate boards accountable for failing to do their part to oversee risks. While the purpose of boards is not to manage risks on a day-to-day basis, they must ensure that proper risk management practices are in place and review relevant risk-related reports on a regular basis. Recognizing that senior management may not be completely objective in their identification or assessment of risk, the board must play a more vigorous role in the process, thereby helping to create a culture that allows for rigorous challenge and spirited debate about important risk matters.[36]

Within family firms, the role of the board in corporate oversight can be even more challenging. In fact, most family firms do not have professional boards of directors or advisors. Boards may be perfunctory (existing only to satisfy the requirements of the by-laws), or they may consist of only family members. There is often little or no separation between the board and management, with the CEO frequently occupying the role of chairperson of the board. When nonfamily members are represented on the board, they are often not truly independent directors; nonfamily directors may at times include the founder's or senior leader's "cronies" or the company attorney or accountant, thereby diminishing the independence of the board. This structure makes achieving effective corporate oversight more difficult because (1) not having outside experience and perspectives lowers the board's overall capacity to be objective and offer novel ideas, and (2) family and close personal relationships can inhibit the development of a climate that welcomes dissenting opinions and push-back on management.

Ultimately, there may be many reasons why family businesses do not plan for the unexpected. For some, planning is ignored because they do not have (or choose not to invest) the time to think through all of the risks and develop plans to deal with them. Such individuals may be "too busy" running the business to consider or discuss the nonimmediate problems or risks. For others, it can be difficult to directly confront risks such as the sudden death of the leader—an event families and individuals would rather not envision. Family businesses also may elect not to form boards of advisors or directors with truly independent voices that can challenge their ideologies, practices, and assumptions about strategies and risks. Finally, in some family businesses, the lack of planning and preparation can be traced back to excessive optimism, overconfidence, and the preservation of the "it won't happen to me" mentality.

CHAPTER SUMMARY

- Lack of planning and preparation affected *Titanic* in four ways: (1) failure to plan for managing and communicating effectively about ice warnings; (2) insufficient planning in regard to the number, size, and equipping of lifeboats; (3) lack of a plan to communicate to passengers and crew in an emergency; and (4) insufficient preparation for conducting a full evacuation.
- In family firms, several kinds of planning should be directed to aspects of business functioning and transitions that are *expected* (business planning, strategic planning, retirement planning, estate planning, succession planning, and wealth planning).
- Other planning activities in family firms should be directed to *unexpected* or lower-probability events (contingency planning, business continuity planning, and risk management planning).
- In planning for both the expected and the unexpected, family business systems may experience resistance to planning or avoid planning for a number of reasons (e.g., not seeing planning as valuable or practical, having difficulty facing risks or changes, or having fears of surfacing conflicts that could disrupt family harmony).
- In the case of both *Titanic* and failed family businesses, proper planning and preparation may have resulted in less catastrophic results, or might have prevented the occurrence of a disaster entirely.

Thomas Ismay. (Titanic Historical Society, Inc., and Titanic Museum)

J. Bruce Ismay. (© Underwood & Underwood/CORBIS)

Lord William J. Pirrie. (Titanic Historical Society, Inc., and Titanic Museum)

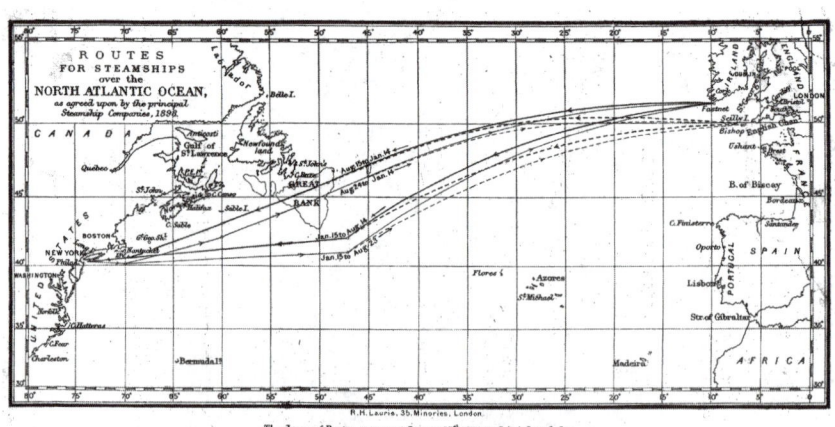

1898 map of routes for steamships over the North Atlantic Ocean. (Courtesy of the National Archives)

Olympic and *Titanic* being built in Belfast (with view of bows in shipyard construction scaffolding). (Courtesy of the Library of Congress)

A view of *Titanic*'s workers standing aside *Titanic*'s central turbine and one of the ship's wing propellers. (Courtesy of the Library of Congress)

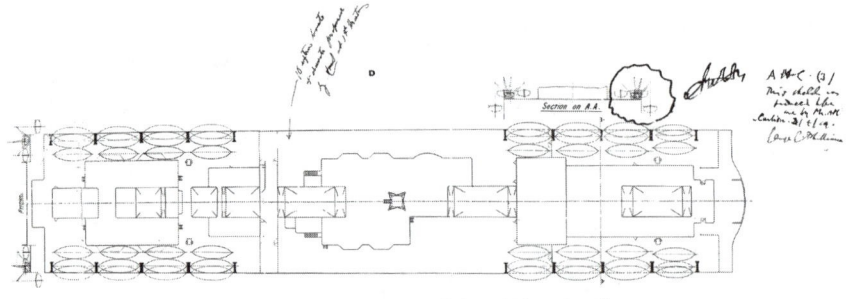

S.S.'s "OLYMPIC" AND "TITANIC," BUILDING BY MESSRS. HARLAND & WOLFF, LTD., BELFAST, FOR
THE WHITE STAR LINE.
EACH VESSEL FITTED WITH THE NEW WELIN DOUBLE-ACTING DAVITS,
HANDLING IN ALL 32 LIFEBOATS.

Harland and Wolff drawing of lifeboat arrangement for *Olympic* and *Titanic*. Places for additional lifeboats were sketched in after the sinking. (Courtesy of the National Archives)

Chief Purser Herbert McElroy (left) with Captain Edward John Smith (right). (Titanic Historical Society, Inc., and Titanic Museum)

Surviving *Titanic* Officers (from left-right): Lightoller, Lowe (seated), Pitman, and Boxhall. (Titanic Historical Society, Inc., and Titanic Museum)

Lifeboats on *Titanic*. (© Hulton-Deutsch Collection/CORBIS)

Titanic wireless operator, Jack Phillips. (Titanic Historical Society, Inc., and Titanic Museum)

Harold Bride, surviving wireless operator of the *Titanic* with feet bandaged, being carried up ramp of a ship. (Courtesy of the Library of Congress)

Titanic lookout Frederick Fleet. (Courtesy of the Library of Congress)

Titanic at sea. (© Underwood & Underwood/CORBIS)

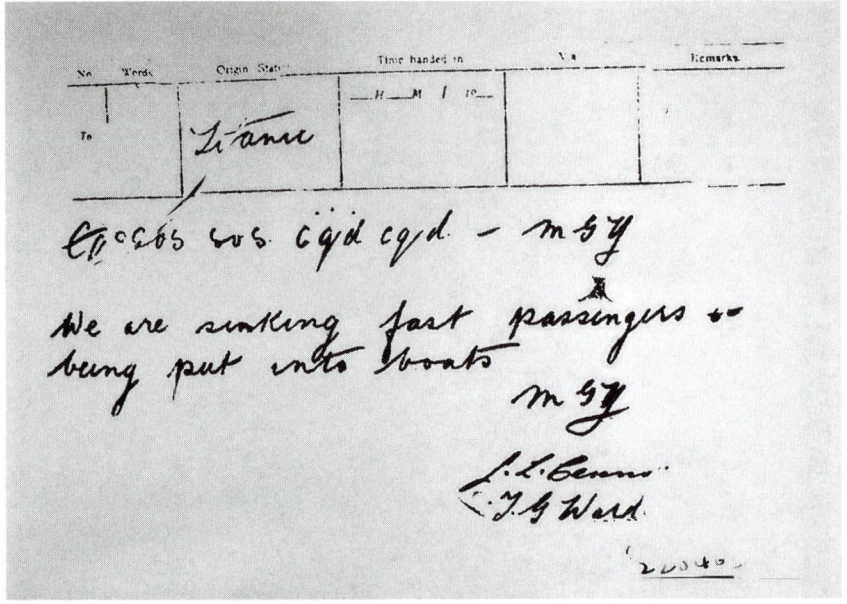

Titanic's final SOS / CQD wireless message sent to *Carpathia* shortly after 2 A.M. on April 15, 1912. (© Bettmann/CORBIS)

Side view of one of *Titanic*'s collapsible lifeboats rowing to *Carpathia*. (Courtesy of the National Archives)

HYDROGRAPHIC OFFICE,

WASHINGTON, D. C.

DAILY MEMORANDUM

N-8.

No. 1013.

April 15, 1912.

NORTH ATLANTIC OCEAN

OBSTRUCTIONS OFF THE AMERICAN COAST.

Mar. 28 – Lat 24° 20', lon 80° 02', passed a broken spar projecting about 3 feet out of water, apparently attached to sunken wreckage.—EVELYN (SS) Wright.

OBSTRUCTIONS ALONG THE OVER-SEA ROUTES.

Apr 7 – Lat 35° 20', lon 59° 40', saw a lowermast covered with marine growth.—ADRIATICO (It. ss), Cevascu.

ICE REPORTS.

Apr 7 – Lat 45° 10', lon 56° 40', ran into a strip of field ice about 3 or 4 miles wide extending north and south as far as could be seen. Some very heavy pans were seen.—ROSALIND (Br ss), Williams.

Apr 10 – Lat 41° 50', lon 50° 25', passed a large ice field a few hundred feet wide and 15 miles long extending in a NNE direction.—EXCELSIOR (Ger ss). (New York Herald)

COLLISION WITH ICEBERG – Apr 14 – Lat 41° 46', lon 50° 14', the British steamer TITANIC collided with an iceberg seriously damaging her bow; extent not definitely known.

Apr 14 – The German steamer AMERIKA reported by radio telegraph passing two large icebergs in lat 41° 27', lon 50° 08',—TITANIC (Br ss).

Apr 14 – Lat 42° 06', lon 49° 43', encountered extensive field ice and saw seven icebergs of considerable size.—PISA (Ger ss).

J. J. K N A P P

Captain, U. S. Navy,
Hydrographer.

Hydrographic Office Memorandum noting *Titanic*'s collision with an iceberg. (Courtesy of the National Archives)

Crowds forming outside of White Star Line offices in New York City awaiting news of the *Titanic* disaster. (© Underwood & Underwood/CORBIS)

Bruce Ismay (at end of table with hand to chin) being questioned by a special subcommittee of the Senate Commerce Committee (chaired by Senator William Alden Smith) on April 19, 1912 at the Waldorf-Astoria Hotel in New York City. (Courtesy of the Library of Congress)

Mrs. James J. ("Molly") Brown presenting a trophy cup award to *Carpathia*'s Captain Arthur Henry Roston for his service in the rescue of the *Titanic*'s survivors. (Courtesy of the Library of Congress)

U.S. Airways flight 1549 crash-lands into New York's Hudson River adjacent to midtown Manhattan on January 15, 2009. (© JUSTIN LANE/epa/CORBIS)

Captain Chesley Sullenberger (left) and First Officer Jeffrey Skiles (right) are applauded at a meeting of the Transportation and Infrastructure Committee at the U.S. House of Representatives on February 24, 2009. Sullenberger's skill is credited with saving the lives of all 155 passengers and crewmembers aboard the plane. (© MICHAEL REYNOLDS/epa/ CORBIS)

6

Frail Architecture

There was too much brag and not enough seaworthy construction.
—Sir James Bisset, on *Olympic* and *Titanic*

Without solid design and construction, any building or business is prone to becoming a "house of cards," vulnerable to collapse even under minimally stressful conditions and providing little stability for those who operate in it. For many, architecture is a game of "trade-offs" and compromise—investing time, energy, and resources in some areas while choosing, perhaps, to cut in others.

Architecture (when related to organizations) means much more than "bricks and mortar." Architecture can also be conceptual, relating to the development, implementation, maintenance, and protection of policies and procedures necessary to survive. This aspect becomes increasingly important when stewarding the firm through the complexities of management succession and ownership succession. Both concepts of architecture are necessary, however, and poor oversight of an organization's design can compromise the stability and future of the business.

For some businesses and structures, frail architecture can lead directly to their demise. *Titanic*'s collapse, of course, was literal—marked by a series of events that went wrong—each of which was critically problematic in and of itself, but not one alone that could have caused the massive loss of life that ensued from the ship's sinking. While *Titanic* was indeed the "best in class" with the highest-quality food and amenities, the same could not be said for her architecture and design. Notwithstanding the fact that *Titanic* was believed to be extremely safe (with watertight bulkheads, a double hull, and a sophisticated wireless system), three key areas with regard to her architecture and construction were found to be contributors to the loss of life: rivet design, engines, and davits.

FRAIL ARCHITECTURE: *TITANIC*

The late nineteenth and early twentieth centuries were periods of enormous change, with immigration to the New World on the rise. To meet the growing demand for transatlantic travel, Harland and Wolff and White Star Line planned to build three enormous Olympic-class ships—a plan that simultaneously created a huge demand for skilled labor. Specifically, a need arose for engineers, riveters, and puddlers.

Puddlers were workers who stirred the molten iron and ensured that it had the perfect balance of iron and slag, a by-product that absorbs impurities in iron and gives iron its fibrous structure.[1] In effect, they were like bakers, charged with ensuring consistency in quality from batch to batch with the exact combination ingredients. Of course, excess slag made the iron weaker, requiring the wrought iron to be "piled"—a process in which rolled wrought iron would be layered in a criss-cross pattern with other rolls of wrought iron, reheated, and rerolled to squeeze out slag remnants. The more the product was piled, the better quality it was.[2] Iron that had been puddled and poured was regarded as Number 1 iron; Number 1 iron that had been piled was regarded as Number 2 iron; Number 2 iron that had been repiled was considered Number 3 iron, or "best"; and Number 3 iron that had been repiled was considered Number 4 iron, or "best best." Harland and Wolff had originally specified that Number 4 "best best" iron be used to make *Titanic*'s rivets, as such rivets would have possessed less slag (and have more strength) than the Number 3 irons that White Star Line ultimately drafted for use in its purchase order. With so many puddlers creating thousands of batches of iron to produce the 3 million rivets used to construct *Titanic*, consistency of iron quality was of utmost importance.

With a lack of qualified workers, Harland and Wolff was well aware of the pressures it faced in completing *Titanic*'s and *Olympic*'s construction on time. The company employed young boys—some as young as 13 years of age—to heat the iron rivets into a cherry-red color (a fairly rudimentary signal for determining whether the iron was appropriately heated), which would make the rivets more malleable when being pounded into *Titanic*'s steel hull. It was a critical process entrusted to the least skilled of employees: heating the rivets too much would make them too malleable and weak, while not heating them up enough would prevent them from forming a watertight seal in the rivet hole.

Not all of the rivets were made of iron, however. Approximately 60 percent of *Titanic*'s rivets were steel, hydraulically driven into place by skilled riveters. The challenge with steel was that it was a more difficult material to work with: when overheated, it became brittle and shattered on impact.[3] By comparison, iron rivets were more supple and predictable in their reaction to heat. Despite the difficulties, steel rivets had been widely used since 1906 by shipbuilders, who noted that "the tendency to use steel rivets in steel ships is increasing, it being found that more satisfactory results are thereby obtained."[4]

White Star Line chose to use steel rivets only amidships the vessel (where most stress would be put on her during travel), with iron rivets being employed to outfit the bow and stern of the ship. The decision against steel rivets in the bow and stern sections was mostly financial, although there were some nonfinancial reasons relating to maneuverability while riveting in cramped areas amid the sloping structure of the bow and stern. Hammering in steel rivets was more difficult work, requiring skilled workers (earning higher wages) who knew how to heat steel correctly. Steel also needed to be tested prior to use, according to the British Board of Trade, causing what White Star Line management saw as an unnecessary delay. Iron rivets, by comparison, were easier (and thus cheaper) to install and did not require skilled labor to the degree that steel rivets demanded. Their use also ensured that no delays would impede construction, as the British Board of Trade (since 1901) no longer required that irons bars be tested prior to rivet use.

Microscopic analysis of *Titanic*'s iron rivets reclaimed from the ocean floor from the 1996 Discovery Channel expedition revealed the following:

> [A] *Titanic* wrought iron rivet contained an average of as little as 1.1 percent and as much as 12.8 percent slag, depending on which rivet was studied. With an average value of over four times the normal slag content, the results were significant. Rivets were full of poorly mixed, abnormally large slag stringers, which created small regions in the heads and shaft that contained as much as 20 to 40 percent slag. With uneven mixtures in a material like this, there will always be localized differences in properties, making weak regions more likely to fail when highly stressed.[5]

Further, once a rivet has stress placed upon it (e.g., with bending of the steel plating that the rivets are holding together), the pressure on the rivet's head can cause it to pop off. Coincidentally, in evaluating *Olympic* following her collision with *HMS Hawke* in 1911, photos show empty rivet holes, lending support to the theory that a catastrophic failure would result from the rivets being unable to maintain their structural integrity under stress.

In the final analysis, the iron rivets that were used aboard *Titanic* consisted of subpar materials and were installed by unskilled workers who were incentivized to work quickly. Even so, Harland and Wolff's unskilled labor was paid less than jobs of similar scope in other shipyards.[6] Further, although White Star Line eschewed Harland and Wolff's recommendation to use "best best" rivets, it remains unclear whether the "best best" rivets would have contained less slag than the "best" Number 3 rivets ordered. As a result of the high level of slag, and its configuration within the rivet itself, the rivets were unusually weak. When put under stress upon *Titanic*'s impact with the iceberg, the heads of the rivets popped off and the seams held together by them opened to the Atlantic and flooded *Titanic*'s belly.

The second architectural flaw that compromised *Titanic*'s integrity as a ship concerned her engines. While White Star Line boasted in postcards, posters, and press kits about *Titanic*'s and *Olympic*'s "triple-screw" engines, little was known at that time about how a ship so large and so heavy would maneuver with engines built using eighteenth-century models. In fact, *Titanic* was the largest human-made moving structure on earth in 1912.

With tall and thin rudders built for speed (versus the short and square rudders built for maneuverability), the Olympic-class ships' design did not mean that White Star Line was completely abandoning its efforts to keep up with Cunard with regard to competing on speed. Nonetheless, it would be the triple-screw engine that would prevent *Titanic*'s officers from maneuvering nimbly around icebergs or other obstacles.

Titanic's engines comprised a large center steam-powered turbine (which could not go into reverse) and two reciprocating steam engines powering the wing propellers (which could go into reverse) on either side of the center turbine. In the post-accident inquiry, Fourth Officer Boxhall claimed that First Officer Murdoch gave orders to the engine rooms to "reverse the engines" in an effort to avoid the iceberg looming ahead. Such an order would have effectively shut down the center turbine, which largely powered the rudder. In effect, the side engines could be reversed, but the ship would not be able to turn. Some have argued that had *Titanic*'s officers simply turned the ship, *Titanic* might have missed the iceberg.[7] It was not just a lack of awareness of the engine's capabilities that contributed to the collision; it was a design flaw in engine configuration that hampered the maneuverability of such a large ship. It has been noted that *Titanic*'s stern was, in effect, "an exact copy of an 18th-century sailing ship" and "a perfect example of the lack of technical development."[8]

To be fair, the construction of *Titanic*'s engines was no cause for alarm with regard to the industry regulations of the day. *Titanic*'s rudder was well within the legal requirements of the time: at 1.9 percent of the hull's underwater profile, the rudder was within the 1.5 to 5 percent proportional requirement, albeit on the low end. Yet, it is important to note that a ship this size had never been built and that the British Board of Trade had not yet updated its rules and requirements to keep up with shipbuilding advancements. In fact, much of the British Board of Trade requirements used a ship's tonnage as the key factor when evaluating issues such as the number of lifeboats to be stowed aboard a ship. It was not until the late nineteenth and early twentieth centuries that passenger steamships became the norm for transatlantic travel; tonnage before this era consisted mostly of goods and not passengers. At the time of *Titanic*'s construction, then, British Board of Trade requirements for lifeboats did not reflect a ship's passenger capacity.

The third architectural flaw dealt with the davits and the lack of information pertaining to how the davits would operate with lifeboats loaded to their full capacity. Recall that *Titanic* held 14 wooden lifeboats with a capacity of 65 people in each, 2 emergency wooden lifeboats with a capacity of 40 people each, and 4 collapsible lifeboats with a capacity of 49 people each. In the end, only 2 lifeboats were lowered with their full capacity of passengers. Notwithstanding the fact that many passengers felt they were safer remaining on the "unsinkable" ship, the officers manning the lifeboats deliberately lowered each lifeboat with fewer passengers than its full capacity, leaving behind passengers on deck who wanted to enter the lifeboats. The reason for this decision was simple: the officers were not sure the davits would hold the lifeboats if loaded to their capacity. The construction of the davits was such that the stress of the weight of the individuals might compromise the davit itself and its ability to be of further use in lowering passengers to safety. Several officers testified to this in the U.S. inquiry following the disaster:

Senator Smith: Who determined the number of people who should go into the lifeboats?

Mr. Lightoller: I did.

Senator Smith: How did you reach a conclusion as to the number that should be permitted to go in?

Mr. Lightoller: My own judgment about the strength of the tackle.

Senator Smith: How many did you put in each boat?

Mr. Lightoller: In the first boat, I put about 20 or 25. Twenty, sir ...

Senator Smith: In a great emergency like that, where there were limited facilities, could you not have afforded to try to put more people into that boat?

Mr. Lightoller: I did not know it was urgent then. I had no idea it was urgent.

Senator Smith: You did not know it was urgent.

Mr. Lightoller: Nothing like it.

Senator Smith:	Supposing you had known it was urgent, what would you have done?
Mr. Lightoller:	I would have acted to the best of my judgment then.
Senator Smith:	Tell me what you would have thought wise.
Mr. Lightoller:	I would have taken more risks. I should not have considered it wise to put more in, but I might have taken risks.
Senator Smith:	As a matter of fact are not these lifeboats so constructed as to accommodate 40 people?
Mr. Lightoller:	Sixty-five in the water, sir.
Senator Smith:	Sixty-five in the water, and about 40 as they are being put into the water?
Mr. Lightoller:	No, sir.
Senator Smith:	How?
Mr. Lightoller:	No, sir; it all depends on your gears, sir. If it were an old ship, you would barely dare to put 25 in.
Senator Smith:	But this was a new one?
Mr. Lightoller:	And therefore I took chances with her afterwards.

On questioning Third Officer Pitman by Senators Smith and Fletcher:

Senator Smith:	Is there any danger in lowering a lifeboat with the davits and other equipment operating? Is there such danger in lowering a lifeboat that you cannot fill it to its capacity?
Mr. Pitman:	I would not like to fill a lifeboat with 60 people and lower it suspended at both ends . . .
Senator Fletcher:	Do I correctly understand you to say that you would not consider it safe to load a boat to its full capacity at the rail before lowering it?
Mr. Pitman:	No; I do not think it would be wise to do it . . .
Senator Fletcher:	Suppose the boat carries 65 people; how many would you feel it is safe to put into the boat before lowering it?
Mr. Pitman:	I think 40 would be a very safe load. I do not think boats are ever intended to be filled from the rail.
Senator Fletcher:	How do you expect to fill them?
Mr. Pitman:	With a side ladder.
Senator Fletcher:	Why was not that course pursued in this instance?
Mr. Pitman:	Well, it was a new ship, and everything new, of course. It takes a certain amount of risk. That was a much quicker way, too.

Senator Fletcher: Which is the much quicker way?

Mr. Pitman: The way we did it.

On questioning Fifth Officer Lowe:

Senator Smith: I want that understood. Do you wish the committee to understand that a lifeboat whose capacity is 65 under the British regulations could not be lowered with safety, with new tackle and equipment, containing more than 50 people?

Mr. Lowe: The dangers are that if you overcrowd the boat the first thing that you will have will be that the boat will buckle up like that [indicating] at the two ends, because she is suspended from both ends and there is no support in the middle.

Senator Smith: These lifeboats were all on the upper deck?

Mr. Lowe: Yes, sir.

Senator Smith: If it is dangerous to lower a boat from the upper deck, filled to the capacity prescribed by the British regulations—

Mr. Lowe: Yes; that is the floating capacity.

Senator Smith: Sixty-five plus is the floating capacity?

Mr. Lowe: That is the floating capacity—that is, in the water, when she is at rest in the water. That is not when she is in the air.

The question remains: what is the purpose of lifeboats if they cannot be filled to capacity while passengers are escaping to safety?

By way of contrast, consider what happened when *Titanic*'s younger sister *Britannic* suffered an explosion in the Aegean Sea (likely due to a mine) in November 1916. When a full evacuation was ordered, no one was left on the ship to perish. Although the ship sank in only 55 minutes (less than half of the time *Titanic* sank), all the lifeboats necessary to hold the 1,066 people on board were launched. With less time to evacuate, the minimal loss of life in this incident can be credited in part to the architectural changes instituted after *Titanic*'s sinking (30 of *Britannic*'s passengers died due to their lifeboats being sucked in by the ship's propellers). Through better davit design, improvements were made on White Star Line ships subsequent to *Titanic*'s sinking that allowed lifeboats to be lowered more effectively when full:

No one admiring the *Britannic*'s massive profile could doubt that lifeboats had become a priority. Five sets of huge gantry davits towered over the boat deck, while two more graced the poop deck, each responsible for launching six of the largest lifeboats ever carried on a ship and, where a funnel did not block the way, capable of reaching across the superstructure to pick up boats from the other side of the ship if it became impossible to launch them there...Each new gantry davit was powered by a special auxiliary electric motor and had its own electric illumination to facilitate nighttime loading.[9]

The inquiry into *Titanic*'s sinking and poor architectural design prompted *Lloyd's Register of Shipping* (the preeminent publication that "describes, classifies, and registers ships based on a series of rules and standards for building vessels"[10] and whose classification is not required, but generally a highly sought-after "seal of approval") to issue the following statement:

> In view of the reports, which have appeared in the Press in connection with the inquiry into the loss of the *S.S. Titanic*, to the effect that the vessel was built considerably in excess of the requirements of *Lloyd's Register*, I am directed to say that these statements are inaccurate. On the contrary, in important parts of her structure the vessel as built did not come up to the requirements of *Lloyd's Register* for a vessel of her dimension.[11]

FRAIL ARCHITECTURE IN FAMILY FIRMS

For many involved in family firms, a common practice is "construction preceding architecture"—the family is involved before the founder has the opportunity to create the policies and practices associated with sound organizational development and good governance. For many, this course of action is simply a matter of survival. When a company is founded, the people who help out while placing fewer demands on the business and the founder are generally family members. Who else will work 12-hour days simply for a "thank you" or pizza and beer? Who else will tolerate the emotional ups and downs of a first customer, a huge investment in equipment, or the loss of a bid? Who else will go for months without being paid for their hard work? In most cases, the family pitches in to help the fledgling enterprise; oftentimes, those same family members remain in the business over time, whether or not they are formally qualified or a good fit for their jobs.

Within family businesses, features of firm architecture account for governance structure and policies related to the following aspects of the firm's operation:

- Finance: how to fund the enterprise and how to make money
- Strategy: how to determine where the firm's best chances for success reside and how to get there

- Personnel: who should be involved and how to keep employees engaged and motivated
- Product/service: what the value-added attributes of the product or service are
- Sales and marketing: how to best reach the target market and what competitive advantages the business has
- Technology: how technology can be best utilized
- Operations management: how to most effectively leverage resources and manage processes to develop the most efficient organization possible

Within family firms, many challenges arise when architecture is overlooked, preventing the successful perpetuation of the business from one generation to the next. In plain terms, this is succession planning. Although many see succession as an "event," it is actually a process of due diligence that begins when the business is founded or in the early formative years.

Succession must be deliberate and ongoing. As former Chairman of General Electric, Jack Welch, said, "Succession is part of the rebirth of an organization."[12] Put simply, if a firm wants to remain competitive, it must evolve. For a family business to be competitive and develop an ongoing plan to position the firm for survival, the business must develop the appropriate architecture and design (by way of policies, procedures, agreements, and plans) as it relates to the succession of ownership and the succession of management.

Features of Organizational Architecture Related to Ownership Succession

Challenges associated with ownership succession in family firms are likely to prevent owners from developing plans to perpetuate the business. The policies and plans can be complex, difficult to understand, and potentially expensive to develop (frequently involving attorneys, accountants, and other trusted advisors). However, the cost of developing plans necessary for the successful transition of ownership is minor compared to the cost of *not* developing these plans.

Businesses are assets—and like all assets, they must be managed, particularly if the business is to finance the retirement of shareholders. Thus all shareholders have a vested interest in seeing the business grow. To this end, if the business is supposed to fund shareholders' retirements, key questions must be answered: How much money is needed for retirement? What are the options for long-term care (and how much will those options cost)? Can the business generate sufficient funds to support that amount while continuing to operate and grow? What is the best way to accurately forecast these financial retirement demands?

The first step in developing any sort of an estate or retirement plan that can facilitate the succession of ownership is to have a good sense of the value of the family firm. Accountants with specialist designations (Accredited in Business Valuation [ABV]) can help to "[determine] the value of a business, business ownership interest, security, or intangible asset."[13] Generally, if a family business owner plans to use the assets of the business as an annuity for retirement, it is important to know what that annuity might reasonably be. Similarly, if a business owner plans to fund his or her estate taxes through life insurance, it is important to have a valuation to determine the amount of estate taxes that may be due, thereby ensuring that adequate life insurance is purchased.

Recognizing this important feature of business architecture, 64 percent of U.S. family business owners state that they have "regular" valuations[14]—but how regular is "regular"? When regional family businesses were questioned on how often a valuation is completed on the business, 20 percent indicated that such analyses occurred every 1 to 2 years, 22 percent stated every 2 to 5 years, and 17 percent said every 5 to 10 years. That leaves 10 percent taking more than 10 years to learn of the true value of the family firm. Of particular note is the 30 percent of respondents who never conducted a valuation.[15] With a little more than half (53.5 percent)[16] of senior-generation family business shareholders having good knowledge of the approximate amount of estate taxes that may come due, and a little less than half (47.7 percent)[17] hoping to fund estate taxes through life insurance, the lack of awareness of the actual value of nearly half of America's family firms may prove devastating to the survival of those enterprises.

In this survey, senior shareholders appeared conflicted about their retirement plans: 50 percent believed that ensuring that the current generation would have enough wealth would be problematic as a new owner took over (27 percent were neutral on this issue, and 23 percent did not foresee it as being a problem). When asked if extracting equity from the business would be a problem as a new owner took over, 48 percent believed it would be problematic (34 percent were neutral, and 19 percent did not foresee any problems). Regarding whether a fair valuation of the business would be problematic as a new owner took control, 41 percent suggested it would be problematic (33 percent were neutral, and 26 percent did not foresee a challenge).

Conducting regular valuations can recalibrate one's expectations for wealth and retirement while ensuring that enough life insurance is purchased (or other financing alternatives are evaluated). These steps ultimately protect the next generation from the burdens stemming from poor planning.

Another feature of business architecture as it relates to ownership is the creation of a comprehensive estate plan (discussed in detail in Chapter 5). An important feature to ensure the sustainable transition of the firm from one generation to the next, a comprehensive estate plan clarifies objectives, ensures the successful perpetuation of family assets (and the business), and minimizes tax obligations through gifting and other planning strategies. Of course, families may want to consider the use of trusts or other gifting strategies to govern the disposition of those ownership assets. Other elements of an estate plan may include prenuptial planning, charitable planning, and planning for family members who have special needs.

Prenuptial agreements are agreements that, by nature, are difficult and cumbersome to discuss. Given the relatively low percentage of family businesses that have shareholder agreements in place, prenuptial agreements may be an important consideration when ownership of the business is up for grabs. Yet, only 9.7 percent of family firms noted that their shareholders had prenuptial agreements in place.[18] For more information on the pros, cons, and alternatives to prenuptial agreements, see Box 6.1.

Box 6.1
Prenuptial Agreements: Pros, Cons, and Alternatives

Henry C. Krasnow—Krasnow Saunders Cornblath, LLP

For some business-owning families, marriage creates unusual anxiety about keeping ownership of the business in the family and family finances secret. Those who think a prenuptial agreement will accomplish these goals are often disappointed.

Prenuptial agreements between young people marrying for the first time require discussions that can question love and commitment. By comparison, previously married individuals who have children or grandchildren to whom they have financial commitments find this negotiation easier and healthy. The usual benefits expected from a prenuptial agreement are that they will (1) prevent exposure of the family's finances, (2) avoid high legal bills or an unfair alimony or support award, and (3) keep the business in the family.

Yet, in bitter divorces, the validity of a prenuptial agreement is often contested, making it almost impossible to keep family finances a secret or save on legal fees. This situation typically arises because prenuptial agreements are enforceable only if entered into after full disclosure of each party's assets. (In some states prenuptial agreements are unenforceable unless fair when signed *and* enforced). Litigation may occur over any of the following issues:

- *Full disclosure.* Parents may not want their in-laws to know how prosperous the business is, and estate planning consultants want to avoid a document that the IRS can use to show that values assumed for the estate plan (the lowest defensible amounts) are incorrect.
- *Child support.* Prenuptial agreements often have no effect on child support, and a legal battle over this issue may expose family finances.
- *Spite.* Insisting on a prenuptial agreement increases the likelihood of a bitter divorce. No better way exists to "pay back" in-laws and ex-spouses for perceived wrongdoing than an embarrassing court battle.

The threat of getting stock in a family business is almost always a strategy to improve a settlement, however, and horror stories about family stock falling into "enemy" hands are often overblown. Few divorcing spouses want their money tied up in the stock of a family business managed by their former in-laws and which they may never be able to sell.

Emotionally neutral ways exist to better address the core issues of secrecy and limited ownership:

- A *buy/sell agreement* signed by all shareholders providing that stock transferred to nonfamily members can be bought back at a set price determined by a formula with a minority discount.
- A *liquidity agreement,* in which the company makes a standing offer to buy the stock of a disgruntled shareholder at a price determined by a formula specified in advance. A divorce judge would likely set the value of the contested stock based on this formula as long as it is applicable to all shareholders and adopted long before the divorce.
- *Maintaining nonmarital property status.* In many states, not all of a couple's property is subject to division upon a divorce. Under many circumstances, stock of the family business may be considered nonmarital property, and not be subject to inclusion in the divorce settlement.

Some parents' insistence on prenuptial agreements may camouflage their underlying desire to control their children's behavior. However, if reducing legal fees, keeping family finances secret, or keeping ownership of the stock among family members is the real goal, better alternatives (with less potential for emotional damage) are available.

Likewise, shareholder agreements (also known as buy-sell agreements and partnership agreements) are critical in holding the business together. They may cover issues ranging from who gets to own stock (e.g., family, nonfamily, in-laws, other requirements for ownership), who gets to vote (e.g., who has voting stock versus nonvoting stock, whether stock should be equalized among family branches), how and when stock is transferred (e.g., whether there is a need for stock to be held in a trust), and which terms and conditions govern the purchase and sale of stock (conditions for a buyback, options to acquire the stock).[19] Notwithstanding the impact ownership and voting stock have on the strategic direction of the business, only 37.4 percent of family firms polled in the United States have implemented buy/sell agreements,[20] and 37.7 percent have a formal redemption/liquidity plan.[21] Box 6.2 provides more information on financing business continuity and the plans needed to sustain family-owned companies.

Box 6.2
Financing Business Continuity

James A. Murphy—de Visscher & Co.

There are many things that family businesses cannot control, but securing adequate financial resources for business continuity—enough to handle unforeseen setbacks and take advantage of sudden opportunities—is not one of them. Family business owners commonly talk in terms of generations and profess to have a longer-term perspective, yet many finance the growth of their businesses, and the eventual retirement of their owners, as if these situations were unpredictable and sudden occurrences. In other words, they remain essentially "reactive" in nature and face problems as they arise, rather than charting their financial course and capital needs and securing them in advance for the journey.

One of the joys of having a family-owned enterprise is the ability to pursue a shared dream and exert some measure of control over one's destiny. A sustainable business, entrepreneurial energy, and personal charisma must be supported, however, by adequate financing resources if the firm hopes to compete in an increasingly complex and globally competitive world.

Family businesses have at their disposal a wealth of capital sources and investors that appreciate the long operating histories, niche business franchises, and strong cultures found in family businesses. Proactive financial planning for sustaining family-owned companies includes the following elements:

- A *strategic plan* that specifies the capital investment funds and working capital needs to sustain and grow the company
- A *liquidity plan* that specifies the capital needed to satisfy retirement obligations or share redemptions of senior-generation, or inactive shareholders
- A *financing plan* that identifies the providers of longer-term, more "patient" resources of both debt and equity capital that are fond of, and anxious to invest in, family-owned companies on a minority ownership basis

With these plans in place, a business owner reduces controllable risk and can focus his or her attention on mitigating some of the other variables that are less under the owner's control.

Features of Organizational Architecture Related to Management Succession

For most enterprising families, the business is the most valuable asset. For there to be an asset to manage, grow, and pass on, a business needs two things: (1) policies in place to bolster management's best efforts at success and (2) a core group of managers and leaders who are capable of executing the organization's objectives and strategy. Of course, this means that family firms need to have a strategy to determine what to aim for and whether they are pointed in the right direction.

As discussed in Chapter 5, building a strategic plan requires an upfront, effective investment of time and human capital. The investment in these areas is worth it. Businesses with a strategic plan will know when and how to allocate resources at the appropriate junctures, and they will spend far less time in upfront planning than the less forward-thinking firms will spend digging out of a mess due to poor foresight and failed execution down the road.

In 2007, only 36.6 percent[22] of family businesses reported that they had a strategic plan—a percentage that is fairly consistent with the results of a national evaluation in 2002 (39.6 percent)[23] and a regional evaluation in 2009 (33 percent).[24] Of family firms with a strategic plan, only 31.1 percent use a formal process to form their plans,[25] leaving one to wonder how else strategic plans are being developed within the family enterprise. While management is often cited as being "very familiar" with the strategic plan, 21 percent[26] to 26.7 percent[27] of those firms with a strategic plan note that management is only "somewhat" familiar with the plan. Because strategic plans allow family business owners to marshal the resources necessary for survival, family firms with strategic plans also are more likely to have shareholder agreements, formal valuations, a formal redemption plan, and a family employment policy—all facets that enable them to earn higher revenues and have more employees than those family firms without a strategic plan.[28]

There are many working parts of a good strategic plan: a fundamental purpose defining why the organization exists and what the organization does; the goals the organization hopes to reach; the strategies by which the organization hopes to reach its goals; tactics and metrics the organization will develop that support each strategy; and the role of all employees involved in the organization in teaching the goals and creating the culture to ensure the goals are achieved. In particular, a strategic plan identifies an organization's SWOT—that is, its internal *strengths* and *weaknesses* and the external *opportunities* and *threats* the business may encounter. A strategic plan also merits another kind of SWOT analysis that considers a firm's internal resources more deeply: *s*uperior products and services; *w*ell-planned strategies, tactics, and metrics; an *o*rganizational culture that is performance driven and committed to employees, customers, suppliers, and community; and *t*alent to see these initiatives through.

Finding the right talent to guide to an organization's strategic plan is essential for success. Firms that search for talent from mostly within the family may find themselves moving from the gene pool to the boiling pot. Family members may be welcomed into the business based simply on their family membership card, and not on performance merit. With most families wishing for the business to remain family owned (as identifying one's business as "family owned" may be a source of competitive advantage), developing a family employment policy does not restrict family members from joining the firm. In fact, this policy can serve to motivate those family members who are qualified, hard working, and earnest in contributing to the business.

Family employment policies belie their simplicity, oftentimes diffusing the harmful conflicts that can arise when family members question one another's competence, merit, objectivity, and judgment. Such policies set expectations with regard to all family members seeking employment at the family firm. Generally, a family employment policy outlines conditions that govern how family members may enter and exit the employ of the family business, addressing expectations related to the following issues:

- Outside work experience and internships (e.g., whether at another company within the same industry, a company in another industry, or another family business)
- Education requirements (e.g., technical degree, bachelor's degree, graduate degree)
- Past promotions (e.g., many outline a desire to see progress and promotion at other firms)
- Supervision (e.g., many outline the reporting structure of family members working in the firm, with particular emphasis on not being supervised by other family members whenever possible)
- Hiring process (e.g., conducted by a nonfamily human resources professional or advisory board members)
- Spousal employment (e.g., some identify that only one member of a spousal union may be employed at the family firm at the same time)

Even though the family employment policy can help to remove ambiguity related to family employment and remedy headaches related to competence, only 28.3 percent of family firms nationwide have developed such a policy,[29] as opposed to 13 percent of regional family firms.[30] Even so, perceived competence of family members is consistently cited as one of the top three sources of conflict for family firms.[31] Other sources of conflict that family business members frequently confront relate to compensation plans and the lack of documented human resources policies.

Compensation can be a very volatile subject as individuals oftentimes equate compensation with "value" or "worth," whether intentionally or not. When roles in the family business system collide, some owners choose to allocate compensation based on maintaining family harmony and loyalty to the detriment of the business. Some compensation ideologies in family firms are identified here:

- "Someday this will all be yours" approach: Successors receive lower compensation (or submarket levels) based on promises of future ownership.
- Market-based approach: Successors receive compensation based on industry benchmarks (similar pay for similar work, whether at the family business or external).
- Performance-based approach: Family members receive compensation that is based on reaching goals (individual goals, departmental goals, and organizational goals).
- Needs-based approach: Family members receive compensation according to their individual needs and requirements to maintain an acceptable family lifestyle (e.g., the divorced parent of four receives more compensation working as a mid-level manager than the single senior-level manager with no children).
- "Golden handcuffs" approach: Family members are compensated well above the industry benchmarks, making it impossible for them to maintain their lifestyles if they leave the family business and seek similar employment elsewhere.

The key to developing a compensation philosophy that supports the integrity of any family organization is to separate business compensation from family compensation. Subjective efforts often cause significant problems, as too much compensation can lead people to have either (1) an over-inflated sense of contribution to the firm or their personal value in general or (2) low self-esteem and an unhealthy dependency on the family firm. Conversely, too little compensation can lead family members to feel angry and entitled, believing that they have earned the right to more compensation after having gone so many years without sufficient pay.

Similarly, irrational compensation can be a recipe for disaster. Consider the following example: Julia is semi-retired and has three adult children working in the business. Daughter A is operating as president, Daughter B is in accounts payable/receivable, and Son is a machinist. Each has varying levels of experience and responsibility: Daughter B and Son work regular 9-hour workdays, while Daughter A puts in 12-hour days (traveling frequently, meeting with customers for dinners, and checking e-mail all weekend). Notwithstanding the fact that each sibling has different levels of responsibility, all are compensated equally—and all are compensated above industry benchmarks for a president operating at a firm of similar size and scope.

How should Daughter A feel? If she voices her displeasure, would she appear greedy, even though she believes, based on her responsibilities, that she should be earning more than her siblings? How might Daughter B feel knowing that she is earning the same amount as her younger brother, who never has to deal with disgruntled customers? How might Son feel knowing his sisters are upset at the compensation arrangement, even though he believes his job is more labor intensive, and sometimes dangerous, and resents the fact that his sisters get to sit in an office? How might Julia feel knowing her children are all unhappy and no longer willing to put up with the "unfair" arrangement when her only wish was to provide for her children and grandchildren? Would she be concerned that her well-meaning attempts have turned the environment she created into an unhealthy one (marked by insidious displays of egotism and entitlement) that threatens the business she has worked so hard to build? Indeed, compensation can be a trigger for harmful competition, and a poorly thought-out or ambiguous compensation plan is not a plan at all.

In family businesses, when it comes to compensation of family members, "fair" does not always mean "equal." To highlight these challenges, the story of one family business that developed a strategy for value-driven compensation is described in Box 6.3.

Box 6.3
Value-Driven Compensation

Mark S. Taub—Kostin, Ruffkess & Company, LLC

As the second generation in my family's business, I look back and fondly recall the importance of learning the "value of the dollar" at an early age. As kids, my brother and I got the same allowance per week and we were rewarded identically when we went to work with mom and dad to clean or perform simple clerical tasks. We weren't overpaid or underpaid; we were equitably paid.

Little did we know, but this was probably a good lesson to learn relative to the importance of fair, equitable, reasonable, and transparent compensation in a family business. After college, my brother and I entered the family business—he joined the accounting and finance department, and I went into sales and marketing.

Our parents determined what our compensation would be based on what they thought was right and what nonfamily members in similar positions were earning. Our basic salary was the same, but with a sales and marketing position, I had the opportunity to earn bonuses based on achieving certain benchmarks. My brother did not. Yet, over time, our compensation program changed as our positions within the company changed (and we became shareholders).

In profitable years, we invested money back into the business and distributed bonuses both to employees and to ourselves based on our equity positions. When there were no profits, there were no bonuses. In some very challenging years, we reduced our salaries. I can even remember my folks reducing their salaries to zero. Our business supported all of us—our families, our employees, and their families. The health of the business was always placed before the financial prosperity of any single family member.

In 2005, we sold the business. I now have the opportunity to work with other family businesses, talking with them about accounting and compensation challenges.

In a family business, the compensation structure will reflect the values and beliefs of the family. If family members are fair, reasonable, and transparent and share common values and beliefs about the business, the compensation structure will support the family's spirit and mission. In the absence of shared values and beliefs, the compensation structure in a family business could lead to animosity, jealousy, anger, frustration, resentment, a lack of trust, and the eventual destruction of the business (and, even worse, the family).

The compensation structure in a family business should reward accomplishments and be flexible enough to adjust to fluctuations in business conditions, the responsibilities of the family members, and the life cycle of the business. A good compensation structure in a family business should be fair, equitable, reasonable, and transparent.

For family businesses thinking about the development of a more formalized compensation plan, I suggest engaging an accountant in the discussion—one who specializes in servicing family businesses and will ask you the right questions, listen to the answers, and share ideas. Ideally, this discussion will yield a compensation plan that balances the unique dynamics of your family with the economic realities of your business.

To illustrate the ambiguity related to family business compensation, consider the frustrated remarks of a 35-year-old president of a family insurance business, when asked to whom he reports:

Are you kidding? Are you *kidding*? Ask the next question: "How are raises determined—particularly for me?" I'll tell you when I got a raise; I got a raise when I got married. I got a raise when I bought a house. I got a raise when my first child was born...My sales have not made a difference. There is *no* performance relationship. And the same thing for everybody else [in the organization].[32]

Undocumented policies and procedures regarding human resources issues also create structural distress within organizations, with many family firms doing without the most basic policies and documents—policies that can ensure that the right people are involved in the business for the right reasons and given the best chances to succeed. Data gathered regionally yielded the following findings in relation to family firms[33]:

- Forty-nine percent do not have written job descriptions outlining responsibilities, minimum qualifications, and reporting structure for every position in the business.
- Eighty-two percent do not have a written job description outlining responsibilities and qualifications for members of the board of directors.
- Seventy-one percent do not have salary grades for each job function or title.
- Eighty-two percent do not have defined career paths by job function, job family, or job category.
- Forty-four percent do not have formal performance reviews for all employees.
- Fifty-nine percent do not have a standardized bonus structure.

The challenge that arises when there is a lack of documented human resources policies ensuring that every employee is motivated, engaged, and competent, and understands the very critical role he or she plays in helping the organization fulfill its mission. Without the aforementioned policies, employees are organizational floaters, lost in a sea of disconnected job functions and organizational ambiguity. Consequently, family businesses risk losing their most valuable assets—engaged employees and family members.

BUILDING A FAMILY CONSTITUTION

A lack of policies that support the business in reaching its goals threatens the very existence of the business and livelihoods of those involved. Whether the concern is getting an estate in order, developing the plans for successful management of the organizational asset, creating a plan for retirement, or ensuring that members of the organization are well trained, mentored, and fairly evaluated, a family business cannot survive without sound organizational architecture.

One effort that has been influential in helping family firms reach their organizational goals through the development of a strong organizational infrastructure has been the emphasis on a "family constitution." In their book *The Family Constitution: Agreements to Secure and Perpetuate Your Family and Your Business*, Daniela Montemerlo and John Ward describe the family constitution as a kind of comprehensive family agreement that helps regulate and guide the family, the owners, and the business. It may comprise a number of different kinds of documents:

- Governance and coordination of the family and the business
- Guiding principles or a family values statement
- Policies (e.g., family employment, board composition, conflict regulation)
- Shareholder's agreement
- Ownership rights and responsibilities
- Strategic plan
- Long-term vision and sustainability plan

The process of developing a family constitution creates an opportunity for family members with different levels of involvement in the business to share their ideas and voice their unique perspectives, resulting in increased buy-in and greater alignment among family members. Such a document, while requiring protracted focus, thought, and effort to develop, helps provide education and clarifies a commonly held set of expectations among family members and other key stakeholders. In addition, it serves a roadmap that can keep the family business system on course toward the bright future they envision.

CHAPTER SUMMARY

- *Titanic* possessed a number of design flaws that contributed to the disaster and loss of life, including: (1) poorly made rivets that failed under stress; (2) an engine system that compromised maneuverability; and (3) a davit system that was incapable of lowering lifeboats when fully loaded.
- Architecture can be both tangible (e.g., bricks and mortar) and conceptual (an intellectual blueprint that leads to the development, implementation, maintenance, and protection of policies and procedures necessary to business survival).
- Policies and procedures necessary for business survival fall into two categories: those relating to management succession and those relating to ownership succession. These policies must hold the

organization together structurally despite unplanned circumstances, ensure smooth operations in progressing toward a goal, and provide for the safe entry and exit of leaders and shareholders.

- Plans and policies relating to ownership succession include retirement plans, valuations, estate plans, shareholder (buy/sell) agreements, and prenuptial agreements.
- Plans and policies relating to management succession include strategic plans, family employment policies, and a human resources infrastructure with plans, policies, and procedures relating to compensation, bonuses, job responsibilities, career paths, required skills, and performance reviews.
- Without a strong infrastructure, the business is apt to collapse under the weight of family expectations, competition within industry, and employee divestment. A lack of infrastructure can cause chaos, panic, and confusion—and the result can be a business and family that are bankrupt financially and emotionally.

7

●

Team Fragmentation

> Individual commitment to a group effort—that is what makes a team work, a company work, a society work, a civilization work.
>
> —Vince Lombardi

If businesses and individuals are to remedy the problems that result from overconfidence, ineffective leadership, poor planning, and frail architecture, it is essential to develop a strong team. Katzenbach and Smith define a team as a small group of people (typically fewer than twenty) with complementary skills committed to a common purpose and set of specific performance goals. Its members are committed to working with each other to achieve the team's purpose and hold each other fully and jointly accountable for the team's results.[1] Real teams are successful because they are challenge driven, members are disciplined and have complementary skills, the team has established processes for communication and the ability to move beyond individual efforts, there are intrinsic social dimensions to membership, and, generally, being a part of a team is fun.[2]

Well-functioning teams are made up of individuals who can hold themselves and one another accountable for meeting team goals and fulfilling a superordinate purpose. Of course, this achievement hinges on having competent team members, a clear mission, defined roles, good communication, and a commitment to monitoring efforts. Developing a true team approach can be complicated, particularly when the effort is overlain by generations of history and complex relationships. Nonetheless, one thing that all teams have in common is that, at one point or another, they are susceptible to fragmentation—erosions of trust, divisions, and being "out of sync."

This chapter first evaluates team fragmentation on *Titanic* with regard to the "officer reshuffle" and the separateness of the Marconi wireless operators. Then, sources of team fragmentation in family businesses are discussed, including: family dynamics, position in the family business system, and demographic differences. Finally, the roles of trust and fairness are explored and high-performing family business teams described.

TEAM FRAGMENTATION: *TITANIC*

In evaluating *Titanic*'s personnel, it is difficult to ascertain whether there was a team approach at all. If there was, what was the team's superordinate goal? What was its purpose? Who was a part of the team? Who was not, and why? How did they hold one another accountable for achieving the team's mission? Was it clear what the mission was?

One might argue that the mission was to transport passengers across the Atlantic to New York City *quickly*—but White Star Line managers themselves had determined that they were unable to compete effectively with Cunard on the basis of speed. One might also argue that the mission was to transport passengers across the Atlantic to New York *luxuriously*—but luxury becomes irrelevant without safety. Thus one might argue that the primary mission was to transport passengers across the Atlantic to New York *safely*—but we know that that was woefully not to be. The lifeboat capacity was about 1,176, or just enough to accommodate roughly half of *Titanic*'s passengers making that fateful journey. Moreover, although the ship was touted as being unsinkable, even Bruce Ismay could not ignore the fact that if there was a fire onboard the ship, passengers would need lifeboats to escape. What happened that led to such an error? What breakdown occurred within the "team"—the same team that passengers presumed would get them to and from New York comfortably, quickly, and safely?

For effective oversight, all team members must be clear about each individual's responsibilities. Just as important, each individual needs to know his or her own role and to understand how that role figures into the larger organizational purpose. Where there is a lack of clarity, confusion reigns.

Recall the events in Belfast on March 31. It was the evening before *Titanic*'s scheduled sea trial, and Captain Smith had just made his way onboard. His first decision was to reschedule the sea trial for the following day (April 2). His second decision was to rearrange the senior officer team by calling for Henry Wilde to serve as the Chief Officer for *Titanic*'s maiden voyage. His reasoning was understandable: he wanted all three senior officers (himself, the Chief Officer, and the First Officer) to have had experience on *Titanic*'s sister, *Olympic*, given that one of the roles of the senior officers would be to help passengers find their way about the ship. Admittedly, it took Charles Lightoller approximately two weeks to learn the layout of *Titanic* and the shortest routes to get from one place to another. *Titanic* was so large, in fact, that one could walk miles upon her decks and spend hours trying to find a particular entryway.

Nevertheless, the "officer reshuffle" had unintended consequences caused by oversight and a lack of protocol, ultimately leading to fragmentation within the team of senior officers. In his 1935 memoir *Titanic and Other Ships*, Lightoller noted:

> Unfortunately whilst in Southampton, we had a reshuffle amongst the Senior Officers. Owing to *Olympic* being laid up, the ruling lights of the White Star Line thought it would be a good plan to send the Chief Officer of *Olympic*, just for the one voyage, as Chief Officer of *Titanic*, to help, with his experience of her sister ship. This doubtful policy threw both Murdoch and me out of our stride; and, apart from the disappointment of having to step back in our rank, caused quite a little confusion. Murdoch from Chief, took over my duties as First. I stepped back on Blair's toes, as Second, and picked up the many threads of his job, whilst he—luckily for him as it turned out—was left behind. The other officers remained the same.[3]

As the officers reviewed their new duties just days, if not hours, before leaving Southampton (Wilde arrived only a few hours before the voyage began), the disappointment and confusion caused by the reshuffle had one severe consequence. David Blair, who had sailed on *Titanic* as Second Officer from Belfast, disembarked in Southampton. While initially saddened that he was not to sail on *Titanic* (he wrote to a relative, "Am afraid I shall have to step out to make room for chief officer of the Olympic. [*Titanic*] is a magnificent ship, I feel very disappointed I am not to make her first voyage"),[4] no doubt Blair was later relieved not to have participated in the voyage. In his haste to leave the ship in Southampton, however, he inadvertently took with him an extremely valuable item: the key to a locker that contained the binoculars for the lookouts.

It remains unresolved as to whether the key Blair took was to the crow's nest locker or to another part of the ship. What is clear is that prior to Blair leaving *Titanic*, the lookouts had binoculars for their use. After Blair left, there were no binoculars. Some speculate that the binoculars were left in his cabin; others speculate that they were his own personal set of binoculars and he naturally took them with him when he disembarked. In this reshuffle, a critical piece of equipment and essential bit of information were taken with Blair—whether the key, the binoculars, or knowledge of the binoculars' whereabouts—and the result was tragic. Upon questioning from Senator Smith at the U.S. inquiry, *Titanic*'s lookout on duty at the time *Titanic* struck the iceberg, Frederick Fleet, noted that if he had the binoculars, he would have seen the iceberg "a bit sooner." When asked, "How much sooner?", his answer was chilling: "Enough to get out of the way."[5]

The clarity of Fleet's response highlights an important component when it comes to team fragmentation: breaking up a team (changing their members, functions, and norms, particularly at the last minute) causes confusion, disappointment, and a breakdown of team cohesiveness and communication. When this disruption is left unmanaged, the team and mission can suffer remarkable, unintended consequences.

Of course, it was not the missing key or lack of binoculars alone that caused *Titanic* to founder. After all, multiple ice warnings had been received throughout the journey that *should* have alerted *Titanic*'s captain to use extra caution when steaming through the Atlantic. In fact, *Titanic* received seven reports advising of ice in or near her track. Notwithstanding their number, only a handful ever made it to the bridge and one (the 9 A.M. warning from *Caronia*) was posted on the navigational chart in the officers' chart room. Certainly, *Mesaba's* warning at 9:40 P.M. on April 14—"Ice report in Latitude 42N to 21–25N. Long. 49 to Long. 50–30W. Saw much heavy pack ice, and great number large icebergs. Also field ice"—would have been a startling message for the officers to receive, as *Titanic* was heading directly into that area.

Lightoller, the only senior officer to survive *Titanic*'s sinking, had the opportunity to speak to Phillips (the operator who took *Mesaba*'s message) moments after the sinking when both were clinging to the Collapsible B lifeboat. In regard to the *Mesaba* message, Phillips explained, "I put the message under a paper weight at my elbow, just until I squared up what I was doing before sending it to the Bridge."[6] With more than 250 passenger messages being transmitted per day[7] (and a backlog of messages to send because the wireless apparatus had broken down on Friday, April 12), Phillips was not able to catch up enough to deliver the message from *Mesaba* to the officers. Lightoller later concluded that the failure to send *Mesaba*'s warning to the bridge "proved fatal and was the main contributory cause to the loss of that magnificent ship and hundreds of lives. Had I as Officer of the Watch, or the Captain, become aware of the peril lying so close ahead and not instantly slowed down or stopped, we should have been guilty of culpable and criminal negligence."[8]

So who is to blame? Phillips and Bride, the wireless operators who neglected to bring the messages to the bridge? The captain, who neglected to develop a procedure whereby messages regarding navigation would be given priority over passenger messages? The Marconi wireless company, Phillips and Bride's employer, which neglected to train its employees on how to handle ice warnings? Or perhaps the blame goes to the officers for not paying closer attention to the dozen-plus ice reports that *Titanic* had received since leaving Southampton, whether the warning was posted on a navigational chart or was relayed to an officer verbally.

Siloism is defined as the condition in which distinct operating units fail to become interdependent and communicate with one another for coordination of efforts. It certainly existed on *Titanic*, and is prevalent among many businesses. Clearly, the officers and wireless operators were performing their duties as instructed—duties that seldom intertwined and were thought to be best left separate. In fact, the idea of being "separate" was an ethos that permeated all of *Titanic*'s operations, work functions, and practices. When Edward John Buley, able seaman aboard *Titanic*, was asked by Senator Smith if he saw any crew arousing people or giving the alarm to board lifeboats, Buley responded, "That was the steward's work, sir. We had nothing to do with that."[9] Classes of passengers were kept separate with separate stairwells and entrances, and even the captain had a separate navigational chart in his own quarters. One can only wonder whether the ice warnings that did reach the bridge were posted on the captain's *own* chart (and not the officers' chart). Recall that, astonishingly, only one warning from *Caronia* (received at 9:00 A.M. on Sunday, April 14) was posted on the chart in the officers' navigational room even though three warnings had been brought to the bridge that day.

Siloism is perhaps best noted in conjunction with the role of the Marconi wireless operators themselves. Employed by the British Marconi Company, Phillips and Bride were not employees of White Star Line. Their role as employees of the British Marconi Company was primarily to provide a service to passengers; consequently, passenger messages were given priority. In addition, Phillips and Bride were well aware that (1) wireless was a novelty, and one of the services that gave *Titanic* a competitive advantage over other ships, and (2) the Marconi Company was paid based on messages *sent*, not messages *received*. Thus the wireless operators focused on transmitting passenger messages quickly and efficiently so that the company could send out the largest number of messages possible and maximize its revenue. With passengers paying such high prices for messages to be sent (and having paid for these messages upfront), the expectation was that all messages would be transmitted regardless of workload, leaving the operators little time to pay close attention to incoming messages.

It was because of this mentality of siloism that Phillips and Bride did not see how their duties contributed to achieving a larger team goal. In fact, this idea is well supported by Phillips' own abrasive response to Cyril Evans, his Marconi colleague working the wireless apparatus aboard the ship *Californian*.

On April 14, at approximately 10:55 P.M., an exhausted Phillips was working Cape Race (a wireless station located on Newfoundland, Canada, which served as a pivot point through which to relay messages from passengers aboard *Titanic* to New York City; being that *Titanic* was too far out of range to connect to New York City directly). Evans, aboard *Californian*, tried to connect with *Titanic* directly. *Californian* was somewhere between 5 and 19 miles away, so when Evans transmitted his message to Phillips, the signal coming through the wireless ear apparatus was deafeningly loud. "Say, old man, we are stopped and surrounded by ice" was the message Evans sent.

Perhaps it was out of exhaustion, frustration, or being overworked, but Phillips' response to Evans was undeniably sharp and curt: "Shut up, shut up, I am busy! I am working Cape Race." Given that the wireless apparatus could send and receive only one message at a time, interrupting his work with seemingly nonessential warnings was taking precious time away from Phillips' ability to transmit passenger messages. With that retort, Evans (the only wireless operator working aboard *Californian*) listened for several minutes longer, shut off the wireless apparatus for the night, and retired to bed. The U.S. inquiry following the disaster found that being so close to *Titanic*, *Californian* was within a close enough distance to potentially save *Titanic*'s passengers and crew.

Dr. Robert Ballard, an esteemed researcher most noted for his work in underwater archaeology and who discovered *Titanic*'s remains in 1985, summarized the outcome of this lack of communication:

> Apart from the slight alteration of course to the south, the closing of the forecastle hatch, and the warning in the crow's nest, the officers of the *Titanic* had taken no precautionary measures to deal with the hazards ahead. It was common practice to rely on lookouts and they seemed confident in their ship's ability to avoid a collision. Because of the lack of coordination between the bridge and the wireless room and the absence of any standard procedure for dealing with ice warnings, they seem to have been under the impression that the main body of ice lay to the north of their path. In the words of Walter Lord, "The result was complacency, an almost arrogant casualness, that permeated the bridge."[10]

Of course, communication works both ways. Although the wireless operators neglected to send vital information to the bridge regarding ice warnings and the position of the threat, officers from the bridge never inquired as to whether further ice warnings were received or gave intermittent or regular updates to the wireless operators as to *Titanic*'s position. This information could have been instrumental. When ice warnings were received, Phillips and Bride might have been able to use the information to deduce that certain ice warnings suggested an imminent threat to the ship and safety of all aboard—and perhaps might have been more proactive in relaying ice warnings to the bridge.

Titanic's crew—if a team at all—was not a high-performing team. Teams cannot grow or survive when working within a culture of siloism, without strong communication and coordinated efforts toward a mutually understood superordinate goal.

TEAM FRAGMENTATION IN FAMILY BUSINESS SYSTEMS

Team fragmentation within family firms happens in various ways, often largely driven by two sources: family dynamics and different positions within the family business system. Issues related to family dynamics may emerge as a normal by-product of living and working closely with others with whom one has deep emotional and historical connections. Shared family experiences oftentimes bring their own baggage (some good, some bad) that inevitably finds its way into the business and unpacks itself in the form of various family conflicts. Given that enterprising families experience a higher degree of involvement among family members, the normative striving to balance the need for autonomy and individual achievement on the one hand and the need for family harmony and close relationships on the other hand can become akin to walking a tightrope.

Recall the family business system introduced in Chapter 4, wherein the roles of owner, family, and manager overlap. Conflicts based on family dynamics or different positions within the family business system often lie dormant for many years—like invisible fault lines that may or may not make their presence known under typical circumstances. In most instances, they do not manifest themselves until the family or business system encounters some source of stress or change. Some of these changes are predictable, such as normal changes associated with the life cycle of family business systems (e.g., adult children entering the business, or "passing the baton" from the incumbent leader to the successor)[11] or expected changes in markets and industry evolution (e.g., increased digitalization and social media's role in the publishing industry). Other changes may be triggered by highly unexpected, "low-probability" events, such as the sudden death of a key family member, the discovery of fraudulent activities, a terrorist attack, or an act of workplace violence. Whether the change is sudden or expected, and whether it is related to the family or the business, events that place the entire system under stress can increase the likelihood that previously invisible fault lines will turn into observable fractures.

The succession process is a prime example of a period of change and reorganization for the family and business. For firms that have enjoyed a longer period of continuity in leadership, the idea of change can feel threatening; whether or not everyone in the system is completely satisfied with how the system "runs" at the moment, at least they know what to expect. In firms where no successor has been identified and no succession plan has been established, anxiety about the future is heightened—particularly as stakeholders become aware of a looming change-up of team members, but no details are shared. Questions abound in the minds of the senior generation (e.g., how will the choice of successor affect the family and the business?), the potential successors (e.g., what will happen if I do, or do not, get selected as the next leader?), employees (e.g., how will things change when the leader leaves?), and customers and suppliers (e.g., how will this change our business relationship?). This process often brings preexisting or new conflicts to the surface. If the process is managed poorly and the conflicts go unaddressed, previously functional relationships and teams can start to erode.

Another example of change resulting in team fragmentation concerns the recession of 2007–2009 and its aftermath. With the United States experiencing unemployment rates hovering around the 9 to 10 percent mark, many family members not previously working in their family's business sought employment there for different reasons (e.g., a layoff or other lost source of income, the need for extra income for paying down debt, or income for added security). In fact, 1 in 10 CEOs of family-owned firms noted that the economic conditions during this period had prompted more family members to become active in the business.[12] When family members enter the family business solely in accordance with values associated with family (e.g., unity, loyalty, and welfare)—without regard to whether hiring family members is in the best interest of the business itself—conflicts between the family and management domains can ensue.

Of note, as boundaries between ownership, management, and family circles become blurred, the system can become difficult to manage, especially during times of economic stress. In evaluating agreement among family members with regard to the best strategy, management structure, and ownership structure, regional survey respondents in mid-2008 noted high levels of family agreement on the best strategy regarding the business (89 percent), best ownership structure of the business (92 percent), and best management structure of the business (91 percent).[13] Just one year later, when asked this same question in mid-2009, 68 percent agreed on the best strategy, 73 percent agreed on the best ownership structure, and 71 percent agreed on the best management structure.[14] While these percentages are still high overall, it is important to observe the approximate 20 percent decline across all three areas following the onset of the economic crisis.

Next, we consider the various ways in which team fragmentations occur, including those associated with family dynamics, those associated with different positions within the family business system (e.g., owners versus managers, family versus nonfamily), and other sources of fragmentation (e.g., generation, gender, and education).

FRAGMENTATION FROM FAMILY DYNAMICS

Fragmentation in families can unfold in many different ways, as families can be diverse with regard to structure, membership, and culture. Nevertheless, there are a few kinds of conflicts within enterprising families that can lead to team fragmentation. These include parent/child conflict, copreneurial clashes, sibling rivalry, and other family divisions. Inability to resolve the animosity that develops from any of these kinds of conflict can be a direct threat to the firm.

Parent/Child Conflict

Discord between parents and children in family firms occurs for a number of reasons. Sometimes it has to do with differences in personality or management styles. Parents may have clear ideas about what it takes for their son or daughter to be successful, and may become angry or critical when their expectations are not met. The son of one business owner described how his father had very specific notions of what running a successful business meant. The father would get extremely upset if he saw his son shut in his office all day, rather than spending time walking around the plant, observing what was happening, and checking in with employees. The son, who was much more introverted than his gregarious father, preferred analyzing production numbers and financial reports as a means of monitoring progress.

Parents who do not fully trust their children to lead oftentimes limit the power their progeny have in making decisions involving strategy, finances, or personnel. In another business, the founder found himself out of options for a family successor after all three of his children tried working in the business and left after a few years because they found working with their father to be unbearable. They felt that their father's tendency to second guess or control every decision undermined their self-confidence, leaving them little room to grow as professionals.

The tensions between parents and children in family businesses can spike during the succession process. Members of the senior generation may feel that they are being unfairly "shoved out" of the business before they are ready to leave. Further, they may feel unappreciated by the succeeding generation for their contributions to the business, the opportunities they are providing, and the guidance they offer successors. For their part, successors may feel frustrated at their parents' unwillingness to entrust the business to them as leaders or to give them the opportunity to be "in charge."

Copreneurs

Fragmentation can also occur among husband-and-wife teams (copreneurs) who manage the business and the family together. Most notable is the effect the work/life balance has on copreneurs who spend all of their time with each other in and out of the business. Given that 67 percent of family business CEOs note that striking a positive balance between work and life is a challenge for anyone running a family enterprise,[15] there is little opportunity for copreneurs to unplug and unwind from the day's activities. Sometimes the stress of managing dual roles takes its toll on the relationship, and something has to give. One woman described her decision to stop working with her husband, with whom she spent 13 years building a business, as follows: "I had to do it. The stress was killing our marriage, and the whole family was suffering for it. It's much better now."

When copreneurs divorce, it can have a devastating impact on the business as well as the personal finances of the couple.[16] Divorces can also lead to wider family rifts, when children or other family members choose sides. Nevertheless, some research indicates that some couples are able to maintain a business relationship even after their marital relationship ends. Copreneurs who maintain a business relationship post-divorce tend to share high levels of trust, a strong commitment to the business, a strong emotional connection to each other, and the ability to compartmentalize and separate work life and personal life.[17]

Box 7.1 evaluates how one copreneurial couple achieves balance and sets healthy boundaries.

Box 7.1
Copreneurs: Achieving Balance and Healthy Boundaries

Lisa Wilson-Foley—All-Star Therapy | Blue Fox Enterprises

He was one of my grad school professors, then my mentor, then my customer, then my husband, then my business partner. He started his first business at age 24. I formed my first company at 29. Both of us love the art of the deal as well as the science and math behind creating a successful business. We are both focused, results-oriented, and driven individuals with a strong fire in the belly.

Partners in life and work, we thrive on seeing our visions become reality. Our playground is the healthcare, sports, and entertainment industries. I bought a golf course; he opened a restaurant and nightclub. I got into mobile diagnostics; he grew a nursing home empire. I got us involved in a co-ed professional team tennis franchise; he bought a minor league basketball team. And the list continues . . . We thrive on the flexible and dynamic nature of our lives, but we also realize that to live at such a fast pace and raise a family, we also need frequent respites and lots of household help.

Copreneurs have major hurdles to overcome to make it work. We have to "turn it off" at times and balance our work/family life with our personal health. Early on, we clearly defined the lines of work and authority. One rule that became critical for our success was that each business has only one final decision maker. Spouse number two can make recommendations, but ultimately doesn't have the final say. That rule has been extremely important in keeping disagreements from getting out of control.

Today, our seven children are in their teens and twenties. They are graduating from college and starting to lead businesses of their own. Soon we will be making next-generation plans, but right now we are still trying to figure which of us will control the new pharmacy.

Sibling Rivalry

Based originally on competition for parental love and attention, sibling rivalries are a "given" in most families. While some level of comparison and competition is normal, some rivalries can become openly hostile when parents compare siblings or when parents try to resolve the conflicts, inadvertently reinforcing the rivalry.[18] In some instances, tensions escalate to the point of physical violence.

Aronoff, Astrachan, Mendoza, and Ward note that sibling partnerships are intense and volatile—and are somewhat more prone to conflict due to a long history of emotional interactions:

As a result of their growing up together, the level of intimacy and emotionality is higher among siblings than, for example, the cousin generation that follows. And because siblings carry into the business all those memories and opinions of each other that they have held since childhood, the possibility for harmful misunderstandings is strong . . . What also sets the siblings apart and can lead to volatility is that there are fewer of them than there are cousins at this cousin stage. Because each sibling may own a substantial minority position in the company, a family business can be threatened when one sibling is angry, disenchanted or unproductive, and isn't functioning as part of the team. Buying that person's shares can wreck the capital structure or the strategic plans of the business.[19]

In one family business, the two brothers running the business functioned as a good team and were both in agreement with regard to their long-range plan: they would build the business and then sell it rather than transition the business to the next generation. But over time, Brother A changed his mind and (having brought several of his children into work at the company) wanted the business to be passed on to his family. Not in agreement with this change in plan, Brother B insisted on being bought out. The battle to reach an acceptable selling price was monumental as the brothers engaged in a costly legal struggle that very nearly severed their family ties.

Birth order can also be a significant contributor to sibling rivalries, particularly when the first-born child is given first "dibs" at opportunities in the business irrespective of merit, leading some siblings to view the eldest as entitled and the parents as narrow minded. Oftentimes, it is the parents who cannot see their "children" as adults and continue this pattern of relying on the first-born child most. In fact, the eldest child is usually perceived as the most responsible and capable as a young child, because he or she likely helped the parents with the younger children and served as a role model for the siblings. Yet, upon reaching adulthood, such differences dissipate in terms of competence and intellectual capability, and each sibling should be evaluated based solely on his or her own merit. Nonetheless, some siblings believe that longevity (being born sooner and having spent more time in the business) merits them having the first shot at opportunities.

Other Family Divisions

In some families, in-laws are kept at a distance and may not be considered "full" members of the family or business. As such, they may be able to occupy management positions, but they may never be offered an ownership stake. Spouses of adult children in the business may be viewed as having less loyalty to the family as a whole, and more allegiance to the spouse or nuclear family. At times, in-laws are faced with issues prohibiting them from ever joining the family business.

In addition, divisions can form according to family branch. As the family grows and relatives become more emotionally distant from the founder(s) and their own cousins, communication between the successive generations can falter, and family branches may grow apart. Over time, the growth and division of family branches may (in the absence of communication) cause multigenerational family fractures, with family branches engaging in competition to win emotional or tangible ownership of the business.

Conflicts often arise when the business lacks a formal approach to family employment, including how to handle (1) employment for extended family members during times of crisis, (2) expectations for younger family members entering the business, and (3) education or experience required for promotion to management. As a typical scenario, consider a family firm with two siblings involved in the firm, each of whom has teenage children. As the children reach age of employment, the eldest is usually the first to work the odd jobs at the business (e.g., working the front desk, washing vehicles, stuffing envelopes). Later, as the younger children reach the age of employment, they may seek opportunities to work at the business during summers and breaks as well. What happens where there is no more work to be done or no further need for seasonal employment? What happens when the company experiences a decrease in sales volume? What happens when the eldest is the child of Sibling A (and has the opportunity to be a part of the family legacy) and the next teenager wanting to enter the business is the child of Sibling B (and will not have the opportunity to be part of the family legacy)? Suppose the child of Sibling A continues in the business: not only can this threaten to breed jealousy among the teenaged cousins, but it can also threaten the relationships among the parent and his or her siblings and cause fractures among family branches (as one family is now seemingly more deeply connected and rooted to the family business than the other family branch). In essence, the question that surfaces along with hurt feelings relates to fairness: "Why your kid and not mine?"

When left unmanaged, fragmentation along family branches can result in all-out, multigenerational family wars. Notably, 18 percent of family firms in one study reported that a family member had left the business due to a conflict.[20]

TEAM FRAGMENTATION FROM POSITION IN THE FAMILY BUSINESS SYSTEM

Managing Owners Versus Nonmanaging Owners

At times, sibling rivalries extend beyond those siblings immediately employed at the business. In fact, 22 percent of CEOs indicated that their estate plans will outline an equal division of ownership among members of the succeeding generation regardless of their contribution to the business (another 33 percent were undecided). Only 18 percent indicated that no ownership would be given to inactive family members.[21] Coincidentally, national survey data also support these regional findings with regard to plans for future ownership: 29 percent of family business owners plan to divide ownership equally, 25 percent are undecided, and 6 percent plan not to give ownership stakes to inactive family members.[22] These figures demonstrate a desire among parents who love their children equally to provide for their children equally with regard to business assets irrespective of the progeny's involvement in the business—the very asset that has allowed the estate to grow. However, tensions can form between those siblings who "show up" every day to grow the business and the other siblings who have less active roles, or who have no role other than shareholder/check collector. The perception in such circumstances can be that the reward is doled out disproportionately to each individual's contribution.

As family businesses move into the third generation and beyond, the level of complexity within the ownership system often increases as the number of family branches and nonmanaging shareholders increases. As familial distance from the business increases, shareholders may grow more distant from the founder and the previously shared value sets become diluted as potentially competing agendas form. Shareholders may become more motivated by their personal gain (e.g., return on investment, dividends) rather than seek to reinvest profits in the business. One correlational study found that increased organizational commitment among shareholders was related to working in the business, a smaller number of shareholders, and fewer family branches involved.[23] In a case study of a fifth-generation family business with 50 shareholders, 86 percent of respondents expressed pride in being a shareholder in the business (and the financial return was the primary motive for holding their shares), but only 38 percent agreed that they were knowledgeable about the company.[24] To keep ownership and management interests in balance, efforts to involve and educate shareholders are extremely important as the size and generational complexity of the family expand.

Family Versus Nonfamily

The distinction between family and nonfamily members is another important "fault line" in many family firms. Sometimes nonfamily employees are innocent bystanders who become caught up in intrafamily rivalries, having to play "referee" or endeavoring to "keep the peace." This can be a very stressful position to occupy.

In addition, family businesses face a number of other challenges when it comes to the development and retention of key nonfamily contributors. In Box 7.2, one anonymous nonfamily president offers his insight into the challenges he faced when working with family employees.

National and regional surveys on family-owned firms have provided data on the challenges that family firms face with regard to attracting

Box 7.2
Diary of a Nonfamily President/Owner

The following excerpts are messages sent over a three-week period by a nonfamily president/owner of a successful family-owned retailer located in the Midwest United States. The author chooses to remain anonymous.

Week 1

Over the past 17+ years, being a nonfamily president/owner of a family business has taken its toll on me. Sometimes I feel like a sacrificial piece of meat. Sibling and cousin rivalries continue, and you know how that works: when I agree with one, the other gets mad at me, and when I agree with their uncle, they all get mad at me. Sometimes I feel like a lame duck president. Being a nonfamily president/owner in a family business leaves you powerless because family members know they can't be fired. Without the fear of being fired hanging over them, how can I get them to act in the demeanor appropriate to their positions?

Our employees love me, and our customers think I'm the next best thing to ice cream, and they have voiced concerns about what will happen if I ever leave (they think I'm the glue that holds everything together). This is why I'm considering going into teaching—so I can feel like someone cares about what I'm saying. I need to get some of my prestige back. Let's face it, I certainly don't know everything, but I have a wealth of knowledge that I gained throughout my career. I'm just frustrated, and it has a way of wearing you down.

Week 2

I'm really distraught. We're close to settling into several new facilities and very shortly I will be signing my life away, and then there's no turning back. If I knew family businesses had all these issues, I never would have joined the company. As I told you before, I never expected any of this when I went through the interview process. They were so nice to me—I really blew it. But, what do I do? There are so many wonderful people here who rely on me.

Week 3

...The dizziness, headache, and blurred vision, may be all due to stress. Now what do I do—"fight or flight"? Nobody ever talks about the medical effects that happen to a nonfamily president in a family business. It would be a good subject to discuss at a meeting only for nonfamily members who are in leadership positions. I would love to hear how they deal or don't deal with issues of being a nonfamily member in a leadership role. It will give everyone an opportunity to gain insight on how they deal with this challenge, and the trickle-down effect it has on the organization. You may be surprised what you hear.

new nonfamily managers, motivating nonfamily managers, and providing advancement for nonfamily managers. Consider the following:

- Nationally, when family business leaders were asked to choose multiple concerns relating to nonfamily management, the key concerns identified were attracting new managers (45 percent), providing advancement opportunities (44.6 percent), and motivating employees (43.8 percent).[25]
- Regionally, the greatest challenges relating to nonfamily employees were providing advancement opportunities (34 percent), motivating employees (25 percent), cohesiveness/team building (14 percent), and differing values/ethics (12 percent).[26]

In fact, the data support what many nonfamily managers feel intuitively: when it comes to working in a family business, nonfamily members tend to encounter a "glass ceiling." In the United States, only 4 to 6 percent of family firms currently have or have had a nonfamily member in the CEO position. In 1997, 87 percent of CEOs in such firms were family members, with an additional 8 percent being related by marriage[27]; in 2002, 80 percent of CEOs were family members, with an additional 14 percent related by marriage.[28] In 2009, only 5 percent of family businesses surveyed had employed nonfamily CEOs,[29] leaving nonfamily employees with the belief that they have little to no chance of becoming chief executive. Nonetheless, there remains some hope for nonfamily employees. Of those firms with a designated successor for the business, 25 percent indicated that family membership was unimportant in determining the key attributes of the firm's next leader. Further, of those family businesses that have had a nonfamily CEO, 75 percent note that it was a successful experience.[30]

With nonfamily management challenges relating to advancement opportunities, motivation, team building, and attracting new managers, some evidence suggests that these challenges can actually lead to nonfamily managers exiting the business for other opportunities. In fact, data show that nonfamily employees generally remain with the family business for as long as 10 years, but noticeably fewer nonfamily employees remain onboard after the 10-year mark.[31]

Family firms typically provide professional development and training opportunities to family members and nonfamily employees alike; approximately 63 percent of CEOs provide professional development and training equally to family and nonfamily employees[32] However, as nonfamily managers progress in their careers at the family firm and enter senior management positions, the investment in education is greater for family members in senior leadership positions.[33] Compared to family employees, nonfamily employees receive higher levels of training in entry-level and middle management positions, but they receive much less training and professional development when entering senior management positions than family employees. This correlation highlights two central themes: (1) the drop-off in investment may be due to nonfamily members' departure from the business or (2) the "glass ceiling" that nonfamily employees hit when entering middle management at approximately the 10-year mid-career mark.

Other challenges related to nonfamily managers that can lead to team fragmentation and siloism (family in one silo, nonfamily in another silo) relate to employment policies that differ between family and nonfamily employees. As most family firms desire to remain family owned, it comes as little surprise that ownership policies and other related practices (such as hiring, compensation, bonus, and retirement benefits) often differ when it comes to family or nonfamily managers. What may be surprising to nonfamily employees are the differences in how policies and practices are evaluated and enforced when it comes to the business's family employees. For example, in a survey of family business CEOs, 25 percent noted that their "termination" policies differed for family and nonfamily employees.[34] Indeed, some nonfamily employees have complained that no matter how badly family members perform or behave, they cannot or will not be fired. This sense—that family members possess special status and are not subject to the same rules as everyone else—can breed animosity and resentment toward the family, and sour the attitudes of nonfamily contributors.

ADDITIONAL SOURCES OF TEAM FRAGMENTATION

In family businesses, many other factors can threaten the unity of teams within the firm and lead to the development of organizational silos. Among them are generation, gender, and education.

Generation

The entry of a new generation into the business brings a new set of norms and practices that sometimes mystify those members of the senior generation. While certain family values are passed down throughout the generations, each generation is also shaped by socioeconomic values (and perhaps religious, political, and cultural values) that change with the times. For example, the Veteran Generation (persons born from 1922 to the early 1940s, also known as the Builders, Traditionalists, and Silent Generation) grew up in a time of war, economic depression, agricultural ruin, and the rationing of scarce resources. Because their lives were generally characterized by core values of sacrifice, duty, conformity, and adherence to rules, it is little wonder why this "do without" generation has trouble seeing eye-to-eye with Generation X (persons born from 1960 to 1980) or Generation Nexters (generally persons born from 1980 to 2000; also called Generation Me, Generation Y, or the Millennials). Members of Generation X grew up in a period marked by distrust of authority (think Watergate, the Iran-Contra scandal, and the Los Angeles riots), so many place a high value on striking a positive work/life balance and establishing independence, eschewing the authority and formality associated with the Veteran Generation.[35]

Other characteristics of the generations may create tensions within organizations that could threaten the viability of teams, particularly when members of several generations are all part of the same team. For example, members of the Baby Boomer Generation (persons born from 1943 to 1960) might characterize members of Generation X as rude, impatient, and having a general disregard for established processes. Similarly, members of the Veteran Generation may see Gen Xers as stubborn, unaware, uneducated, and disrespectful. While Veterans may believe the Baby Boomers are self-absorbed, members of Generation X may believe that Boomers are workaholics, self-righteous, clueless, and too political.[36]

Within family firms, these generational values may surface with regard to concerns about commitment to the family business. Data from national and regional surveys show a concern among CEOs regarding the next generation's commitment level to the business. In particular, when asked the question "How confident are you that your next generation of leadership will show the same level of commitment as the current leadership?" only 19 percent of respondents to a survey noted that they were extremely confident; more than half (51 percent) were unsure or not confident that the next generation would show the same level of commitment.[37] In following year's survey, 31 percent of respondents indicated that when the current management of the business retired and a new owner took over, concerns regarding the next generation's commitment level to long-term ownership would be a challenge (38 percent were unsure if the successor's commitment level would be a challenge).[38]

Some family businesses develop generational silos, wherein members of the same generation communicate with one another, but do not communicate across generations. This approach frequently results in the succeeding generation being left in the dark about what the senior generation plans to do with regard to estate planning or the future of the business.

Gender

Gender biases in families can lead to differential treatment of female managers or owners. Sometimes female owners are not taken seriously by their husbands, brothers, or sons, and are left out of important decision-making tasks or ignored. Some women are left out of the business completely. As one (male) successor said, "My father had absolutely no interest in including my sister [in the business]. For him, the business was kind of an all-boys club, and only my brother and I were welcome." On the management side, male successors may be deemed better suited for top management or financial positions, while female successors may be directed into career paths that have been traditionally viewed as more female oriented (e.g., human resources, purchasing, accounts payable, or marketing), regardless of their true capabilities or merits.

Not surprisingly, most CEOs of family firms are male, although the numbers are shifting quickly. In 2007, 24 percent of U.S. family businesses surveyed employed a woman as CEO or president, and 31.3 percent noted that it was likely a female will emerge as the family firm's successor.[39] These percentages reflect a substantial increase from 2002[40] and 1997[41] surveys, wherein just 10 percent and 5 percent of family firms, respectively, employed a female president or CEO.

Education

Education level can also cause fissures within the team and family unit. In fact, having a formal education and business qualifications[42] is seen as nearly as important as working at least 10 years in the family business.[43] For some families, this issue poses an interesting challenge: how to evaluate those successors who have learned about the business from the ground up and invested time working for the business relative to those successors who have interned at the company and gone off to college or graduate school to develop the skills necessary for business management. Both types of potential successors have invested their resources and time with the goal of earning the top management positions, and both may believe that their investment is of equal or greater value to the future success of the business. Oftentimes in family firms, this divergence leads to a "book sense" versus "common sense" argument and the ensuing jealousies (e.g., who had more opportunities, who has more commitment and stayed at the business through rough patches, or who has closer family ties) create a no-win situation that can be destructive to any team.

TRUST AND FAIRNESS

When team fragmentation occurs, deep-seated issues related to trust and fairness are often at the core of the dispute. Trust has been defined as "a psychological state comprising the intention to accept vulnerability based on the positive expectations of the intentions or behavior of another."[44] Many different kinds of questions related to trust commonly emerge in family firms: Can I trust you to do your part? Can you trust me to make good decisions or to make mistakes from which I can learn and grow? Can I trust that you will take care of me and help me if I am in trouble? Can I trust you to be a good steward of assets or wealth entrusted to you? Can I trust you to run the management team competently and ethically? Can we trust the board to perform their oversight duties?

One model of trust for family firms incorporates three types of trust: interpersonal trust, competence trust, and system trust.[45]

- Interpersonal trust is based on a shared experience that allows for deep knowledge and understanding of personal characteristics, behaviors, thoughts, and feelings. It is thought to be high in the early stages of family firm development and is a key source of competitive advantage over nonfamily firms.
- Competence trust is the belief that people are capable of performing the jobs they are entrusted to do. Especially during the middle stages of family firm development, this type of trust may be enhanced by increased openness to outside input and expertise.
- System trust is impersonal, referring to a broader trust in an organizational system (how it is structured and how it functions) that helps the family business function as family growth diminishes the capacity for interpersonal and competence trust. Considered particularly important for later stages of family firm evolution, system trust is fostered by organizational transparency and the development of clear policies and guidelines that help manage expectations for present and future stakeholders.

In this model, trust is viewed as a kind of asset that, if properly managed, can be sustained over time, facilitating optimal health and functioning of the family business system.

In addition to mistrust, perceived unfairness or injustice in family firms is a problem that promotes team fragmentation. Questions pertaining to fairness include these: Why should I have to wait until I am 50 years old to lead the company? Why does my brother get paid more than me? Why wasn't my daughter hired, and is my nephew truly qualified for that job? Why did the CEO's brother-in-law get (or not get) fired?

Research shows that improvements in procedural justice (or fair processes) in family firms can lead to reduced conflicts, improved performance, and increased commitment and trust from the organization's members. Van der Hayden, Blondel, and Carlock observe that distributive justice (fairness of decisions, outcomes, and distribution of resources) in family firms is guided by different criteria: the needs of family members, the performance or merit of employees or managers, and equality among shareholders.[46] These different criteria for fairness give rise to conflicts, because each represents a different point of view within the system. According to Van der Hayden et al., if a system has a fair decision-making process in place, members may more readily accept those decisions that they do not like. This "increases the performance of the 'family-firm team': the team will execute decisions superbly because they have contributed to shape them, have been given a chance to make them 'their own,' and hence appreciate them much more."[47] Conversely, continual violations of fair process can lead members of the system to seek revenge in ways that can prove very destructive to the family or the business.

By their very nature, family business systems possess fault lines that can lead to team fragmentation. However, if members of a family business system possess (1) the will to build trust, (2) the processes to promote fairness, and (3) the skills to resolve conflicts as they arise, then the stage is better set for those members to become a part of a high-performing team. For the family business owner whose experience is highlighted in Box 7.3, team performance was enhanced by his family's ability to forgive one another and move past their differences.

BUILDING A HIGH-PERFORMANCE FAMILY BUSINESS TEAM

Family businesses can use a number of tactics to break down the culture of siloism and ensure that the core management team remains vibrant, strong, and intact. However such tactics alone quickly lose traction if they are not deployed within a context that emphasizes five key factors: a common purpose, competent membership, loyalty to the team, communication, and measurements.

Box 7.3
It's Not in the Books

John S. Santa—John Santa Consulting | Santa Energy

It is a late winter weekday afternoon when the Harvard research assistant and I are pondering a most perplexing question. We are working on a case study of our 2nd generation family business, and we are trying to figure out the way in which my three brothers and I have been operating together as a team. We are equal partners with an age span of about 15 years—and here is the amazing thing: we are still partners, we still speak to one another, and we have not committed either physical or mental mayhem on one another. And yet we have an arguably successful and rapidly growing enterprise on the brink of welcoming yet another generation of family to leadership and ownership.

It certainly was not for a lack of disagreement and arguing. It was not for a lack of caring or devotion to the general cause of the family business or our devotion to whatever aspect of the enterprise for which we assumed personal responsibility. And then it became clear. Perhaps it was a discovery by default, but there it was plain as day: *we had survived because we learned how to forgive one another.* What a strange business concept (certainly one never found in the prodigious tomes of any business school library). But there it was: simply the ability to forgive one another so that we might move on to bigger and better things.

And yet, upon reflection, we realize how uniquely suited that dynamic is to a family business because, as family member partners, we are always related. And even if we battle and spar, we are always related. And even if we make mistakes, there is an opportunity for forgiveness because we are, after all, always related. Unlike unrelated partners and associates who may come and go over sundry issues, our brother/sister partners are always our siblings. We always share parents and we always cherish their children as our nephews and nieces as they cherish ours. So welcome to the world of forgiveness in family business. And God bless our parents for all the blessings they bestowed on us—but especially the ability to forgive one another and move on.

Perhaps one of the more crucial aspects of a high-performance team is the idea of a "common purpose" or a superordinate goal. For family businesses, developing a shared vision is not always as simple as it seems. In some family enterprise systems, the primary reason that the business exists is to support the family's needs and its potential. In others, this idea is reversed: it is the *family* that serves the business. In the former example, the business is available to family members because the business supports the family's lifestyle. In the latter, the family members are available to the business, but only if the business needs them and if the skill set is the right match. In effect, the business belongs to the community and the family serves as its stewards. Understanding the nuances—and why the family and the business coexist—is essential to developing a shared vision and common purpose.

Loyalty to the team is vital to its functioning, but it is oftentimes not reliable being that individuals are usually a part of many different teams at one time and experience conflicting demands for time and resources. For example, an individual may be part of a vertical team in overseeing the marketing division of a business, but also part of a horizontal team that includes all division heads. Then there are the other "teams" to which an individual belongs: a spousal team, a recreational sporting team, a member of a volunteer emergency medical team, and so on. Bride and Phillips, *Titanic*'s wireless operators, likely felt this tension. Were they part of a team onboard *Titanic*, or were they a part of a team of wireless operators who worked in concert with one another to send and receive messages? During periods of stress, when time is at a premium and the relative costs of inefficiency are high, team members must know where one another's allegiance is and feel solidarity in achieving the common purpose. If a member of a top management team does not have loyalty to that team, fragmentation can result. For example, if a warehouse fire or some other dire emergency occurs, the top management team must know that each team member will be dedicated to resolving that emergency.

It is critical that family teams, when they also constitute the top management team, have competent members who can hold one another accountable for meeting the common purpose. Family members involved in the top management team must have the appropriate skills, knowledge, attitude, aptitude, and values that will give the team its best chance for success. Members who want to belong to the top management team because of extrinsic factors (such as compensation or the status associated with a senior management title) can hurt team performance.

Family teams must also work to establish metrics for success—otherwise, how will the team know if it has been successful in reaching its common purpose? Metrics in the way of individual performance metrics, divisional performance metrics, and organization-wide performance metrics can help to ensure that the team is working properly, is accountable, and has the right members onboard. Metrics can also play a crucial role in determining who the top management team successors should be. In the end, the use of metrics will (1) give the successors an objective goal to work toward, (2) instill a culture of meritocracy within the organization, and (3) ensure that the top and most appropriate performers become members of the top management team. The goal when such measurements are used is not to shut out family members or successors, but rather is to develop family members personally and professionally.

High-performing family teams cannot realize their full potential unless considerable efforts are devoted to communicating with one another. It is essential to foster good communication through practices such as active listening, clarification, and considered response. At a minimum, communication is the glue that holds teams together—building trust, encouraging proactive thinking and constructive criticism, enhancing commitment, motivating members, and weeding out members not committed to the team by keeping a focus on the common purpose. At its best, communication can help a family business succeed over generations.

CHAPTER SUMMARY

- On *Titanic*, team fragmentation was evidenced by unfortunate results of the "officer reshuffle" and the manner in which the wireless operators functioned as their own silo, lacking awareness of their vital role in preserving the ship's safety.
- Team fragmentation and siloism in family business systems can develop as a result of family dynamics, position within the family business system, or demographic differences. In attempting to balance family needs with good business decisions, family business owners may unknowingly weaken the ties that hold family business teams together.
- Fragmentation and siloism stemming from family dynamics can occur as a result of parent/child conflict, copreneur disharmony, sibling rivalry, and other family divisions (e.g., conflicts relating to in-laws or family branches).
- Conflicts stemming from position within the family business system itself (where the roles of family, owner, and manager coalesce) can result in fragmentation and siloism between managing owners versus nonmanaging owners and family versus nonfamily employees.
- Other sources of team fragmentation (and causes of siloism) relate to different generational values, gender, and education level.
- When team fragmentation occurs, deep-seated issues related to trust and fairness are often at the core.
- High performing family business teams are characterized by a common purpose, competent membership, loyalty, use of metrics, and communication.

PART III

●

Listening to and Learning from *Titanic*

> I still think about the 'might have beens' about the *Titanic*, that's what stirs me more than anything else. Things that happened that wouldn't have happened if only one thing had gone better for her. If only, so many if onlys. If only she had enough lifeboats. If only the watertight compartments had been higher. If only she had paid attention to the ice that night. If only the *Californian* did come. The 'if only' kept coming up again and again and that makes the ship more than the experience of studying a disaster. It becomes a haunting experience to me, it's the haunting experience of 'if only.'
>
> —Walter Lord, *Titanic* historian and author

This final part of the book consolidates the learning that the *Titanic* disaster offers, in hopes that family business owners will not have to look back on the memory of their firm and say to themselves, "If only . . ." Part III takes *Titanic*'s lessons and considers them in a broader perspective, helping readers understand how to build an environment that minimizes the possibility of tragedies from occurring in their businesses.

Chapter 8 evaluates how the five fatal flaws discussed in Part II of this book are interconnected—and how too much or too little emphasis on each domain (confidence, leadership, planning, architecture, and teams) can cause inertia and debilitate organizations. Seven strategies are given to help family businesses navigate the journey of transitions, such that the passage of the business from one generation to the next is a safe one.

In Chapter 9, the concept of legacy is explored from the perspective of the *Titanic* story and from the perspective of family enterprise systems, including the desire to pass on a business, material wealth, values, or a way of life. Final consideration is given to the kinds of legacies owners hope to create and the kinds of legacies that matter most.

8

Establishing Safe Passages

> It is not the strongest of the species that survive, nor the most intelligent, but the one most responsive to change.
>
> —Charles Darwin

For most of the people aboard *Titanic*, the passage across the Atlantic was anything but safe; and for most family firms, the safe passage of the business from one generation to the next fails to occur. In this chapter, the five fatal flaws that led to failure for *Titanic* and that threaten family firms are considered as a group. They are examined in terms of both how optimal levels of each domain produce the best chances for survival and how the flaws are interrelated. Based on this analysis, seven strategies are offered for establishing "safe passages" for family firms, and the important aspects of managing the change process are discussed.

The fatal flaws introduced in preceding chapters offer a framework whereby family business members can evaluate the trigger points that might potentially derail their firm's survival and identify areas that are in need of redress. Keeping "in check" the confidence of the organization's owners, team dynamics, organizational infrastructure, and leaders, and ensuring that the firm is prepared for the changes and challenges that inevitably lie ahead can be a stressful and time-consuming process that requires ongoing attention. It comes as little surprise that the same resource constraints that may lead to the development of the firm's organizational flaws are the same resource constraints that may compromise its ability to monitor them.

The goal with regard to the fatal flaws is to identify potential areas of danger for the organization, isolate the threats, disable them, and marshal the resources to ensure that they do not recur. However, as with most things in life, moderation is key. Low self-esteem is harmful, as is having too much self-esteem. Too much infrastructure is restrictive, while too little infrastructure is unstable. How can family business leaders benchmark where their organization falls relative to its flaws?

OPTIMAL RANGES FOR EFFICACY AND INTERCONNECTEDNESS

Within any system, tolerance must be exercised with regard to ranges of confidence, leadership, planning and preparation, architecture, and teams, and with regard to the importance assigned to each domain. Sometimes, leadership may be more necessary than teams; at other times, architecture may be more necessary than confidence. It is unlikely that each domain will be assigned equal weight given the needs of the business and the competitive environment. Moreover, the importance of each domain will probably change as the family business transitions through the founding generation to the second generation, third generation, and beyond. For example, more resources will likely be devoted to building the organizational architecture that will enable the family business to survive in earlier generations compared to succeeding generations. In contrast, succeeding generations may require more resources for building effective leaders and teams as the organization becomes more complex than the business shepherded by preceding generations. No doubt every organization experiences fluctuations within the competitive environment that can put stress on leaders and teams, causing even the most steely of teams to weaken. Figure 8.1 outlines a conceptual model that illustrates optimal ranges for all domains (which, for purposes of discussion, are given equal weight) with a corresponding table (Table 8.1) identifying the attributes and optimal scope within each.

The overconfidence demonstrated by *Titanic*'s captain and owners is legendary, as they sped through an ice field on a ship promoted as completely safe, if not unsinkable. Chapter 3 explored how an excess of confidence can surface in family firms, leading to denial, narcissism, entitlement, insular thinking, and unrealistic perceptions of individuals' skills and contributions. However, the goal is not for businesses to err on the side of too much caution, thereby depleting confidence to levels that are counterproductive. In fact, too little confidence when it comes to management of a family firm leads to poor decision-making processes, as key decision makers may feel a sense of inertia stemming from anxiety and low self-esteem. Low levels of confidence can also lead to stagnation (at the cost of innovation); poor execution and follow-through on decisions; poor marketing and positioning of the business, its assets, and its products and services; too much external influence in decision making; low employee

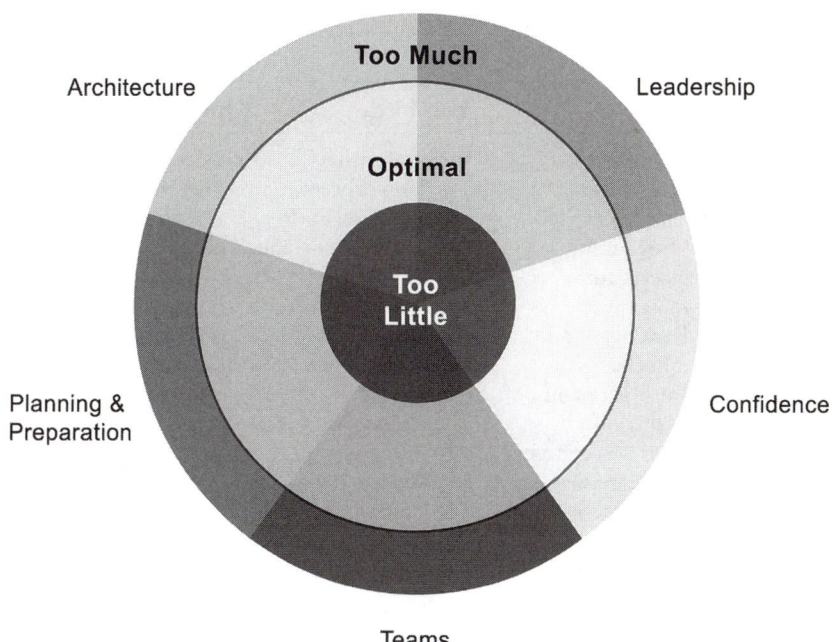

Figure 8.1
Conceptual model for optimal ranges for confidence, leadership, planning and preparation, architecture, and teams

morale; and abandonment of the business by family members and employees who lose confidence in the business's ability to survive.

When a firm experiences too much leadership—as evidenced by either too many leaders (making for a top-heavy organization), too much emphasis placed on the abilities and importance of a solitary leader, or a leader who neglects to "let go" of responsibilities—the result can be equally destructive. Among the challenges of too much leadership, organizations can suffer from internal distrust, lack of employee empowerment, poor mentoring of succeeding generations, power struggles among family owners, demoralized employees (particularly nonfamily employees who experience the "glass ceiling" phenomenon), and inertia in decision making due to "too many chefs in the kitchen." In one family business, the lack of consensus building and power struggles among three members of the senior generation led to a complete failure in building appropriate estate and succession plans. The result: the first to die will be "luckier" because there will be enough liquid capital to cover the costs of that person's estate taxes. The next two to die will have less fortunate legacies, as their deaths (and subsequent estate tax burdens) will force a sale of the business, as all of the liquid assets needed to pay the taxes will have been depleted.

Table 8.1
Optimal and Suboptimal Ranges for Confidence, Leadership, Planning and Preparation, Architecture, and Teams

	Too Much	Too Little	Optimal
Confidence	• Denial • Narcissism • Entitlement • Over-optimism, inaccurate forecasting • Lack of outside influence • Little focus on adaptability • Poor perception of individuals' abilities as related to compensation and responsibilities • Taking too many uncalculated risks	• Poor decision-making processes • Lack of execution • Poor marketing and positioning • Too much outside influence • Low employee morale • Abandonment of the business • Pessimism, fear, insecurity • Lack of innovation or appropriate risk taking	• Balanced approach whereby employees are valued for their skills, knowledge, attitudes, and aptitude • Employees are empowered to make decisions and promote change from the ground up • Senior managers and owners make decisions with input from outside advisors and employees • Growth is measured, monitored, and transparent • Managers and employees have the ability to embrace weaknesses and leverage one another's strengths
Leadership	• Autocratic • Lack of employee empowerment • Inertia in decision making • Poor mentoring of future generations • Power struggles among family owners • Demoralized employees uncertain of where or who to turn to for guidance • Glass-ceiling phenomena among non-family employees • Limited adaptability	• Confusion • Lack of vision • Lack of building external networks • Poor ability to plan strategically • Uncertainty relative to the firm's future • Inability to manage conflict • Absence of trust • Counterproductive and unhealthy flexibility	• Leaders establish a vision and empower managers and subordinates to develop strategies and tactics • Tasks are delegated and employees are given training to succeed in their positions • Leader candidates (family and nonfamily) are continually developed and given appropriate feedback • Leaders communicate primarily by listening and guiding

Table 8.1 (Continued)

	Too Much	Too Little	Optimal
Architecture	• Inflexible organizational structure • Focus on transactions and/or transactional relationships • Focus on conforming • Inordinate focus on maintaining the existing structure	• Weak monitoring systems with which to gauge effectiveness • Poor job-person fit • Breeding ground for conflict stemming from ambiguity	• Emphasis on firm transformation rather than transactions • Roles clarified with articulated guidelines on how to manage firm-level strategic decisions
Planning and preparation	• Rigidity • Poor ability to quickly adapt to changing conditions • Getting bogged down because of overemphasis on process and procedure	• Chaos, confusion • Reactive versus proactive • Anxiety, uncertainty • Poorly managed processes for communication, which lead to conflicts • "Generational shadow" constraints	• Analysis of the best/worst/most likely scenarios relative to major firm decisions • Firms are both exploratory and exploitative of current and future opportunities • Firms engage in forecasting with industry experts and build internal bench strength
Teams	• Lack of an identifiable leader • Poor individual accountability • Inertia in decision making • Conformity and loss of individual creativity • Power struggles within and between teams • Focus on team dynamics instead of the firm's products and services	• Loneliness and boredom • Focus on self-preservation • Lack of external perspective • Perception of nepotism • Culture of star performers and individual achievement	• Environment in which individuals are accountable for meeting individual and team goals and are evaluated on and compensated for meeting those goals

Similarly, when companies experience too little leadership, the result can be a lack of vision, confusion and uncertainty, poor ability to plan strategically, inability to manage conflict, and (as in the situation characterized by too much leadership) distrust. In addition, too little leadership jeopardizes the firm's ability to create external networks and strategic partnerships—a key component of the tasks addressed by leaders and top management teams. Top management is responsible for carrying out a number of different functions:

- Influencing the perceptions and actions of various other constituencies[1]
- Operating at the boundary of the organization and its environment[2]
- Monitoring and interpreting external events and trends, dealing with external constituencies, and formulating, communicating, and monitoring the organization's responses to the environment[3]
- Implementing those responses[4]

Without leaders who can effectively manage at the interface of the organization and its external environment, the business cannot mitigate the obstacles ahead and develop an appropriate and implementable strategy.

When firms are struggling to adapt to change, too much architecture can be prohibitive, leading to inflexible management and organizational structures, a focus on transactions and transactional relationships, a focus on conformity, and an inordinate amount of resources spent on maintaining the existing structure. Within family systems, the firm's architecture may repeat the behavioral patterns that family members demonstrate at home and work, with individuals continuing to perform the roles they were supposedly "born into." For example, the eldest son may "inherit the reins" while female family members play supporting roles. Conversely, without strong architecture, family businesses are likely to suffer from having poor job-person fit, weak monitoring systems to measure firm effectiveness, and conflict among employees and family members stemming from too much ambiguity.

Similar to having too much architecture, an inordinate amount of planning and preparation can slow progress so that attempts to plan for the future become an exercise in futility. While some family businesses build a strategic plan that looks out 15 years, the general recommendation is to build a plan that is executable over a 3- to 5-year period (a more realistic plan, given that industries tend to change dramatically over decades). However, too much planning and preparation can build a rigid organizational structure that is incapable of adapting to changing market conditions and that demonstrates a lack of innovative thinking. For instance, one study of planning in family firms found that firms rich in innovative capacity experienced slightly lower performance when they had high levels of strategic planning, as opposed to when they had lower levels of strategic planning.[5]

When family firms have not engaged in planning or preparation, changes in industry can catch these businesses off-guard and ill prepared to deal with change. The ensuing chaos, anxiety, and focus on being "reactive" rather than "proactive" can freeze family firms in their tracks. When too little planning and preparation is done in the family domain, senior-generation family members often lack the confidence in the next generation's abilities, largely because of the lack of preparation in developing talent. The chaos and anxiety that result from poor planning frequently lead to ineffective communication and internal conflicts.

Teams also play a crucial role in the family business, whether they are teams within the business, family teams, or family members and employees working together. Too much emphasis on teams can lead to the lack of an identifiable leader, loss of individual accountability, inertia in making progress toward a goal, conformity and reduction in individual creativity, power struggles among team members, and a focus on maintaining good team dynamics rather than fulfilling the team's purpose. Yet, as discussed in Chapter 7, teams bring an important dimension to any business. Generally, the "we're all in this together" ideal brings about unity and mutual accountability—but only if teams are properly managed. When overemphasis on teams debilitates a business's ability to progress, the result can prove fatal for a business. Conversely, in firms where a team approach is not embraced, employees and family may suffer from loneliness and boredom, resort to self-preservation, and lack external perspectives and fresh ideas. The culture may reward "star performers" while creating unhealthy competition and silos within the organization. Also, without the chance to work with nonfamily employees, family members may not have the opportunity to "prove" themselves to colleagues and peers, thereby perpetuating the perception of nepotism.

It is important to note that the five flaws do not occur in isolation; rather, these domains are intimately interconnected. Figure 8.2 demonstrates hypothesized relationships among the five fatal flaws. The model starts with overconfidence and associated ideas (e.g., narcissism, entitlement, and over-optimism), which are viewed as characteristics of individuals, families, or firm cultures that (reciprocally) lead to and result from ineffective leadership. Overconfidence can also lead to frail architecture as well as poor preparation and planning. To the extent that business owners assume that "everything is going to be fine," they may fail to perceive risks or devote enough time and money preparing for them. Similarly, they may view the development of agreements, policies, and plans as too bureaucratic and unnecessary. As described previously, destructive narcissism and over-optimism are associated with problems in leadership (e.g., inaccurate forecasting, taking bold risks, and lack of mentoring).

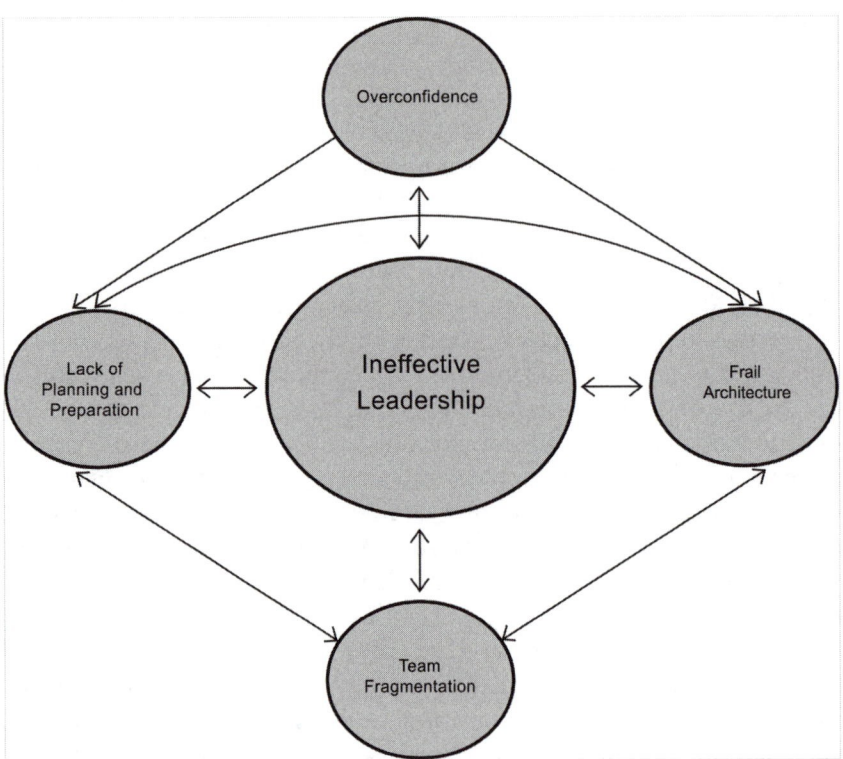

Figure 8.2
Proposed relationships among the five fatal flaws

At the center of the model is leadership, which has reciprocal links to all
other flaws. Effective leadership is expected to be related to optimal levels
of planning and preparation and to development of an appropriate level of
firm architecture. Planning and architecture are also expected to be positively correlated, as planning activities often result in the development of
plans, policies and procedures, and agreements. In contrast, poor planning,
ineffective leadership, and lack of firm architecture are all expected to result
in team fragmentation—with team fragmentation (via divisions within the
family system or the organizational system) then disabling a team's ability
to plan, prepare, lead, and develop the strong architectural systems necessary for business survival. One of the important functions of leadership is
to build strong teams that work together efficiently toward a common goal,
so it makes sense that problems with leadership will have a negative effect
on healthy team development. Teams are also expected to suffer when planning and preparation are minimal, and when firms lack adequate policies
and procedures to help clarify roles and expectations. Box 8.1 further

explores the role of leaders as "cultural torch bearers" who can create an environment that can breed success or failure.

What might an organization that embraces optimal levels of confidence, leadership, planning and preparation, architecture, and teams look like—and how does one get there? How can leaders effectively manage the interconnectedness inherent in governing employees, family, and

Box 8.1
Cultural Torch Bearers

Patrick Terrion—Founders Capital Management

The role of today's company leaders has evolved, primarily into that of "torch bearers" who set the values and culture for the organization. These individuals lead with a servant's mentality, providing the organization with what it needs to be successful. Servicing, as opposed to controlling the company, creates an environment for the organization to anticipate and adapt to an ever-changing business landscape. But how does a leader create this environment?

1. By identifying and constantly nurturing the cultural aspects of the company that led to its success, including a passion for the business and a dream for its future.
2. By encouraging constant learning, and cheering failure that can lead to future success.
3. By showing determination to succeed at every level of the company, and caring for all stakeholders as part of the family—employees, suppliers, customers, and the community.
4. By "listening" and "understanding" the customers and giving them what they want—that is, seeking to be different and unmatchable.
5. By allowing for "interdependence" versus "independence." Interdependence with customers, suppliers, and employees develops and strengthens the business network, while independence separates people from the business.

If business leaders follow this deep cultural recipe for building a business, the potential for organizational failure will be significantly reduced. Employees who are passionate about the business will be zealous about their jobs. They will share the dream about the business future, and be determined to be part of its success, including allowing innovation to take place and learning from their experiences. Individuals in this environment listen to and understand one another, and work interdependently toward a common goal.

Ultimately, failures due to overconfidence, inability to innovate, or inability to develop new leadership are failures of cultural development. Leaders who "become the culture" and associate the company's success with their own success (instead of allowing the culture to belong to the company) can tragically debilitate performance and create a recipe for business disaster.

owners, while ensuring that the business continues to develop high-quality products and services?

Optimal ranges of confidence, leadership, architecture, planning and preparation, and teams can take many shapes, and will undoubtedly require different resources. Nevertheless, the overarching vision when establishing what a family firm can achieve when striking the right balance is applicable to all firms. Optimal balances promote a culture with the following characteristics for employees, leaders, and family members:

All Employees

- Are empowered to suggest and promote change from the ground up.
- Are given the tools to succeed in their roles and are encouraged—through appropriate mentoring, education, and training—to take on additional responsibilities. Employees are also given a "safe haven" in which to discuss challenges and problems within the company without fear of retaliation.
- Are valued for their skills, knowledge, attitudes, and aptitudes, and are given appropriate feedback in a way that is not threatening and given from individuals who want to see them succeed.
- Are accountable to individual and team goals, and are evaluated and compensated on successful achievements with regard to each.

Leaders

- Make key strategic decisions after having considered input from outside advisors (and sometimes from customers, suppliers, and employees).
- Embrace one another's and employees' weaknesses, provide assistance to overcome weaknesses, and leverage one another's strengths without permission, thanks, or apology.
- Establish a vision for the company that is rooted in innovative thinking.
- Delegate tasks and develop future leaders by incrementally increasing the responsibilities related to those tasks.
- Communicate primarily by listening and guiding.
- Engage in forecasting with industry experts and make building bench strength a core initiative within the business.

Family

- Defines growth in a way that is acceptable to both the family and the business, with growth being measured and monitored transparently.

- Clarifies roles with articulated guidelines on how to manage (and how the family should be involved in) major firm-level strategic decisions.
- Emphasizes transformation rather than transactions.
- Evaluates best-case, worst-case, and most likely scenarios relative to major firm decisions.
- Sees the necessity for the firm to be both exploratory (in new ventures and initiatives) and exploitative (with current opportunities).
- Encourages change as a necessary ingredient to promote the success of both the family and the business.
- Respects the opinions of others and works to develop a superordinate goal.

Of course, for family businesses, change can be difficult to undertake. When perceived as a task, change can be quick, painful, and fear inducing. When welcomed as a long-term cultural value, it can be reinvigorating. How change will affect the family firm and its employees depends on how the balance is struck between embracing change and retaining core values.

Establishing a superordinate goal may not be as simple as it seems. More likely than not, people will have different ideas about why the business exists and where it should go in the future. Further, "success" can have many definitions. What does it mean to have "business success"? Is success based on profitability or growth in profit margins, number of locations, number of employees, time and costs saved by making processes more efficient, or the firm's ability to give back to the community? Would that definition still hold if the profitability came about through reductions in staff vis-à-vis layoffs or replacement of current employees with lower-wage employees in developing economies? And what does it mean to have "family success"? Is family success based on time spent at home, income growth, religious faith, growth in educational attainment across generations, longevity in marriage, philanthropic contributions, or ability to access quality healthcare and enhance quality of life? Does family success relate to family "togetherness," whether measured by the *amount* of time spent together at home or at work or the *quality* of the time together? The larger question, then, is this: When the family and business are taken together, what determines "family business success"?

For many, the overwhelming desire is for both the family and the business to survive, with the family continuing to give and receive love and support to its members, and the business continuing to provide for the well-being of the family and the community (including employees). Conflicts can arise, however, when the prospect of "well-being" becomes defined as "unconditional welfare," whereby the business provides for those who have little investment (personal or financial) in the company's operation or survival.

Tagiuri and Davis analyzed independent "objectives" (aggregated from 74 specific goals) that family owners and managers of successful firms typically seek to fulfill.[6] Relative to the business, family business owners aim to have a business that meets the following criteria:

- Is a place where employees can be happy and productive
- Makes its employees proud by promoting an image and commitment to excellence in its field
- Provides the owner(s) with financial security and benefits
- Develops new and quality products
- Provides a means of personal growth, social advancement, and autonomy
- Is a good corporate citizen
- Offers job security

How can family firms welcome and facilitate the changes required to build a balanced business that reaches these objectives?

STRATEGIES FOR ESTABLISHING SAFE PASSAGES

Family firms find themselves dealing with crises as they arise, including unexpected crises due to changes in the family, the business, or the environment. However, the best method of managing crises is to develop an environment that minimizes the chances of unanticipated problems from surfacing in the first place. This section profiles seven strategies for establishing safe passages that are never too soon or too late to implement: (1) create a sense of urgency around business survival; (2) embrace outside counsel; (3) develop the policies and procedures necessary for business survival; (4) invest in human capital; (5) create a process for strategic planning; (6) promote an entrepreneurial orientation; and (7) communicate, communicate, communicate.

Strategy #1: Create a Sense of Urgency Around Business Survival

Paramount to any strategy for establishing safe passage is the need to create a sense of urgency around business survival. Oftentimes, urgency is confused with "panic" or "disorder"—an interpretation that does an injustice to urgency's intent. Urgency means making business survival *the* number one priority. Procrastinating, waiting to focus on important tasks until another day, and hoping that difficulties will be resolved on their own are unacceptable ways of managing if survival is truly of paramount importance. Managing a business—a family business, no less—is demanding, but owners are negligent toward that enterprise when they turn a blind eye to problems.

One of the challenges that interferes with the ability to create urgency is failure to prioritize appropriately. Steven Covey has described the importance of distinguishing between the issues that are *urgent* (requiring immediate attention) and the issues that are *important* (the things that truly matter most).[7] Business leaders often come to view the day-to-day "fires" as the urgent matters that deserve all of their attention, which results in the more important matters (such as planning for survival) getting delayed or knocked off their agendas. Creating and sustaining urgency around survival must begin with a clear change in priorities.

Urgency means that owners also must communicate what the business needs from all stakeholders to ensure that the business is given its best chance for survival. It means being transparent, allowing employees to see for themselves how each person is an important part of the business's success, and doing what is necessary to keep the goal of survival first and foremost in everyone's mind while making sure that morale stays up. Everybody needs to be onboard with making survival the top priority; thus, for family business leaders, this strategy can mean making difficult decisions about those individuals who do not embrace the urgency to survive. It is incumbent upon the leaders to measure performance, align performance with outcomes, map low performance to the appropriate causes, and make the necessary changes without delay.

Strategy #2: Embrace Outside Counsel

Family business owners must also be open to and ready for outside perspectives. This statement does not mean that everyone's ideas must be implemented; rather, it means that alternative viewpoints are heard and given due consideration. There are a number of resources that family business owners can leverage when it comes to hearing alternative perspectives on managing family, intrafirm, and industry dynamics.

Many family business owners listen to the perspectives of spouses, close friends, and close industry allies. But more likely than not, these groups of individuals will have ideas, beliefs, and experiences similar to those of the family business owner —so their perspectives may not be entirely different from the owner's viewpoint. For this reason, it is important for the family business owner to break out of his or her network and hear new information that could challenge that individual's ways of thinking.

Perhaps the easiest method for gaining alternative perspectives is through those parties to whom the business owner has more immediate access—employees, customers, and suppliers. In fact, many improvements come from the ground up as employees have ideas for new ways to streamline processes for increased efficiency. Customers' demands for new solutions are often a primary driver of positive changes and innovation. Suppliers may anticipate changes on the industry's horizon before they appear in mainstream awareness. In fact, Roy Kroc, the visionary who made Dick and Mac McDonald's restaurant a household name, saw McDonald's success as a three-legged stool supported equally by the strength of the McDonald's corporation, franchisees, and suppliers. Other business owners (particularly as start-up entrepreneurs) also take this three-legged stool approach in building their businesses based on equal input in the form of the voices of customers, enterprise, and industry.

Involvement in local or regional associations is also critical to gather outside perspectives. Networking allows business owners to learn from peers who represent different industries, have met different challenges, or have developed different organizational structures. Likewise, leaders should listen to other family businesses that face similar challenges when it comes to managing intrafirm or family dynamics. Participating in university-sponsored family business programs is a source of great inspiration to leaders or successors who require support in their efforts to navigate difficulties specific to family enterprises. No doubt every family business scenario is unique; however, most of the underlying reasons for the challenges that emerge are common among family firms. Learning how others have managed certain challenges is crucial to getting ideas. In addition, the chance to network with others in different industries can open the possibility of thinking creatively about new products and services extending into new industries. It is also an opportunity to brainstorm on new needs not currently met in market(s), new business models, new opportunities to expand through joint ventures, or new ways to partner in promoting corporate social responsibility efforts.

While it is important to gain perspectives from various industries, it is, of course, still important to remain involved in associations specific to the business owner's industry. The idea is for a family business leader to look at his or her role multidimensionally—both horizontally (networking with others in the same industry or field) and vertically (networking with others who are family business owners and/or share other personally relevant attributes such as gender, age, position, firm size, generational standing, and location), and representing various industries. In effect, being a part of these other organizations may open the doors to networking with other business owners who, in some cases, may serve as a quasi-advisory board.

Of course, being involved in business or industry associations is not necessarily a substitute for having a formal advisory board made up of individuals who represent diverse competencies. As businesses become more complex (e.g., as they introduce another generation into the business, experience growth, or face changes in the competitive environment), an advisory board can be monumentally helpful in preparing the owners and managers for the challenges ahead. One thing should be clear: the implementation of an advisory board does not mean that the business owners are "weak" or are incapable of running the business. Indeed, advisory boards do not tell leaders how to run their businesses; rather, they offer advice and wisdom earned though experience, and the owners are free to "take it or leave it."

Advisory boards typically are composed of three to eight individuals who may (1) have backgrounds or competencies lacking in the business, such as marketing, branding, product development, or human resources; (2) have experience growing a business; and (3) have experience managing a family business or understand how to manage the family relationships. Sometimes this means the advisory board will include the following types of members:

- Psychologists specializing in family business dynamics
- Human resources professionals who can help the firm develop creative compensation and bonus programs to increase employees' effectiveness
- Lean transformation specialists to drive efficiency
- Sales consultants who can improve a firm's ability to negotiate with potential customers and close deals effectively
- Marketing experts to help articulate the firm's competitive advantage and position that in the marketplace
- Environmental experts to consult on energy and waste
- Wealth advisors
- Consultants who can help to manage major change initiatives
- Executive coaches who can help with developing talent

The list of potential advisory board candidates is endless, and will differ for each organization depending on where the firm is in its life cycle and what it needs to support its growth.

Strategy #3: Develop the Policies and Procedures Necessary for Business Survival

It is never too late to begin developing the policies or procedures necessary for business survival. Making an appointment to talk with an accountant and attorney about developing a formal succession and estate plan can happen within days, if one so chooses. The process will not necessarily be complete in a matter of days, however; a "good" succession can take a minimum of three to five years to complete, and that timeline assumes that the process happens quickly and without strong dissenting opinions. The process is likely to move more rapidly when all parties agree and can communicate effectively, the business is not overly complex, and there are fewer shareholders and family branches involved. However, picking up the phone or composing an e-mail is an important first step to initiate the succession process.

It is also never too late to develop a family employment policy, draft a buy/sell or shareholder agreement, get a valuation of the business, and write out job descriptions. Some of these matters may require more of an upfront investment of time or money than others (such as a valuation or shareholder agreements), but developing a family employment policy and job descriptions can be fairly simple and relatively inexpensive. Some family businesses have hired business interns to interview employees and establish an outline for job descriptions that can then be further developed by managers within the business or consultants hired for the purpose of establishing an infrastructure for career development. The critical thing is to get started. The firm should then celebrate the "small wins" when even just one initiative—no matter how large or small—reaches the next stage toward completion. In fact, celebrating small wins is necessary for team morale and ensuring that everyone remains focused on the goal.

In the end, the question is not "How much will it cost us?", whether the measurement is in time, money, or other resources. Instead, the question becomes "Can we afford *not* to do this?"

Strategy #4: Invest in Human Capital

Investing in human capital always generates a positive return. For family businesses, investing in employees may help family firms achieve a number of positive results: increased buy-in from employees, higher loyalty to the firm, lower turnover rates, an ability to become a better adapted and more competitive organization, and better measurement of the capabilities of the firm's most important asset (its employees). Family business leaders must focus on developing competencies and communication skills that make them accessible to employees. Nonetheless, building the knowledge and skill base of all employees (family and nonfamily), and empowering them, helps businesses to better compete within a global environment where technical changes are prevalent.

Having a smarter workforce never hurts, but suppressing the capabilities of the employees will. Investing in human capital does not necessarily mean providing tuition assistance and flex-time (although both are terrific benefits to offer). Instead, investing in human capital means that family firms can offer ongoing development opportunities to employees. For example, the firm might bring in speakers on topics that are personally relevant to employees:

- Managing personal finances and retirement plans
- Healthier eating, weight-loss techniques, or smoking-cessation strategies
- The benefits of meditation to relieve stress
- Ways to evaluate colleges for those employees with children
- Ways to better communicate with family members to ease tension within one's home

Issues pertinent to employees on a professional level may involve discussions of time management, developing "leaner" or more efficient processes, giving back to the community (as part of a corporate effort), and other types of training (e.g., new technology platforms, desktop publishing programs, forensic accounting, languages, social media, etc.) that should be open to those employees willing to invest the effort. Of course, one of the best ways to determine which kinds of training will be most valued is to ask the employees about their interests. Finding creative ways to develop employees personally and professionally builds a more satisfied and loyal workforce.

Another type of development opportunity is allowing employees to cross-train within departments or to shadow others within the different business units (e.g., a lathe operator interested in marketing or an accounting employee interested in sales). This practice has several benefits. Primarily, it builds a team approach as employees gain a more sophisticated understanding of everyone's role in "the big picture." Further, it allows employees to develop other capabilities that may be useful if they are needed to "fill someone's shoes" on a temporary basis. A flu epidemic, a natural disaster, or other crisis-invoking event may require that employees pitch in to perform functions outside of their core duties. The result of cross-training and providing other opportunities for employee development can be happier, more engaged and intellectually stimulated workers who can have great things to say about where they work—and that kind of positive publicity cannot be bought.

Strategy #5: Create a Process for Ongoing Strategic Planning

As a living document, a strategic plan is a critical undertaking that can help point the business in the right direction. Unbeknownst to many, a strategic plan does not need to be lengthy. In fact, for many family business owners, the lengthier the plan is, the more cumbersome it is to implement and monitor (and the more dust it gathers on the shelf). In its simplest form, a good strategic plan that is clear and articulate does not need to be measured in pages (its length varies widely from business to business), but rather can be developed and monitored through a number of online resources. One useful tool is the One Page Business Plan®; it is easy to develop, is transparent and shared with others, has built-in methods to monitor and hold others accountable, and evaluates progress toward a series of goals.[8]

Developing a strategic plan takes an upfront investment in time, and it is generally best when the plan is built with input from advisors, employees, customers, and family members. The beauty of a strategic plan is that it forces leaders to consider the best-case, worst-case, and most likely scenarios. It allows business owners to determine the best path for the business to pursue while outlining contingencies to manage possible unexpected developments.

Among the key elements of strategy formulation is the development of a mission that identifies target customers, markets, and geography; products or services; core technologies; and key components of a family firm's business philosophy, such as commitment to survival, growth and profitability, and desired public image.[9] Another important element is a company "situation analysis"[10] that discusses the firm's ability to grow by asking about (1) the effectiveness of the current strategy in meeting corporate goals, (2) the firm's internal strengths and weaknesses, and (3) the company's competitive position and competitive strength.[11] Some companies also identify critical success factors—those few key areas that, when things go well, allow the business to flourish.[12] The last part of the strategy formulation process is the consideration of global or international positioning—that is, choosing the most viable means of competing globally.[13] This component helps business owners come to terms with antiquated systems, techniques, or practices that worked in the past, but may not necessarily work for a future that is increasingly competitive internationally and places high demands on technology.

Ward articulated a cyclical, ongoing process that family-owned businesses must go through when developing a strategic plan for the business. He observed that a number of steps must be taken to balance the interests of the business and the family[14]:

1. Securing family commitment to the future of the business
2. Assessing business health
3. Identifying business alternatives
4. Considering family and personal goals
5. Selecting a business strategy
6. Assessing the family's interests and capabilities

In their book *Strategic Planning for the Family Business*, Carlock and Ward described a comprehensive approach to strategic planning called the "parallel planning process." In this model, for family business planning to be most effective, planning for the family should accompany business planning. Strategic thinking and commitment from the family and from management then lead to the development of a "shared future vision" that drives the planning process. This planning process integrates the perspectives of the family/owners (who create a "family enterprise continuity plan") with those of the firm's management (who create the "business strategy plan"). Carlock and Ward's model recognizes and addresses the complexities of balancing the long-term needs of both the family and the business in the planning process.[15]

When specific metrics are identified during its development, a strategic plan lets business owners, managers, and key stakeholders know whether the business is progressing toward a pre-determined goal or veering off track. At times, businesses will meet obstacles along the way (such challenges are not at all uncommon). However, if developed correctly (after considering the risks of moving toward a particular goal), the strategic plan should outline the obstacles that may arise and exactly what should be done to overcome them.

Strategy #6: Promote an Entrepreneurial Orientation

For family firms to succeed beyond the founding generation, it is imperative for the business and its members to develop an "entrepreneurial orientation," relating to the firm and its members' propensity for innovation, risk taking, and proactivity.[16] However, research has shown that a firm's entrepreneurial orientation dwindles in latter stages of the founding generation,[17] and it may continue to subside in succeeding generations for several possible reasons:

- Growth is less of a priority in the founding generation, which may be more concerned with other objectives related to survival.[18]
- Succession can cause firm stagnation as firms adopt a more conservative financial structure, thereby limiting their growth rate.[19]

- Family firms may become more concerned with preserving wealth than with creating additional wealth, leading to a culture of risk aversion[20] and less of an orientation toward firm growth.[21]
- Family firms may adopt a conservative, risk-adverse, and change-resistant orientation, leading them to become less proactive and innovative.[22]

Developing an entrepreneurial orientation and achieving firm growth, therefore, become more of a priority for succeeding generations in a family firm.[23] In fact, embracing an entrepreneurial mindset positively influences growth of the firm more so in the second generations and beyond compared to the founding generation.[24]

For family businesses, a core strength relative to becoming more innovative and proactive lies in the centralized organizational structure that co-locates owners and managers in the family business system.[25] With fewer layers between managers and owners, decisions can be made in less time, which represents a source of competitive advantage when the "window of opportunity" for launching new products and services into the marketplace is narrow. To create a culture whereby intergenerational entrepreneurial activity can thrive (termed *interpreneurship*[26]), family business owners must welcome ideas (and potential challenges) related to the following areas: (1) exploring new strategies; (2) restructuring the organization so that some processes or business units have more autonomy and exposure to the competitive environment; (3) restructuring finances (possibly through developing trusts, undergoing a recapitalization, and other measures); and (4) bringing change to the family business system itself.[27] Poza suggests that creating an interpreneurial culture may be achieved in several ways[28]:

- Diversifying into other businesses, services, products, or industries (or alternatively, specializing and becoming more of a niche player)
- Developing venture capital firms or new ventures divisions within the family firm
- Developing cross-functional task and business teams composed of various departmental representatives and top management
- Implementing new reward systems
- Establishing an integrated information system
- Reevaluating ownership equity structures (perhaps allowing for some equity to be held by employees)
- Modernizing human resources policies to allow for gain sharing and psychological ownership

As business-owning families attempt to balance tradition with innovation, promoting an entrepreneurial orientation may also mean finding ways to enhance creativity, perhaps by entering alternative global markets. In fact, most family firms do not generate international sales (although many, such as local restaurants and automotive repair shops, are not necessarily aiming or positioned to do so). Nonetheless, even businesses with a local focus (e.g., that serve only the immediate surrounding community) can learn from firms with a global perspective by considering how the customer experience is managed globally, how similar global firms manage efficiency, or how similar firms in different parts of the world utilize different resources and techniques. Consider the following:

- In 2002, 31 percent of U.S. family business owners surveyed indicated that they generate international sales, with the vast majority (88 percent) of those firms collecting less than 11 percent of their total revenues from these global customers.[29]
- In 2009, 35 percent of regional family business owners surveyed indicated that they generate international sales, with 46 percent of those firms collecting more than 50 percent of their total revenues from these global customers. Notably, 15 percent collected 25 to 49 percent of their total revenues from global sales; 26 percent collected 10 to 25 percent of revenues from global sales; 11 percent collected 5 to 9 percent of revenues from global sales; and only 2 percent collected less than 5 percent of revenues from global sales.[30]

These data highlight the increasing importance of maintaining a global focus. For family firms with an entrepreneurial orientation, there is a world of possibility for growth. Box 8.2 highlights how family firms can build an entrepreneurial orientation through incremental creativity.

Box 8.2
Creativity in the Family Firm

Lucy L. Gilson, PhD—University of Connecticut

Creativity is often described as key to the founding of a new business, with the entrepreneurial spirit generally defined in terms of innovation and proactivity. Indeed, starting a business is said to be dependent upon an idea for a new product, service, or process that is both novel and useful. What is interesting, then, is that family business owners, when asked about creativity, oftentimes shy away and say things like

"We can't afford to be creative" or "We are so busy with our day-to-day work that we have no time for creativity." Such demurrals suggest that after the original creative period involved in establishing a business, business owners start to think about creativity only in terms of radical breakthroughs—forgetting that creativity exists along a continuum.

On this continuum, creativity ranges from the radical highly novel breakthrough idea (a departure from existing knowledge or capabilities; major changes to the status quo) to the more incremental, less novel, and often more useful idea that centers on changing product features, seeking out new customers for existing services, or looking at new processes for how work is to be done. Incremental creativity (based on existing knowledge or capabilities and/or minor changes to the status quo) is by no measure less creative than radical creativity—it just has different foci. While radical creativity brings with it big rewards, it is also associated with big risks. Thus it is the more incremental creative ideas that actually keep a business "in business."

Creativity is not easy: it takes time and involves risk and divergent thinking. In fact, research I have conducted with colleagues[1] has shown that creativity is directly linked to improved performance. Specifically, individuals, teams, and organizations that are more creative have higher levels of performance, regardless of whether that performance is measured in terms of sales volume, time between equipment failures, reduced expenditure on parts, or product reliability. However, we have also found that customer satisfaction is not improved when individuals or teams are more creative; in fact, on occasion, the opposite relationship has been found.

Family business owners *must* be creative to survive, but creativity at all points along the continuum is necessary to generate the interest and excitement needed if a firm is to innovate, compete, and ultimately survive. Not every creative idea needs to be a radical one.

[1] Gilson, "Why Be Creative"; Gilson et al., "Creativity Standardization."

Strategy #7: Communicate, Communicate, Communicate

An obstacle that many family businesses encounter when attempting to build a lasting organization (and engaging in succession planning, in particular) is communication. To some, succession or estate planning means talking about "death"—a touchy topic for anyone to navigate. In particular, senior-generation family members may not want to talk about these issues for numerous reasons: fear of change; the feeling of "finality"; financial anxiety; complexity or lack of knowledge about the process; the perception of losing identity, power, control, and perquisites; uncertainty about what to do in the future; or concerns about the effect of equity redistribution on the family. Similarly, succeeding-generation family members may neglect to bring up issues related to succession and business survival due to concerns about appearing greedy, self-centered, aggressive, or disloyal to the parents or senior-generation family members.

Communication is usually difficult for family business members to do well, regardless of firm size, industry, or location. Consider the following research findings:

- Communication was ranked as the most serious threat to long-run survival of family firms.[31]
- Communication was ranked as the most important step a business-owning family must take ensure the firm's survival.[32]
- Communication was ranked number 3 among the most significant issues facing family businesses.[33]
- Forty-four percent of family business owners reported that communication is challenging in managing the family firm (only 27 percent said it was unchallenging).[34]

Tagiuri and Davis noted that family business members can have "private language," which (on the one hand) can lead to more efficient communication with greater privacy, but (on the other hand) can be disadvantageous as it may cause sensitivity, distortion, and conflict.[35] For some members of a family business, communication can be muddied when confused with role identity. For example, is it your boss who wishes to meet with you to talk about a poor sales report, or is it your mom waiting to reprimand you for not meeting her expectations? The purpose of the meeting may be the same, but how it is interpreted has a significant effect on the expectation relative to the communication patterns used and the effectiveness of that communication.

Although family firms are often bursting with emotionally charged issues, the inertia related to putting off difficult conversations benefits no one—especially the business and employees. To provide the framework for effective communication, family business members must first be aware that communication goes beyond dialogue to include written materials, nonverbal signals and cues, body language, and behavior. Moreover, good communication is as much about listening as it is about speaking. Family business owners must learn to welcome constructive conflict, thereby ensuring that collaboration is the outcome (rather than competition, compromising one's position, or avoiding the conflict entirely).[36] Productive communication is facilitated by the presence of emotional resources such as trust, a willingness to be vulnerable, and the courage to take the risk of raising emotionally loaded topics. To prevent "emotional scarcity," it is helpful for family business members to start conversations by expressing appreciation, recognition, and support.[37] Ensuring effective communication may mean bringing in outside facilitators who can diffuse sensitive issues and ensure that meetings remain productive. Sometimes, ensuring effective communication means developing different skills, such as active listening (e.g., before responding, the listener demonstrates an understanding of the speaker's position, by reflecting back what was heard and asking clarifying questions).[38]

Successful family firms implement two practices that enhance communication: (1) they form an independent board of directors and (2) they begin a regular process of family meetings.[39] Independent boards allow for regular communication about the future of the business—engaging with people who possess valuable knowledge and experience. But even more important is the independent director's ability to ask the difficult questions and promote communication where it is most needed. Regular family meetings bring opportunities to discuss the future of the family and its members, including the meaning and role of the business in their lives. It is often helpful to begin by developing communication charters or agreements that delineate the "ground rules" for communication within meetings, which can increase participants' sense of emotional safety. For some families, this process can be awkward or daunting at first, but over time the practice of regular meetings builds a kind of "fitness" that allows family members to communicate more easily about even the most challenging issues.

MOTIVATING FOR AND MANAGING CHANGE

For family businesses to survive, change is inevitable—whether that involves change in strategy or change in leadership. Each change moves through a sequence of six steps:

1. Developmental pressures (e.g., age or family changes) signal the need for change.
2. Triggering events force change (e.g., mandatory retirement, unforeseen incidents).
3. Disengagement occurs (recognizing the need to change and evolve).
4. An exploration of alternatives is undertaken.
5. The best alternative is selected.
6. The organization commits to the new structure.[40]

Through all these steps, it is important to communicate the change clearly and effectively. This involves speaking to all employees in a candid manner. It means finding change agents who will champion the change and build internal loyalty. It entails motivating employees and family members for the change and helping them move past their barriers to change. And finally, it means measuring the results and communicating about the results of change. In fact, Mento, Jones, and Dirndorfer conceptualized how the change management process occurs in both theory and practice, and were able to break the process down into 12 distinct steps[41]:

1. Highlighting what is prompting the change
2. Defining the change initiative that isolates the scope of the effort
3. Evaluating the climate for change to assess the readiness of change recipients and potential obstacles to adoption
4. Developing a change plan that outlines specific goals and responsibilities for strategists, implementers, and recipients of the change
5. Finding and cultivating a sponsor—someone who can commit to the change and legitimize the change effort to others
6. Preparing the audience and recipients of the change to overcome resistance and let go of the status quo
7. Creating the cultural fit to ensure that the change lasts and remind recipients that the change is not just a fad, but the new reality of the organization
8. Developing and choosing a leadership team with diverse skill sets that can inspire others
9. Creating small wins to keep everyone motivated and energized
10. Communicating the change in a way that is candid and regular
11. Measuring progress of the change effort
12. Integrating the lessons learned from the process

Among some family business cultures (e.g., those with low risk tolerance and low entrepreneurial orientation), change can breed fear and cynicism. Cynicism has many negative effects stemming from lack of information, lack of communication, and lack of opportunity to participate in decisions (or be "heard"). It can lead to employees and family members experiencing lower levels of morale, desire to work hard, job satisfaction, commitment to the business, "faith" in the firm's senior leadership team (or a view that senior family members are "beyond their shelf life"), morale, and desire to work hard.[42] Overall, the inability to manage the change effort itself can be a recipe for disaster if not handled with sensitivity and sensibility. Box 8.3 explores strategies that can successfully motivate change in family firms.

Indisputably, bringing about effective change requires at least one change agent—someone within the family, someone within the senior management team, someone close to all employees, or even an outside individual who is genuinely committed to the best interests of the company and its employees (such as a customer or a supplier that is encouraging and

Box 8.3
How to Motivate Change in Family Business

Michael V. Pantalon, PhD—Yale University

I grew up in a family business, watching my uncle grow his electrical contracting business into a multimillion-dollar endeavor. While I did not go into the business, I had the opportunity to watch the business mature with the addition of each of his sons. But it was not until I became a management consultant and coach that I realized how effectively my aunt and uncle had managed the business *and* the family dynamics inextricably entwined within it.

But what if your family business doesn't have motivated leaders or successors? How, then, do you motivate or influence positive change? More challenging yet, how do you motivate such change when you're dealing with openly resistant family members? There are no easy answers, of course, but the science of motivation and influence tells us two things very clearly:

1. You cannot make or force anyone to change, and the more you try to, the worse the outcomes. There is no sustainability in pressure.
2. People only listen to one person, and no, it's not their boss or parent—not even if their boss *is* their parent. People only listen to themselves.

Thus the reasons or motives for change cannot be given or told to someone—and technically, you can't directly motivate or influence someone. Instead, you need to get them to motivate or influence themselves by helping them state their own reasons for change. The way these two research-based principles of motivation can be translated into action strategies is by reinforcing autonomy and asking a motivational question.

Reinforcing Autonomy

Very simply put, you reinforce autonomy when you stop telling people what they *have* to do and instead tell them it's up to them. This technique is an excellent way to get a resistant person to stop resisting long enough to seriously consider your proposal. Also, given that autonomy, independence, separation, and identity formation are so important to the development of a strong family business, this first step fits in nicely with those dynamics. This strategy pays off by encouraging the person you're speaking with to really think about what he or she genuinely wants to do—and that's what *you* want. You don't want your family members to simply do as they're told. Rather, you want them to do things because *they want to*, because they see the value of doing them and have a personal desire to do them well.

A Motivational Question

Once you've reinforced the autonomy, you need to ask a very specific type of motivational question to actually move the person to articulate his or her genuine reasons or motives for change. It is critical to *not* ask why the person is *not* willing to change.

> As reflexive as this may be, do not ask, "Why *won't* you consider my proposal," because it merely reinforces reasons *not* to change. The better question is "Why might you change (or consider my proposal)?" As contrarian as this question might sound, if you persist with it while continuing to reinforce autonomy, the person will start to think about what's in it for him or her to do what you're asking. That's what creates breakthroughs in performance, goal attainment, true engagement, and sustainability.

supportive of the change). Regardless of their position, it is important for change agents to be accessible, open-minded, skilled in communication, diplomatic, dedicated, and respected by peers. Family business leaders who recognize the need to bring about change will find an invaluable ally in the change agent. Other qualities desired in change agents relate to being visionaries and risk takers, passionate, patient, persistent, loyal, challenge driven, thick skinned to criticism, sensitive to others, committed to the process, and good team builders. More importantly, change agents are courageous, possessing the courage to fail, the courage to try something new, the courage to experiment and take risks, and the courage to do what is morally right.[43]

Change is difficult. But for firms that want to make survival the number one business priority, change will undoubtedly be part of the process. To prevent the derailment of the change effort, it is important to build in change as a cultural norm within the firm. Change should be a constant effort within the business so that employees and family members become used to the process. And during the entire process, leaders must remember to allow, affirm, support, and advocate for positive changes that will ensure the survival of the family and the business.

CHAPTER SUMMARY

- Within family firms, there are optimal ranges of confidence, leadership, planning, architecture, and teams. Too little or too much of each domain can lead to problems in the culture that can undermine adaptability and lower the business's chances of survival.
- The five fatal flaws do not exist in isolation with regard to one another, but rather are connected in predictable ways.
- Seven strategies can help family businesses navigate the journey of transitions, such that the passage of the business from one generation to the next is a safe one. These strategies call for family business leaders to do the following:

- ○ Create a sense of urgency around business survival
- ○ Embrace outside counsel
- ○ Develop the policies and procedures necessary for business survival
- ○ Invest in human capital
- ○ Create a process for strategic planning
- ○ Promote an entrepreneurial orientation
- ○ Communicate, communicate, communicate.
- Change can be managed through a series of steps aimed at mitigating ambiguity and motivating others for change. Leaders must prepare stakeholders for change, and the process requires the assistance of change agents (internal or external) who can champion the cause.

9

Legacies

> I am ever mindful of the legacy of my grandfather, the founder of this Kingdom, who had said to me that he perceived his life as a link in a continuous chain of those who served our nation and that he expected me to be a new and strong link in the same chain . . . I wish democracy and peace to be my legacy to my people and the shield of generations to come.
>
> —King Hussein I

Family enterprises begin with the entrepreneurial dream of the founders. When that dream becomes a tangible reality—a source of livelihood, pride, and meaning—many desire to pass that dream onto the next generation. Parents and other family leaders start with the best of intentions and want only good things for their children, grandchildren, and kin. But good intentions are not enough to ensure that the desired legacy is what actually gets passed on. The choices and decisions people make, the way they conduct themselves in the world, and the results of their actions have consequences (for good or for ill) that ultimately determine an individual's legacy.

This chapter begins by exploring the legacies of *Titanic*—legacies that she and some of the people related to her story have left behind. *Titanic*'s tragedy stands in bold contrast to the triumph of Captain Chesley Sullenberger and the crew of U.S. Airways Flight 1549, whose calm professionalism proved critical when the plane was forced to land in New York's Hudson River after a catastrophic failure of the plane's engines. An analysis of this averted disaster shows how the presence of a number of "protective" factors (contrasted with "risk" factors, which lead to fatal flaws) resulted in a triumphant outcome. The different aspects of the legacies of family enterprises are explored with respect to the business itself, material wealth, values, and ways of life.

TITANIC'S LEGACIES

There is not just one legacy that the *Titanic* story has left to the world; there are many. In the wake of the sinking, a number of changes were enacted in an effort to prevent this kind of disaster from recurring. For example, U.S. laws were modified to require that any ship using an American port meet the following criteria:

- Carry enough lifeboats to hold everyone on board
- Ensure that lifeboats are adequately staffed with well-trained crew members
- Equip lifeboats with necessary survival tools and materials
- Hold a lifeboat drill for each person on every voyage
- Have a wireless system staffed 24 hours a day
- Give precedence to wireless traffic regarding the ship's navigation over passenger communications[1]

The sinking also led 17 nations to found the International Ice Patrol at the first Safety of Life at Sea (SOLAS) convention in 1914. The Ice Patrol's mission is summarized here:

> [T]o monitor the movement of icebergs and oceanographic conditions in the Grand Banks region of the North Atlantic Ocean and warn the transatlantic mariner of iceberg dangers. While this charge may sound simple, it requires a litany of tasks to accomplish. These tasks include: the periodic searching of nearly 500,000 square miles of ocean; an in-depth understanding of the dynamic weather and ocean currents on the Grand Banks; monitoring and predicting the movements of thousands of icebergs; continuous operation of a sophisticated computer model known as the Berg Analysis and Prediction System (BAPS); transmission of warnings and ice charts to ships at sea in a host of different formats; and nearly daily cooperation with over 30 organizations and agencies in the United States, Canada, and Europe.[2]

Fittingly, every April since 1923, the Ice Patrol has honored the people whose deaths led to its establishment, by dropping wreaths by ship or by air near the site of *Titanic*'s sinking.

As for the leadership legacies of the *Titanic* story, some are heroic, others are shameful, and others are somewhere in between. Chief among the publicly identified rogues was Captain Stanley Lord, whose failure to act upon the sighting of signal rockets would haunt him for the rest of his life. Within months of being condemned by both the U.S. Senate and British Board of Trade inquiries for not coming to *Titanic*'s aid, Lord lost his job with the Leyland Line, and he ultimately spent the rest of his career taking on smaller and smaller commands. Lord and his supporters made repeated requests to open an inquiry to exonerate him, but these were denied. Even after his death in 1962, Lord's family spent decades trying to clear his name.

Like Lord, Bruce Ismay never quite recovered from the disaster. Murmured accusations of cowardice were heard on both sides of the Atlantic, suggesting that the owner (like the captain) had a moral obligation to go down with his ship and give up his seat for another, especially while women and children were still on board. Ismay was sharply ridiculed by the press in America (who referred to him as "J. Brute Ismay"), but the British public and media response were less critical. His reputation severely damaged, Ismay resigned as president of the International Mercantile Marine and chairman of White Star Line in June 1913. For the remainder of his life, he stayed out of the public eye, moving to an estate in western Ireland. To his credit, Ismay contributed financially to establish some charitable organizations, including one for the widows of lost seamen. When he died due to complications from diabetes in 1937, he was survived by his wife Julia, who was often heard saying that, "The *Titanic* ruined our lives . . ."[3]

Captain Smith's legacy is less clear. Initially, he was cast as a superhero—a popular rumor circulated that his last act was to swim with a child in his arms, bringing the youngster safely to a lifeboat before swimming off to die. He had been lauded for his character, patriotism, and self-sacrifice. Others have viewed Smith as culpable for making poor decisions that led to the accident, despite his otherwise celebrated career. Some more recent stories of *Titanic* portray Smith as a tragic figure. As one biographer noted, "Despite its many inaccuracies, the sympathetic modern image of Captain Smith as the rather lonely King Lear-like figure on the bridge of his last command, filled with despair, perhaps driven mad with grief, deserted by fortune, watching the green water slowly creeping up the glass in front of him, has proven popular and is likely to endure."[4] But whether evaluated based on how he lived or what happened the night that he and many others died, Smith will be most remembered as having been the man in charge during one of the worst peacetime shipping disasters in history.

There were some heroes whose actions that night were exceptional, embodying the noblest aspects of the human character. First among them was the captain of *Carpathia*, Arthur H. Rostron, who heeded the call for aid and rushed to assist *Titanic*, pushing his ship as fast as was safely possible. For his swift action, efficient planning, and thoughtful attention to the survivors, Rostron was honored by the U.S. and British governments. After World War I, he was made a Knight Commander of the Order of the British Empire, and was later promoted to Commodore of the Cunard fleet before retiring in 1931. On the tombstone shared by Rostron and his wife, the epitaph reads, "Their bodies are buried in peace, but their name liveth for evermore."[5]

Another individual who was responsible for leading some 58 people to safety was third-class steward, John Hart. He guided two groups of women and children through the confusing maze of passages and stairwells that separated the third-class cabins from the boat deck where the lifeboats were loaded. Fifth Officer Harold Lowe was one of the only sailors to direct his lifeboat to return to where *Titanic* sank, searching for survivors and overriding fears of being swamped by the desperate souls in the water. Both men took risks, putting their own lives on the line in an attempt to save others.

Other heroes that night remained faithful to their duties, continuing to do their jobs in the service of others right to the very end. The engineering staff remained at their posts so as to maintain power for the lights and wireless system, and bandmaster Wallace Hartley and his orchestra continued playing their instruments until the ship went under. Their deep sense of commitment, service, and duty (even at the darkest hour) stand as humbling and inspiring examples that have endured over time.

Still other heroes were observed for their loyalty and self-sacrifice. Macy's department store owner Isidor Straus declined a seat in a lifeboat, refusing "any distinction in favor not granted to others."[6] His wife Ida and other women also refused lifeboat seats, preferring to stay with their husbands, dying together as they had lived together. There were also unusually benevolent people like Edith Evans, who volunteered to step out of a lifeboat so that others would live.

> When [one] boat was about to be lowered it was found that it contained one more passenger than it could carry. Then the question came as to who should leave. Miss Evans, who was a splendid girl of 25, said to Mrs. Brown that she [Mrs. Brown] had children at home and should be the one to remain ... Miss Evans left the boat, saying that she would take a chance of getting in a boat later. It seems that this brave girl never got that chance, but went down to her death with the other heroes and heroines on the *Titanic*.[7]

No doubt there were many heroes that fateful night whose names will not be remembered by history. Their actions revealed the possibility that ordinary people can make extraordinary choices and that humankind's potential for altruism and self-sacrifice is unlimited.

FROM TRAGEDY TO TRIUMPH: THE CASE OF U.S. AIRWAYS FLIGHT 1549

A contemporary story of leadership and heroism, which stands in stark contrast to the tragedy of *Titanic*, was the triumph of Captain Chesley Sullenberger and the crew of U.S. Airways Flight 1549. On January 15, 2009, First Officer Jeff Skiles was at the controls when Flight 1549 lifted off from New York's LaGuardia Airport bound for Charlotte, North Carolina. In addition to the 2 pilots, there were 150 passengers and 3 flight attendants aboard the Airbus A-320 aircraft. Before the plane reached 3,000 feet, approximately 95 seconds into the flight, the aircraft unexpectedly encountered a large flock of Canadian geese. The birds hit the plane in several places, including the nose, the wings, and both engines. Within a few seconds, it became clear that the plane had lost power to both of its engines—and both pilots were aware that they were facing an extremely grave emergency.

Luckily for all those on board, their captain was an expert in airline safety. A former U.S. Air Force (USAF) fighter pilot, Sullenberger was also an instructor who served as safety chairman of the Air Line Pilots Association (ALPA). An accident investigator and national technical committee member, he participated in several USAF and National Transportation Safety Board accident investigations and made many technical and academic contributions to the field of aviation safety:

- His safety work with ALPA led to the development of a Federal Aviation Administration Advisory Circular.
- Working with National Aeronautics and Space Administration scientists, Sullenberger coauthored a paper on error-inducing contexts in aviation.
- He was instrumental in the development and implementation of the Crew Resource Management course used at U.S. Airways, teaching the course to hundreds of his colleagues.

Sullenberger also runs his own safety consulting business, Safety Reliability Methods Inc., which provides (among other services) emergency management, safety strategies, and performance monitoring to the aviation and other industries.[8]

Sullenberger's first action after striking the flock of geese was to assume control of the plane by issuing the command, "My aircraft." Skiles acknowledged this change of control, responding, "Your aircraft." Skiles began managing the emergency checklist and consulted the Quick Reference Handbook for the most appropriate procedure for this particular emergency. Skiles attempted to regain engine power while Sullenberger glided the plane, which was now dropping at a rate of 1,000 feet per minute. At the same time, the captain communicated the plane's predicament to air traffic control and began to evaluate his options.

Vital to this process was Patrick Harten, the air traffic controller who maintained contact with Flight 1549. Harten contacted LaGuardia and other nearby airports to clear runways for an emergency landing, working with Sullenberger to provide him with as many options as possible. The captain had to quickly weigh the critical questions: *How long could he keep the plane in the air? How far were the runways? What were the obstacles? How densely populated were areas below the flight path? Were there emergency or rescue services nearby?* It was not an easy decision to make, given that water landings are extremely difficult to train for and rarely end well. However, Sullenberger concluded that the best option for a safe landing was the Hudson River, because (1) it was wide and long enough, (2) he could reach it, (3) there would be minimal risks to people on the ground, and (4) there would be police, ambulances, and ferry boats nearby to assist with the rescue.

With that crucial decision made, the next step was preparing for the landing. Ninety seconds before the plane hit the water, Sullenberger spoke to the passengers and crew: "This is the captain. Brace for impact." He explained his choice of words:

> There was no time to give the flight attendants a more complete picture of the situation we faced. So my first priority was to prevent passenger injury on impact. I did not yet know how well I'd be able to cushion the touchdown. I said "brace" and then chose the word "impact" because I wanted the passengers to be prepared for what might be a hard landing. The flight attendants—Sheila, Donna, and Doreen—immediately fell back on their training...I could hear [them] shouting their commands in response to my announcement, almost in unison, again and again: "Brace, brace! Heads down! Stay down! Brace, brace! Heads down! Stay down!" As I guided the plane toward the river, hearing their words comforted and encouraged me. Knowing that the flight attendants were doing exactly what they were supposed to do meant that we were on the same page. I knew that if I could deliver the aircraft to the surface intact, Donna, Doreen, and Sheila would get the passengers out the exit doors and the rescue could begin. Their direction and professionalism would be the keys to our survival, and I had faith in them.[9]

Sullenberger later acknowledged that his initial reaction was fear and incredulity: "It was the most sickening, pit-of-your-stomach, falling through the floor feeling I had ever experienced... two thoughts went through my mind, both rooted in disbelief: *This can't be happening. This doesn't happen to me.*"[10] But as his focus rapidly shifted to the tasks at hand, his feelings changed. "I did not think I was going to die. Based on my experience, I was confident that I could make an emergency water landing that was survivable. That confidence was stronger than any fear."[11]

It was a rough landing. After the plane came to a complete stop, the officers and crew quickly and safely evacuated every last passenger through an orderly process: initially to the aircraft's wings and life rafts, and later to the boats that had rushed to the plane's aid. After a final check of the craft, which was filling with water from the tail section, Sullenberger was the last person off the plane.

Speaking with news anchor Katie Couric, Sullenberger said, "One way of looking at this might be that for 42 years, I've been making small, regular deposits in this bank of experience, education, and training. And on January 15 the balance was sufficient so that I could make a sudden large withdrawal."[12] Indeed, Sullenberger demonstrated the inverse of the fatal flaws in the *Titanic* disaster: displaying confidence in his abilities (but not over-confidence), providing effective leadership (making quick, careful decisions and communicating clear, assertive instructions), valuing safety training and preparation, and acting with the assurance that a strong, well-trained team could work in concert to execute his orders. As a leader, Sullenberger created for himself a different legacy than *Titanic*'s leaders. Captain Sullenberger, like Captain Smith, had a great deal of experience. But the difference between them—and what sealed each of their legacies— is that one minimized the risks and the other did not.

LEGACIES IN FAMILY ENTERPRISE SYSTEMS

In family enterprise systems, there are different dimensions to the notion of legacy. The kinds of legacies that family business owners hope to achieve include the transfer of (1) the business itself or other sources of material wealth and (2) a set of values. While values are less tangible than a business or wealth, they are perhaps the most important aspect of a legacy, because they represent deeper sources of meaning in life (including dreams and ways of life, the meaning of carrying the family name, and what the family hopes to be to their communities and to the world). Without values and a shared commitment to seeing those values preserved, a family cannot sustain the business or material wealth for very long. This section explores both the material and values-based dimensions of legacy.

The Legacy of a Business

The business often becomes the focus of legacy for the enterprising family, because in most cases the business constitutes the most significant component of the senior generation's wealth and represents the promise of wealth creation for generations to come. It is also a very visible entity in the life and history of the family—a centerpiece for the family's energy and activity. For members of the second generation, the idea of carrying a parent's legacy is meaningful and participation in the business becomes a way to retain a sense of closeness or connection to the parent(s) who founded it. Said one family business successor, "If it wasn't a family business, I probably wouldn't be doing this job in another field ... I'm definitely here because it's something my dad started and something I want to continue doing."

Scholars and researchers who have examined factors that promote success (or failure) of family business transitions have identified numerous factors that inhibit or promote family business succession. Factors that promote business succession transitions include the presence of the following assets:

- Incumbents who can "let go" of the business because of an ability to delegate, and who have outside interests and an identity that is not overly connected to the business[13]
- Trustworthy, committed, capable, and well-prepared successors[14]
- Trusting, genial, mutually respectful relationships among family members (particularly between incumbents and successors)[15]
- A shared common vision and superordinate goals among family members[16]

Other factors tend to inhibit business successions from happening:

- Lack of strategic, estate, or continuity planning[17]
- Changes in business (i.e., lower performance, decreased scale, loss of key customers/suppliers)[18]
- Insufficient funds to sustain tax burdens, liquidate the exit of heirs, or absorb the costs of hiring professional managers[19]
- An inappropriate relationship between the firm's past and future (i.e., "evidenced by excessive attachment to the past by an overly dependent and conservative successor, a rejection of the past by a rebellious one, or an incongruous blending of past and present by a wavering new leader")[20]

Families that wish for their business to be passed on have a complex array of legal, interpersonal, financial, and management concerns, each of which must be carefully addressed for the business to continue.

The Legacy of Wealth

In addition to the passage of the business, enterprising families may seek to pass on wealth to their children and grandchildren. Similar to the orchestration of a business transition, wealth preservation requires coordination of estate and financial planning along with maintaining family cohesion and preparation of heirs. While both legal/financial and family/interpersonal aspects of wealth preservation are important, some evidence suggests that success or failure hinges mainly on the family side of the equation. In one study of failed wealth transitions, 60 percent failed because of a breakdown in trust and communication; 25 percent failed because heirs were not prepared; and 15 percent were attributed to other causes, including tax and legal issues and lack of a clear family mission.[21]

To prevent a breakdown in trust and communication, families must endeavor to find ways to build and maintain family ties. Creating forums for the family to come together is essential. Formal structures (such as a family council, regular family meetings, or retreats) are needed to assure that time is set aside to discuss substantive issues related to wealth and the family's future. Using a facilitator for formal family meetings is advantageous because it enables all family members to participate fully and have their voices heard. An outside moderator can also help establish ground rules and a sense of safety, as well as ensure that the meeting remains focused and productive, while extracting and summarizing the important themes. Regular meetings can build family norms for increased transparency, which helps sustain trust. Meetings can also promote the development and use of methods for airing and resolving disagreements in a proactive manner so they do not erode cohesion, trust, and goodwill. In addition to formal meetings, informal or less structured times together that allow family members to enjoy one another's company and have fun can strengthen their foundation of shared positive experiences and memories.

An important facet of preparing heirs involves anticipating and developing strategies for combating the deleterious effects of wealth. The dysfunctions associated with affluence—or "affluenza"[22]—can erode a family's ability to preserve its wealth across generations. The corrosive effects of wealth are plentiful[23]:

- Workaholism and lack of consistent or steady caregiving can create trust and abandonment issues that affect personality development.
- Inherited wealth can create a sense of entitlement, lower motivation to achieve, and poor ability to tolerate frustration or delay gratification.
- Wealth can lead to problems being financially responsible (e.g., spending within one's means) or problems appreciating the value of money.
- Inherited wealth can damage self-confidence and self-esteem.
- Wealthy people can become the target of other people's resentment, envy, jealousy, or opportunism.
- Those persons who are most affluent oftentimes insulate themselves from other communities and become less in touch both with the world and with their own blessings.
- Wealth can lead to overemphasis on material items and poverty in nonmaterial domains (such as poverty of spirit, dearth of trust, and lack of compassion).

Perhaps the best strategy for preparing heirs so they do not succumb to the detrimental aspects of wealth largely involves imparting a strong set of values.

The Legacy of Values

Particularly as family enterprise systems become generationally advanced, the perpetuation of family wealth or a family business must be undergirded by a strong foundation of values. Put simply, a family has to find other motivations to stay connected to the business besides money. Also, if families want their wealth to be used in ways that are productive for their members and for the larger society, they must develop values to help guide their stewardship. Values are the principles that underlie decisions made and actions taken. Invoking values is a powerful way to lead, as values can "inspire people to do things that are difficult, to make commitments that require discipline, to stick to plans for the long haul."[24]

Articulating values helps families solidify an underlying source of meaning and purpose that bridges family and business goals, and can become an important source of competitive advantage for family firms. As Keith Campbell, a fourth-generation chairman of a flooring company, explained, "There must be a solid commitment from the vast majority of owners that the company will serve a purpose beyond income and will be managed with the next generation in mind. Some companies do this through a mission statement. We incorporated our family values—which we view as our legacy—into nearly every aspect of our business."[25]

Family philanthropy is an excellent way for enterprising families to express their values while building family cohesion and carrying forth a sustainable legacy. Family firms, which are frequently well connected to the communities in which they are embedded, often place a strong emphasis on philanthropy and giving back to their communities. Charitable giving in family firms takes a variety of forms:

- Supporting national or international causes financially
- Fundraising for local community groups (e.g., bake sales, athletic fundraising events)
- Giving employees time off to volunteer
- Allowing nonprofit organizations to use company space or other organizational resources
- Family and business leaders volunteering their time on nonprofit boards

A philanthropic spirit also brings benefits to the company. Said one family CEO, "It allows employees to get involved [and] builds teamwork and a sense of purpose ... It gives us a greater reason for being other than putting groceries on the table. It helps us think about the bigger picture."[26] In a similar vein, family firms show greater levels of environmental responsibility than nonfamily firms,[27] perhaps because of tighter linkages to family values and because they are more responsive to the values of their internal stakeholders.[28] Some family enterprise systems establish a family foundation that can create excitement for family members not involved in the business and offer a renewed focus for family who are transitioning out of active business involvement. Family foundations account for half of all independent foundations, and they were responsible for giving away more than $21 billion in 2008.[29] Box 9.1 describes the experience of one family member's experience of legacy through family philanthropy.

Box 9.1
Dad's Legacy

Anonymous

When I was seven years old, my father started a tradition. A few days before Thanksgiving and Christmas, he took me and my four siblings shopping. Each of us got our own shopping cart and a set dollar amount, and we could buy whatever we wanted—for other people. My father explained that some kids and families were not as lucky as we were. They might not get a nice meal at Thanksgiving or presents under their Christmas trees, so it was important for us do what we could to help them by getting them some things they might want or need. He also explained that whenever you give to others, it will come back to you 100 times over. Dad avoided any public recognition, and he instructed us that our annual shopping trips were not something to tell people about, but something we did quietly, just because it was the right thing to do. Each year our secret trips were a source of fun that we all looked forward to.

My father did not like giving to charities because he didn't know whether the money was being used wisely. Instead, being the consummate entrepreneur, he started his own charitable organization. It was funded mainly through the profits from his business, plus contributions from friends, relatives, or business associates. Throughout the year, anytime he heard about people who needed help (especially people who were trying to improve their own situations), my father would get them what they needed. And at the end of the year, whatever money was left over went toward our holiday shopping trips.

Nearly 45 years have passed since our shopping trips started, and the family has not missed a single year. My dad has stepped back and let us take the lead—my siblings and I being the charity's officers. The tradition has also been passed on to my children, nieces, and nephews. We taught them, the same way our father taught us. What started as a tradition became one of his important legacies to our family: the importance of generosity toward less fortunate members of our community.

When a family's business and values are inextricably connected, the legacy that gets passed on is something greater and more meaningful. The legacy is a way of life, which exists at the intersection of "what we do," "who we are," and "how we live." Family farms represent an excellent example of the passage of a way of life; indeed, some of the oldest family businesses in the United States are family farms. In fact, 15 of the top 20 oldest U.S. businesses are agricultural, livestock, or related businesses.[30] Most farmers farm not because it is an easy or profitable business, but rather because working the land involves a deep love for the history and heritage associated with it. Of all U.S. farms in 2007, 98 percent were family farms, with the majority (88 percent) identified as small family farms with annual sales less than $250,000. Small family farms accounted for 16 percent of U.S. agricultural output, while larger family farms (sales more than $250,000) provided 66 percent of total production.[31] For smaller farms, carrying on the tradition of farming is becoming increasingly difficult, as there are a number of challenges to overcome:

- Keeping children interested in and passionate about farming, instead of pursuing other careers in more urban centers
- Competition from larger or corporate farms
- Costs of the fuel and equipment required to farm larger acreage with less help

- Inability to control the prices of the commodities they sell
- Unpredictability of the weather and other environmental factors that can affect production

To mitigate these challenges, most small family farmers must supplement their income with off-farm employment or other sources (Social Security, pensions, dividends, or rental income).[32] Rollin and Sandra Fogle, of Shelby County, Indiana, wanted their farming lifestyle to continue for at least another generation. Darin, age 37 and the youngest of their three adult children, had always wanted to maintain their heritage; the question was how to find a way to supplement his farm income. Darin took auto-body classes during high school and has created a robust winter business that focuses on restoring antique tractors, cars, and trucks. He and his father converted an old barn into a modern shop. Thanks to the body shop, the Fogles found the means for Darin to stay on the farm and continue the family legacy.[33]

Values are typically transmitted to the next generation inadvertently. In many instances, parents do not give ample consideration to or instructions about the values they are hoping to impart. In this scenario, the process of learning values is unspoken and learned primarily by children watching how their parents and other family members behave. In addition, teaching values can be done more explicitly though parenting, early and ongoing education, the intentional modeling of behaviors that are in alignment with desired values, and communicating frequently about people's choices and their reasons for making them. Enterprising families often create values statements to capture and communicate their values to others in the family or their business (see Box 9. 2).

Box 9.2
Creating a Values Statement

Dennis T. Jaffe, PhD—Saybrook University

Values are part of the legacy that founders want to pass on, implicitly or explicitly, to their families, employees, customers, and community. At the time of transition, the company defines these values as a guide for successors. With great expectations and enthusiasm, many families in business have begun to create values statements, but too often the glow fades as they come up with a wonderful statement that seems to go no further.

Values are not *created* by a values statement. Instead, such a statement merely recognizes the values that exist and emphasizes them. Values are created by people's behavior, although they aren't always clear or explicit (and, therefore, may be difficult to define). Values are principles that underlie the way people treat one another and make important decisions.

Having clearly defined values sets the stage for difficult discussions in the family about what it does and how it does things. Coming up with a values statement for a company, or a family, is not an end, but rather the first step along a difficult path. If you have a public values credo—either within the family or within the community—you will be held to it. Also, different people will see these values differently.

A good exercise that companies and families can engage in is to think of tough issues where a value is challenged, and then to have a discussion about how the person or company can uphold the value in the face of a particular challenge. One family holding company looks at each acquisition not just through a financial lens but by considering whether the venture fits its family values. Another family gives an annual report of its family holdings and adds a report on the family values, specifying how the businesses are doing measured against this yardstick.

The values of one generation sometimes need to be revised over time, as more people become part of a family. The original values may not be held by everyone in the family, or may be interpreted differently. Given this diversity, a family with a values credo must place its values in a living framework that can evolve through the generations.

Some important caveats about values should be observed:

- Values must never become an excuse not to change and innovate.
- Values differ from traditions. Traditions are customs or patterns that are passed from one group to another; they may be emblematic of values, but they are not the values themselves.[34]
- Values may be articulated with words, but are taught, tested, and evaluated through actions—particularly in situations that incur some personal cost in service of the value.
- If values are publicly stated, every effort must be made to honor them—especially by family members and those in leadership positions. If the firm fails to "walk the talk," it can lead to a culture of resentment and cynicism.

RICHES VERSUS ENRICHMENT

An astute CEO from a (formerly family-owned) *Fortune* 100 company made an interesting observation about the relationship between wealth and legacy—that wealth in and of itself cannot buy a legacy. He recalled a trip to Florence, Italy, where he visited the Basilica di Santa Croce (Basilica of the Holy Cross). Inside the church, elevated for all to see, were beautifully carved sarcophagi of some of the world's most brilliant and creative thinkers—Michelangelo, Galileo, Machiavelli, Foscolo, Gentile, and Rossini—whose remains were gloriously entombed by their patrons and supporters. Under his feet, in the floor of the basilica were worn, faded stones that marked the burial places of some of the wealthy individuals of the time, who revered the enlightened thinkers and chose to be buried close to them. They admired these "illuminati" not for their monetary contributions to society (as most of them died penniless), but rather for their contributions to the betterment of humanity. The people who flock to visit this famous site come to honor the visionaries who elevated the human spirit and changed the world, not the wealthy citizens buried below. In concluding this metaphor for what endures, the CEO noted that material wealth is ephemeral, whereas intellectual and creative contributions to humanity form the most timeless legacies.

For us, his story raises the final consideration for this book. We ask you: what kind of legacy do you wish to leave? Few people will achieve the scientific breakthroughs of a Galileo, possess the artistic vision of a Michelangelo, or accumulate the wealth of the Rockefellers. Not everyone will be in a position to make intellectual or financial contributions to the world. But that does not mean that their legacies will be short in duration, impact, or worth. Legacy is not about traditions, for in the absence of the values behind their creation, traditions can be rendered meaningless. We submit that legacy is about giving the world happy, confident, and value-driven individuals who contribute to causes that are meaningful to them. It is about providing family members with an environment in which they prosper not just financially, but intellectually, spiritually, and emotionally. It is about bestowing upon them the blessing to follow their own dreams and leave their own marks on the world. It is about giving family members love, freedom, and confidence to stand on their own and believe in themselves—for those are the greatest gifts of all. It is what makes the founder of a legacy a legend.

In sum, legacy is about enrichment, not riches. Family enterprise systems can be a source of tremendous enrichment for individuals, families, communities, and societies. For those family firms that beat the odds to survive through the decades or centuries, the dreams of the founder will have endured and evolved—and the family will have learned how to be stewards of values that bring enrichment. We hope that another of *Titanic*'s legacies will be to inspire stakeholders within family enterprises to be aware of and watchful for icebergs and to do all they can to prepare for a safe passage across the generations.

CHAPTER SUMMARY

- *Titanic*'s legacy included the enactment of changes that increased the safety of transatlantic ocean travel. The legacies of the various people associated with this disaster range from shameful to sublime.
- *Titanic*'s tragedy stands in stark contrast to the triumph of Captain Chesley Sullenberger and the crew of U.S. Airways Flight 1549. An analysis of this averted disaster reveals how the inverse of fatal flaws (e.g., appropriate confidence, effective leadership, training and preparation) led to a safe outcome.
- Family firms pass on different legacies, including those associated with businesses, wealth, and values. Values can be critical for helping families in business remain cohesive enough to sustain their activities over generational transitions.
- Family firms may participate in philanthropy in a variety of ways, which can be a unifying force for family members and employees.
- In the final analysis, the most important legacies for family enterprise systems comprise the ways they *enrich* the people and communities associated with them rather than the *riches* they generate.

Appendix: National and Regional Survey Data

National survey data include the results of the 2002 and 2007 American Family Business Surveys (AFBS).

- The 2002 AFBS was conducted by the MassMutual Financial Group and the George and Robin Raymond Family Business Institute. The research was directed and supported by the Loyola University Chicago Family Business Center, the Cox Family Enterprise Center at Kennesaw State University, and Babson College. The survey yielded responses from 1,143 firms. Of those, only firms that were at least 10 years old and had at least $1 million in sales were included in the study.
- The 2007 AFBS was interpreted by Kennesaw State University and underwritten by Massachusetts Mutual Life Insurance Company (MassMutual) and the Family Firm Institute. The 2007 survey yielded responses from 1,035 firms. Of those, only firms that were at least 10 years old and had at least $1 million in sales were included in the study. Of the 650 firms that met these criteria, the median age of the companies was 22 years old.

The 2007–2010 Connecticut Family Business Surveys (CFBS) were developed and interpreted by the University of Connecticut Family Business Program and the Connecticut Business and Industry Association.

- The 2007 CFBS was sent to approximately 4,200 family firms; 641 returned surveys, giving a response rate of 15 percent. The percentages quoted relate to the number of respondents answering each question; thus the sample size for each question varies. In addition, all figures are rounded to the nearest whole number, so they may not total to 100 percent. The margin of error is ± 3.9 percent. The 2007 survey was underwritten by Blum Shapiro and Citizen's Bank.

- The 2008 CFBS was completed by 573 family businesses. The percentages quoted in the report relate to the number of respondents answering each question, and all figures are rounded to the nearest whole number, so they may not total 100 percent. The margin of error is ± 4.1 percent. The 2008 survey was underwritten by Blum Shapiro.

- The 2009 CFBS was completed by 521 family businesses. The percentages quoted in the 2009 survey relate to the number of respondents answering each question; thus the sample size for each question varies. In addition, all figures are rounded to the nearest whole number, so they may not total 100 percent. The margin of error is ± 4.4 percent. The 2009 survey was underwritten by Farmington Bank and Kostin, Ruffkess & Company, LLC.

- The 2010 CFBS was completed by 503 businesses, 424 of which indicated that they were family-owned. The report is a review of those 424 family firms. The percentages quoted throughout the 2010 survey analysis relate to those firms that responded to each question. In some cases, the figures were rounded to the nearest whole number, so they may not total 100 percent. The margin of error is ± 4.5 percent. The 2010 survey was underwritten by Comcast and Farmington Bank.

Notes

INTRODUCTION

1. http://www.cincymuseum.org/explore_our_sites/special_exhibits_events/current_exhibits/titanic_spiritual_heroes.pdf
2. Lightoller, *Titanic and Other Ships*, 99.
3. http://www.brainyquote.com/quotes/quotes/k/karlmarx382655.html
4. Shanker and Astrachan, "Myths and Realities."
5. Ibid.
6. Beckhard and Dyer, "Managing Continuity."

PART I

1. These sources were the transcripts from the U.S. Senate Hearings ("U.S. Inquiry"); the transcripts from the British Board of Trade Investigation ("BOT Inquiry"); Butler, *"Unsinkable"*; Matsen, *Titanic's Last Secrets*; and Merideth, *1912 Facts about Titanic*. Transcripts from both U.S. and British Board of Trade inquiries can be found online at http://www.titanicinquiry.org.

CHAPTER 1

1. http://www.jfklibrary.org/Asset+Tree/Asset+Viewers/Audio+Video+Asset+Viewer.htm?guid={897B68E1-9DCA-46FF-B38E-51C541272ABA}&type=Audio . JFK's Address at Rice University on the Nation's Space Effort, Houston, Texas, September 12, 1962.
2. Maddison, *The World Economy*, 256–262.
3. Wells, *Recent Economic Changes*, preface.
4. http://en.wikipedia.org/wiki/Gilded_age#cite_note-10
5. Matsen, *Titanic's Last Secrets*, 78.

6. Lansberg, *Succeeding Generations.*

7. Bork, *Family Business, Risky Business*; Lea, *Keeping It in the Family.*

8. Nelton, "Father and Sons."

9. Handler, "The Succession Experience."

10. Davis and Harveston, "In the Founder's Shadow."

11. Venter et al., "The Influence of Successor-Related Factors."

12. Merideth, *Facts About Titanic*, 111; Hall and Beveridge, Olympic & Titanic, 5.

13. Butler, *"Unsinkable,"* 18.

14. Dollars in 1912 were converted to dollars in 2010 using Robert Sahr's method (Sahr, 2010; http://oregonstate.edu/cla/polisci/faculty-research/sahr/sahr.htm).

CHAPTER 2

1. www.captainedwardjohnsmith.co.uk

2. http://www.encyclopedia-titanica.org/titanic-biography/edward-john-smith.html; http://www.mytitanic.co.uk/people/ejsmith.php

3. http://www.titanicinquiry.org/images/charts/Chart1.gif

4. Lightoller, *Titanic and Other Ships*, 100.

5. British Board of Trade Inquiry, 73.

6. Ibid.

7. Ibid., 355.

PART II

1. Butler, *"Unsinkable,"* 180–186.

2. Beesley, *The Loss of the S.S* Titanic, 48.

3. Survey data refers to the American Family Business Surveys (AFBS) and Connecticut Family Business Surveys (CFBS) which are described in the Appendix.

CHAPTER 3

1. www.wordnetweb.princeton.edu/perl/webwn

2. Bandura, *Self-Efficacy.*

3. Merideth, *1912 Facts About Titanic*, 49.

4. Ibid.

5. Lightoller, *Titanic and Other Ships*, 97.

6. Cooper, *E.J.*, 138.

7. http://www.encyclopedia-titanica.org/disaster-at-last-befalls-capt-smith.html

8. Merideth, *1912 Facts About Titanic*, 6, 50.

9. http://www.titanicuniverse.com/titanic-the-unsinkable-ship/1443

10. Butler, *"Unsinkable,"* 11.

11. British Board of Trade Inquiry, 452.

12. Ibid., 440–41.

13. "London Press Critical," *New York Times,* July 31, 1912; http://query
.nytimes.com/gst/abstract.html?res=FA0B17FA395813738DDDA80B94DF405B
828DF1D3.

14. British Board of Trade Inquiry, 450.

15. Lightoller, *Titanic and Other Ships,* 97.

16. Ibid.

17. Merideth, *1912 Facts About Titanic,* 119.

18. Butler, *"Unsinkable,"* 39; Lord, *A Night to Remember,* 73; Merideth, *1912
Facts About Titanic,* 119.

19. Butler, *"Unsinkable,"* 168; Lord, *A Night to Remember,* 177.

20. Beesley, *The Loss of the S.S.* Titanic, 47–48.

21. Lord, *A Night to Remember,* 73.

22. 2007 AFBS, 6.

23. 2008 CFBS.

24. U.S. Bureau of Labor Statistics, "Business Employment Dynamics," 17.

25. Smith, "Red Flags," 85.

26. Lovallo and Kahneman, "Delusions of Success," 58.

27. Barnard, "Narcissism," 422–23.

28. Lovallo and Kahneman, "Delusions of Success," 58.

29. 2007 AFBS.

30. 2009 CFBS.

31. Ibid.

32. http://www.businessweek.com/smallbiz/content/apr2007/
sb20070416_589621.htm

33. 2009 CFBS.

34. Ibid.

35. 2007 CFBS.

36. American Psychiatric Association, *Diagnostic and Statistical Manual,* 661.

37. Maccoby, "Narcissistic Leaders," 4–5.

38. Kets de Vries, *Reflections on Leadership,* 18–19.

39. Chatterjee and Hambrick, "It's All About Me."

40. Maccoby, "Narcissistic Leaders," 6.

41. Gordon and Nicholson, *Family Wars,* 96–104.

42. 2002 AFBS.

43. Lubit, "The Long-Term Organizational Impact of Destructively Narcissistic Managers," 134–35.

44. Downs, *Beyond the Looking Glass.*

45. Schwartz, *Narcissistic Process.*

46. Rappaport, "Co-narcissism," 3–4.

47. Lansberg, "Narcissism," 2.

48. Haynes et al., "The Intermingling of Business and Family Finances."

49. 2007 AFBS.

50. Hubler, "Ten Most Prevalent Obstacles," 118–19; Jaffe and Brown,
"Entitlement to Stewardship," 1–3.

CHAPTER 4

1. http://captainedwardjohnsmith.co.uk/2679.html
2. British Board of Trade Inquiry, 15778–87.
3. Butler, *"Unsinkable,"* 248.
4. http://www.titanicscience.com/TSci-ActivityGuideFinal.pdf
5. Butler, *"Unsinkable,"* 250.
6. Cooper, *E. J.*, 290.
7. Butler, *"Unsinkable,"* 91.
8. Merideth, *1912 Facts About Titanic.*
9. British Board of Trade Inquiry; Meredith, *Facts About Titanic.*
10. Vallejo, "Is the Culture of Family Firms Really Different?"
11. Denison et al., "Culture in Family-Owned Enterprises."
12. Bluedorn and Lundgren, "Culture-Match Perspective."
13. Aronoff and Baskin, *Effective Leadership*, 24.
14. Jehn, "A Qualitative Analysis of Conflict Types and Dimensions."
15. Tagiuri and Davis, "Bivalent Attributes."
16. Kaye, *The Dynamics of Family Business*, 103–104.
17. Cosier and Harvey, "The Hidden Strengths in Family Business"; Kellermanns and Eddelston, "Feuding Families."
18. 2007 AFBS; 2008 CFBS; 2009 CFBS.
19. 2008 CFBS; 2009 CFBS.
20. 2002 AFBS; 2008 CFBS.
21. http://en.wikipedia.org/wiki/John_Rigas; http://query.nytimes.com/gst/fullpage.html?res=9402E3DC163EF93BA15755C0A9619C8B63&ref=johnjrigas
22. Chrisman et al., "Important Attributes of Successors."
23. Sharma and Rao, "Successor Attributes in Indian and Canadian Family Firms."
24. Chrisman et al., "Important Attributes of Successors"; Sharma and Rao, "Successor Attributes in Indian and Canadian Family Firms."
25. Vallejo, "Is the Culture of Family Firms Really Different?," 271.
26. Chrisman et al., "Important Attributes of Successors."
27. Goldberg, "Research Note."
28. Chrisman et al., "Important Attributes of Successors."
29. DeMassis et al., "Factors Preventing Intra-family Succession"; Handler and Kram, "Succession in Family Firms."
30. Cater and Justis, "The Development of Successors"; Churchill and Hatten, "Transfers of Wealth"; Handler, "Succession in Family Firms."
31. Aronoff and Ward, *Another Kind of Hero*, 15.
32. Goldberg, "Research Note"; Venter et al., "The Influence of Successor-Related Factors."
33. 2007 AFBS.
34. Sonnenfeld, *The Hero's Farewell.*
35. Sonnenfeld and Spence, "The Parting Patriarch."
36. Cadieux, "Succession in Small and Medium-Sized Businesses."
37. Ibid.
38. Aronoff, *Letting Go*, 2.

39. Lansberg, *Succeeding Generations*, 236–37.

40. Blumentritt et al., "Creating an Environment for Successful Nonfamily CEOs," 321.

41. Ibid.

42. Poza, *Family Business*, 138.

43. Gersick et al., *Generation to Generation*, 237–38.

44. Moore and Juenemann, "Good Governance," 66.

45. Salovey and Mayer, "Emotional Intelligence."

46. Goleman, *Working with Emotional Intelligence*.

47. Petrides and Furnham, "On the Dimensional Structure of Emotional Intelligence."

48. Burns, *Leadership*.

49. Bass, *Leadership and Performance*.

50. Vallejo, "Analytical Model of Leadership."

51. Ibid.

52. Sorenson, "The Contribution of Leadership Style and Practices."

53. Ibid.

54. Gardner and Stough, "Examining the Relationship Between Leadership and Emotional Intelligence"; Rosete and Ciarrochi, "Emotional Intelligence."

CHAPTER 5

1. Encarta Dictionary: http://encarta.msn.com/encnet/features/dictionary/dictionaryhome.aspx

2. Schwenk and Shrade, "Effects of Formal Strategic Planning."

3. U.S. Inquiry, Affidavit of Catherine E. Crosby, http://www.titanicinquiry.org/USInq/AmInq18Crosby01.php

4. U.S. Inquiry, Affidavit of Imanita Shelley, http://www.titanicinquiry.org/USInq/AmInq18Shelley01.php

5. Lord, *A Night to Remember*, 54.

6. Meredith, *Facts About Titanic*, 145.

7. Lord, *A Night to Remember*, 75–76.

8. Butler, "*Unsinkable*," 58.

9. Lord, *A Night to Remember*, 90.

10. U.S. Inquiry, Affidavit of Emily Ryerson, http://www.titanicinquiry.org/USInq/AmInq16Ryerson01.php

11. U.S. Inquiry, Testimony of Mrs. J. S. White, http://www.titanicinquiry.org/USInq/AmInq12White01.php

12. Rue and Ibrahim, "The Status of Planning"; Upton et al., "Strategic and Business Planning Practices."

13. http://www.sba.gov/category/navigation-structure/starting-managing-business/starting-business/writing-business-plan

14. http://www.family-business-experts.com/business_plan_template.html

15. http://www.entrepreneur.com/encyclopedia/term/82470.html

16. Eddelson et al., "Resource Configuration."

17. Mazzola at al., "Strategic Planning."

18. Ward, "The Special Role of Strategic Planning."

19. abanet.org
20. File and Prince, "Attributions for Family Business Failure."
21. Poza, *Family Business*, 96–97.
22. 2002 AFBS.
23. 2007 AFBS.
24. 2009 CFBS.
25. Yogev, *For Better or for Worse*.
26. Sonfield and Lussier, "A Comparison."
27. Blumentritt, "The Relationship Between Boards and Planning."
28. Sharma et al., "Succession Planning as Planned Behavior."
29. Lansberg, "The Succession Conspiracy."
30. Ibid.
31. Handler and Kram, "Succession in Family Firms."
32. Jarvis and Mandell, *Wealth Protection*.
33. Collier, *Wealth in Families*; Hughes, *Family Wealth*; Jaffe, "Six Dimensions of Wealth."
34. http://www.ready.gov/business/
35. Dorfman, *Introduction to Risk Management and Insurance*.
36. Ferguson, "Challenges and Changes."

CHAPTER 6

1. McCarty and Foecke, *What Really Sank the* Titanic, 25–26.
2. Ibid., 29–30.
3. Ibid., 41.
4. Thearle, "The Modern Practice of Shipbuilding."
5. McCarty and Foecke, *What Really Sank the* Titanic, 147–148.
6. Ibid., 5.
7. Barczewski, Titanic: *A Night Remembered*.
8. http://www.bbc.co.uk/history/british/britain_wwone/titanic_01.shtml#two
9. Ballard and Archbold, *Lost Liners*.
10. McCarthy and Foecke, *What Really Sank the* Titanic, 17.
11. *Lloyd's Register*, Infosheet No.18; www.lr.org/Images/18% 20Titanic_tcm155-173529.pdf
12. http://www.businessweek.com/1998/23/b3581001.htm
13. aicpa.org
14. 2007 AFBS.
15. 2009 CFBS.
16. 2007 AFBS.
17. 2002 AFBS.
18. Ibid.
19. Aronoff et al., *Developing Family Business Policies*.
20. 2007 AFBS.
21. 2002 AFBS.
22. 2007 AFBS.
23. 2002 AFBS.

24. 2009 CFBS.

25. 2007 AFBS.

26. 2009 CFBS.

27. 2002 AFBS.

28. Ibid.

29. Ibid.

30. 2009 CFBS.

31. 2007, 2008, 2009 CFBS.

32. Handler, "The Succession Experience," 302.

33. 2010 CFBS.

CHAPTER 7

1. Katzenbach and Smith, *The Wisdom of Teams*, 61–64.

2. Ibid.

3. Lightoller, Titanic *and Other Ships*, 98.

4. http://www.telegraph.co.uk/news/main.jhtml?xml=/news/2007/08/29/ntitanic129.xml

5. U.S. Inquiry, 324.

6. Lightoller, Titanic *and Other Ships*, 100.

7. http://www.keyflux.com/titanic/facts.htm

8. Lightoller, Titanic *and Other Ships*, 100.

9. U.S. Inquiry, 607.

10. Ballard and Archbold, *Robert Ballard's* Titanic, 24.

11. Gersick et al., *Generation to Generation*.

12. 2010 CFBS.

13. 2008 CFBS.

14. 2009 CFBS.

15. Ibid.

16. Galbraith, "Divorce and the Financial Performance of Small Family Business."

17. Cole and Johnson, "An Exploration of Successful Copreneurial Relationships."

18. Friedman, "Sibling Relationships."

19. Aronoff et al., *Making Sibling Teams Work*.

20. 2010 CFBS.

21. 2009 CFBS.

22. 2002 AFBS.

23. Vilaseca, "The Shareholder Role."

24. Thomas, "Attitudes and Expectations."

25. 2002 AFBS.

26. 2009 CFBS.

27. 1997 AFBS.

28. 2002 AFBS.

29. 2009 CFBS.

30. Ibid.

31. 2010 CFBS.
32. Ibid.
33. Ibid.
34. Ibid.
35. Zemke et al., *Generations at Work*.
36. Ibid.
37. 2008 CFBS.
38. 2009 CFBS.
39. 2007 AFBS.
40. 2002 AFBS.
41. 1997 AFBS.
42. 2008 CFBS.
43. 2009 CFBS.
44. Rousseau et al., "Not So Different After All," 395.
45. Sundaramurthy, "Sustaining Trust."
46. Van der Hayden et al., "Fair Process."
47. Ibid., 21.

CHAPTER 8

1. Hambrick and D'Aveni, "Top Team Deterioration."
2. Mintzberg, *The Nature of Managerial Work*.
3. Ancona and Nadler, "Top Hats and Executive Tales."
4. Andrews, *The Concept of Corporate Strategy*; Miles and Snow, *Organizational Strategy*.
5. Eddelson et al., "Resource Configuration," 45.
6. Tagiuri and Davis, "Bivalent Attributes."
7. Covey, *The Seven Habits;* Covey at al., *First Things First*.
8. Horan, *The One Page Business Plan*.
9. Pearce and David, "Corporate Mission Statements."
10. Andrews, *The Concept of Corporate Strategy*.
11. Harris et al., "Is Strategy Different."
12. Leidecker and Bruno, "Identifying and Using Critical Success Factors."
13. Harris et al., "Is Strategy Different."
14. Ward, "The Special Role of Strategic Planning."
15. Carlock and Ward, *Strategic Planning*.
16. Casillas et al., "A Configurational Approach."
17. Cruz and Nordqvist, "Entrepreneurial Orientation."
18. Hoy, "The Complicating Factor of Life Cycles."
19. Molly et al., "Family Business Succession."
20. Cromie et al., "The Management of Family Firms"; Dunn, "Success Themes"; Kaye and Hamilton, "Roles of Trust"; Reid et al., "Family Orientation."
21. Molly et al., "Family Business Succession."
22. Naldi et al., "Entrepreneurial Orientation"; Zahra, "Entrepreneurial Risk Taking."

23. Salvato, "Predictors of Entrepreneurship."
24. Casillas et al., "A Configurational Approach."
25. Salvato, "Predictors of Entrepreneurship."
26. Poza, "Managerial Practices."
27. Ibid.
28. Ibid.
29. 2002 AFBS.
30. 2009 CFBS.
31. Habbershon, "Improving the Long-Run Survival."
32. Ibid.
33. Ibid.
34. 2009 CFBS.
35. Tagiuri and Davis, "Bivalent Attributes."
36. Cosier and Harvey, "The Hidden Strengths."
37. Hubler, "Ten Most Prevalent Obstacles."
38. Kaye, *Workplace Wars*.
39. Ward, *Perpetuating the Family Business*.
40. Gersick et al., "Stages and Transitions."
41. Mento et al., "A Change Management Process."
42. Reichers et al., "Understanding and Managing Cynicism."
43. Furnham, "Managers as Change Agents."

CHAPTER 9

1. Merideth, *1912 Facts About Titanic*, 215.
2. http://www.titanichistoricalsociety.org/articles/ice-patrol.asp
3. Butler, "*Unsinkable*," 233; http://en.wikipedia.org/wiki/J._Bruce_Ismay
4. Cooper, *E. J.*, 384.
5. http://en.wikipedia.org/wiki/Arthur_Henry_Rostron, http://www.encyclopedia-titanica.org/titanic-biography/arthur-henry-rostron.html
6. Merideth, *1912 Facts About Titanic*, 159.
7. *New York Times*, "Women Revealed as Heroines," April 20, 1912; http://www.encyclopedia-titanica.org/women-revealed-as-heroines-wreck-3.html
8. http://safetyreliability.com/index.html
9. Sullenberger and Zaslow, *Highest Duty*, 235–36.
10. Ibid., 210–11.
11. Ibid., 237.
12. http://www.youtube.com/watch?v=nThQpsCo0_0&NR=1
13. Handler, "Succession in Family Firms"; Lansberg, "The Succession Conspiracy."
14. Morris et al., "Correlates of Success"; Sharma et al., "Succession Planning as Planned Behavior."
15. Morris et al., "Correlates of Success"; Venter et al., "The Influence of Successor-Related Factors."
16. Dyer, *Cultural Change in Family Firms*.

17. File and Prince, "Attributions for Family Business Failure;" Ward, *Keeping the Family Business Healthy*.

18. DeMassis et al., "Factors Preventing Intra-family Succession;" Getz and Petersen, "Identifying Industry-Specific Barriers."

19. Ibid.

20. Miller et al., "Lost in Time."

21. Williams and Preisser, *Preparing Heirs*, 49.

22. O'Neill, *The Golden Ghetto*, 37.

23. O'Neill, *The Golden Ghetto*; Williams and Preisser, *Preparing Heirs*.

24. Aronoff and Ward, *Family Business Values*, 1.

25. Campbell, "Money Can't Buy Legacy," 36.

26. Pearl, "Giving Back," 69.

27. Craig and Dibrell, "The Natural Environment."

28. Huang et al., "Salient Stakeholder Voices."

29. http://foundationcenter.org/gainknowledge/research/pdf/keyfacts_fam_2010.pdf

30. Kristie, "America's Oldest Family Businesses," 53–62.

31. USDA, "Structure and Finances of U.S. Farms."

32. Ibid.

33. http://www2.indystar.com/articles/9/187163-5679-157.html

34. Aronoff and Ward, *Make Change Your Family Business Tradition*, 15.

Bibliography

Transcripts from both the U.S. and British Board of Trade inquiries can be found online at http://www.titanicinquiry.org. Information about the American Family Business Surveys (AFBS) and the Connecticut Family Business Surveys (CFBS) is found in the Appendix.

BOOKS

American Psychiatric Association. *Diagnostic and Statistical Manual for Mental Disorders* (4th ed.). Washington, DC: American Psychiatric Association; 2000.

Andrews, Kenneth. *The Concept of Corporate Strategy* (3rd ed.). Homewood, IL: Dow Jones-Irwin' 1987.

Aronoff, Craig. *Letting Go: Preparing Yourself to Relinquish Control of the Family Business*. Marietta, GA: Family Enterprise Publishers; 2003.

Aronoff, Craig, Joseph H. Astrachan, Drew S. Mendoza, and John L. Ward. *Making Sibling Teams Work: The Next Generation*. Marietta, GA: Family Enterprise Publishers; 1997.

Aronoff, Craig, Joseph H. Astrachan, and John L. Ward. *Developing Family Business Policies: Your Guide to the Future*. Marietta, GA: Family Enterprise Publishers; 1997.

Aronoff, Craig, and Otis W. Baskin. *Effective Leadership in the Family Business*. Marietta, GA: Family Enterprise Publishers; 2001.

Aronoff, Craig, and John L. Ward. *Another Kind of Hero: Preparing Successors for Leadership*. Marietta, GA: Family Enterprise Publishers; 1992.

Aronoff, Craig, and John L. Ward. *Family Business Values: How to Assure a Legacy of Continuity and Success*. Marietta, GA: Family Enterprise Publishers; 2001.

Aronoff, Craig, and John L. Ward. *Make Change Your Family Business Tradition*. Marietta, GA: Family Enterprise Publishers; 2001.

Ballard, Robert, and Rick Archbold. *Lost Liners: From the* Titanic *to the* Andrea Doria *The Ocean Floor Reveals Its Greatest Ships.* Alexandria, VA: PBS Online; 2000.

Ballard, Robert, and Rick Archbold. *Robert Ballard's* Titanic. New York: Barnes & Noble; 2007.

Bandura, Albert. *Self-Efficacy: The Exercise of Control.* New York: W. H. Freeman; 1997.

Barczewski, Stephanie. Titanic: A Night Remembered. London: Hambledon Continuum; 2006.

Bass, Bernard M. *Leadership and Performance.* New York: Free Press; 1985.

Beesley, Lawrence. *The Loss of the S.S.* Titanic: *Its Story and Its Lessons.* Boston: Houghton Mifflin Company; 1912.

Bork, David. *Family Business, Risky Business* (2nd ed.). Aspen, CO: Bork Institute for Family Business; 1993.

Burns, James M. *Leadership.* New York: Harper and Row; 1978.

Butler, Daniel A. *"Unsinkable": The Full Story of the RMS* Titanic. Mechanicsburg, PA: Stackpole Books; 1998.

Carlock, Randel S., & John L. Ward. *Strategic Planning for the Family Business: Parallel Planning to Unify the Family and Business.* New York: Palgrave; 2001.

Collier, Charles. *Wealth in Families.* Cambridge, MA: Harvard University Press; 2003.

Cooper, Gary. *E. J.: The Story of Edward John Smith, Captain of the* Titanic. 2009. www.lulu.com

Covey, Stephen. *The Seven Habits of Highly Effective People.* New York: Simon & Schuster; 1994.

Covey, Stephen, A. Roger Merrill, and Rebecca R. Merrill. *First Things First.* New York: Simon & Schuster; 1990.

Dorfman, Mark S. *Introduction to Risk Management and Insurance* (9th ed.). Englewood Cliffs, NJ: Prentice Hall; 2007.

Downs, Alan. *Beyond the Looking Glass: Overcoming the Seductive Culture of Corporate Narcissism.* New York: AMACOM; 1997.

Dyer, Wayne G. *Cultural Change in Family Firms: Anticipating and Managing Family Business Transitions.* San Francisco: Jossey-Bass; 1986.

Gersick, Kelin, John A. Davis, Marion McCollom, and Ivan Lansberg. *Generation to Generation: Life Cycles of the Family Business.* Boston: Harvard Business School Press; 1997.

Goleman, Daniel. *Working with Emotional Intelligence.* New York: Bantam; 1998.

Gordon, Grant, and Nigel Nicholson. *Family Wars: Stories and Insights from Famous Family Business Feuds.* London: Kogan Page; 2008.

Hall, Steve, and Bruce Beveridge. Olympic *and* Titanic: *The Truth Behind the Conspiracy.* Haverford, PA: Infinity Publishing; 2004.

Horan, Jim. *The One Page Business Plan.* Berkeley, CA: The One Page Business Plan Company; 1997.

Hughes, James E. *Family Wealth: Keeping It in the Family.* New York: Bloomberg Press; 2004.

Jarvis, Christopher R., and David B. Mandell. *Wealth Protection: Build and Preserve You Financial Fortress.* Hoboken, NJ: John Wiley & Sons; 2003.

Katzenbach, Jon R., and Douglas K. Smith. *The Wisdom of Teams: Creating the High-Performance Organization.* New York: Harper; 1994.

Kaye, Kenneth. *The Dynamics of Family Business.* New York: iUniverse; 2005.

Kaye, Kenneth. *Workplace Wars and How to End Them: Turning Personal Conflicts into Constructive Teamwork.* New York: AMACOM; 1994.

Kets de Vries, Manfred. *Reflections on Leadership and Career Development.* San Francisco: Jossey-Bass; 2010.

Lansberg, Ivan. *Succeeding Generations: Realizing the Dream of Families in Business.* Boston: Harvard Business School Press; 1999.

Lea, James. *Keeping It in the Family: Successful Succession in the Family Business.* New York: Wiley; 1991.

Lightoller, Charles H. Titanic *and Other Ships.* London: Ivor, Nicholson and Watson; 1935.

Lord, Walter. *A Night to Remember.* New York: Holt, Rinehart, and Winston; 1976.

Maddison, Angus. *The World Economy: Historical Statistics.* Paris: Development Centre, OECD; 2003.

Markopolos, Harry. *No One Would Listen.* Hoboken, NJ: John Wiley & Sons; 2010.

Marshall, Logan. *On Board the* Titanic: *The Complete Story with Eyewitness Accounts.* New York: Dover Publications; 2006.

Matsen, Brad. Titanic*'s Last Secrets.* New York: Twelve; 2008.

McCarty, Jennifer Hooper, and Tim Foecke. *What Really Sank the* Titanic: *New Forensic Discoveries.* New York: Citadel Press; 2008.

Merideth, Lee W. *1912 Facts About* Titanic (2nd ed.). Sunnyvale, CA: Rocklin Press; 2003.

Miles, Raymond E., and Charles C. Snow. *Organizational Strategy, Structure, and Process.* New York: McGraw-Hill; 1978.

Mintzberg, H. *The Nature of Managerial Work.* New York: Harper & Row; 1973.

Montemerlo, Daniela, and John L. Ward. *The Family Constitution: Agreements to Secure and Perpetuate Your Family and Your Business.* Marietta, GA: Family Enterprise Publishers; 2005.

O'Neill, Jessie H. *The Golden Ghetto: The Psychology of Affluence.* Center City, MN: Hazelden; 1997.

Poza, Ernesto J. *Family Business.* Mason, OH: Thomson Southwestern; 2004

Schwartz, Howard S. *Narcissistic Process and Corporate Decay: The Theory of the Organizational Ideal.* New York: New York University Press, 1990.

Sonnenfeld, Jeffrey. *The Hero's Farewell: What Happens When Chief Executives Retire.* New York: Oxford University Press; 1988.

Sullenberger, Chesley, and Jefferey Zaslow. *Highest Duty.* New York: HarperCollins; 2009.

Thearle, S. J. P. *The Modern Practice of Shipbuilding in Iron and Steel.* London: W. Collins; 1891.Ward, John L. *Keeping the Family Business Healthy.* San Francisco: Jossey-Bass; 1987.

Ward, John L. *Perpetuating the Family Business: Fifty Lessons Learned from Long Lasting, Successful Family Businesses.* New York: Palgrave MacMillan; 2004.

Wells, David A. *Recent Economic Changes and Their Effect on Production and Distribution of Wealth and Well-Being of Society.* New York: D. Appleton and Company; 1890.

Williams, Roy, and Vic Preisser. *Preparing Heirs: Five Steps to a Successful Transition of Family Wealth and Values*. San Francisco: Robert D. Reed Publishers; 2003.

Yogey, Sarah. *For Better or for Worse ... But Not for Lunch: Making Marriage Work in Retirement*. New York: McGraw-Hill; 2001.

Zemke, Ron, Clair Raines, and Bob Filipczak. *Generations at Work*. New York: AMACOM; 2000.

JOURNALS, PERIODICALS, AND REPORTS

Ancona, Debora G. and David A. Nadler. "Top Hats and Executive Tales: Designing the Senior Team." *Sloan Management Review*, Fall (1989): 19–29.

Barnard, Jayne W. "Narcissism, Over-Optimism, Fear, Anger, and Depression: The Interior Lives of Corporate Leaders." *University of Cincinnati Law Review* 77 (2008): 405–30.

Beckhard, Richard, and W. Gibb Dyer. "Managing Continuity in the Family–Owned Business." *Organizational Dynamics* 12 (1983): 5–12.

Bluedorn, Allen, and Earl Lundgren. "A Culture-Match Perspective for Strategic Change." *Research in Organizational Change and Development* 7 (1993): 137–79.

Bluedorn, A., and E. Lundgren. "A Culture-Match Perspective for Strategic Change: Research Framework for Family Businesses." *American Journal of Small Business* 11 (1987): 51–64.

Blumentritt, Timothy. "The Relationship Between Boards and Planning in Family Businesses." *Family Business Review* 19 (2006): 65–72.

Blumentritt, Timothy P., Andrew D. Keyt, and Joseph H. Astrachan, "Creating an Environment for Successful Nonfamily CEOs: An Exploratory Study of Good Principals." *Family Business Review* 20 (2004): 321–35.

Cadieux, Louise. "Succession in Small and Medium-Sized Businesses: Toward a Typology of Predecessor Roles During and After Instatement of the Successor." *Family Business Review* 12 (1999): 311–23.

Campbell, Keith. "Money Can't Buy Legacy." *Family Business Magazine*, Summer (2005): 36–38.

Casillas, Jose C., Ana M. Moreno, and Jose L. Barbero. "A Configurational Approach of the Relationship Between Entrepreneurial Orientation and Growth of Family Firms." *Family Business Review* 23 (2010): 27–44.

Cater, John James III, and Robert T. Justis. "The Development of Successors from Followers to Leaders in Small Family Firms: An Exploratory Study." *Family Business Review* 22 (2009): 109–24.

Chatterjee, Arijit, and Donald C. Hambrick. "It's All About Me: Narcissistic CEOs and Their Effects on Company Strategy and Performance." *Administrative Sciences Quarterly* 52 (2007): 351–86.

Chrisman, James J., Jess H. Chua, and Pramodita Sharma. "Important Attributes of Successors in Family Businesses: An Exploratory Study." *Family Business Review* 11 (1998): 19–34.

Churchill, Neil C., and Kenneth J. Hatten. "Non-market-Based Transfers of Wealth and Power: A Research Framework for Family Business." *Family Business Review* 10 (1997): 53–67.

Cole, Patricia, and Kit Johnson. "An Exploration of Successful Copreneurial Relationships Postdivorce." *Family Business Review* 20 (2007): 185–98.

Cosier, Richard A., and Michael Harvey. "The Hidden Strengths in Family Business: Functional Conflict." *Family Business Review* 11 (1998): 75–79.

Craig, Justin, and Clay Dibrell. "The Natural Environment, Innovation, and Firm Performance: A Comparative Study." *Family Business Review* 19 (2006): 275–88.

Creswell, Julie, and Landon Thomas Jr. "The Talented Mr. Madoff." *The New York Times*, January 25, 2009. http://www.nytimes.com/2009/01/25/business/25bernie.html

Cromie, Stanley, Ben Stephenson, and David Monteith. "The Management of Family Firms: An Empirical Investigation." *International Small Business Journal* 13 (1995): 11–34.

Cruz, Cristina, and Mattias Nordqvist. "Entrepreneurial Orientation in Family Business: A Generational Perspective." Paper presented at the 8th annual International Family Enterprise Research Academy conference, Nyenroede, the Netherlands.

Davis, Peter S., and Paula D. Harveston. "In the Founder's Shadow: Conflict in the Family Firm." *Family Business Review* 12 (1999): 311–23.

DeMassis, Alfredo, Jess H. Chua, and James J. Chrisman. "Factors Preventing Intra-family Succession." *Family Business Review* 21 (2008): 183–93.

Denison, Daniel L., Colleen Lief, and John L. Ward. "Culture in Family-Owned Enterprises: Recognizing and Leveraging Unique Strengths." *Family Business Review* 17 (2004): 61–70.

Dunn, Barbara. "Success Themes in Scottish Family Enterprises: Philosophies and Practices Through the Generations." *Family Business Review* 8 (1995): 17–28.

Eddelson, Kimberly A., Franz Willi Kellermanns, and Ravi Sarathy. "Resource Configuration in Family Firms: Linking Resources, Strategic Planning, and Technological Opportunities to Performance." *Journal of Management Studies* 45 (2008): 26–50.

Ferguson, Brian. "Challenges and Changes: Guidance for Boards on the Oversight of Risk." *Director Journal*, 148 (2010): 6–8.

File, Karen M., and Russ A. Prince. "Attributions for Family Business Failure: The Heir's Perspective." *Family Business Review* 9 (1996): 171–84.

Friedman, Stewart D. "Sibling Relationships and Intergenerational Succession in Family Firms." *Family Business Review* 4 (1991): 3–19.

Furnham, Adrian. "Managers as Change Agents." *Journal of Change Management* 3 (2002): 21–19.

Galbraith, Craig G. "Divorce and the Financial Performance of Small Family Business: An Exploratory Study." *Journal of Small Business Management* 41 (2003): 296–306.

Gandel, Stephen. "Wall Street's Latest Downfall: Madoff Charged with Fraud." *Time*, December 12, 2008. http://www.time.com/time/business/article/0,8599,1866154,00.html

Gardner, Lisa, and Con Stough. "Examining the Relationship Between Leadership and Emotional Intelligence in Senior Level Managers." *Leadership & Organizational Development Journal* 23 (2002): 68–78.

Gersick, Kelin, Ivan Lansberg, Michele Desjardins, and Barbara Dunn. "Stages and Transitions: Managing Change in the Family Business." *Family Business Review* 12 (1999): 287–98.

Getz, Donald, and Tage Petersen. "Identifying Industry-Specific Barriers to Inheritance in Small Family Businesses." *Family Business Review* 17 (2004): 259–76.

Gilson, Lucy L. "Why Be Creative: A Review of the Practical Outcomes Associated with Creativity at the Individual, Group, and Organizational Levels," in *Handbook of Organizational Creativity*, edited by C. Shalley and J. Zhou. New York: Lawrence Erlbaum Associates; 2007: 303–22.

Gilson, Lucy L., John E. Mathieu, Christina E. Shalley, and T. M. Ruddy. "Creativity Standardization: Complementary or Conflicting Drivers of Team Effectiveness." *Academy of Management Journal*, 48 (2005): 521–31.

Goldberg, S. "Research Note: Effective Successors in Family-Owned Businesses: Significant Elements." *Family Business Review* 9 (1996): 185–97.

Habbershon, Timothy. "Improving the Long-Run Survival of Family Firms: LEADS Research Project." 2000. http://www3.babson.edu/ESHIP/ife/upload/Improving-the-Long-Run-Survival-of-Family-Firms.pdf

Hambrick, Donald C., and Richard A. D'Aveni. "Top Team Deterioration as Part of the Downward Spiral of Large Corporate Bankruptcies." *Management Science* 38 (1992): 1445–66.

Handler, Wendy C. "The Succession Experience of the Next Generation." *Family Business Review* 5 (1992): 283–307.

Handler, Wendy C. "Succession in Family Business: A Review of the Research." *Family Business Review* 7 (1994): 133–57.

Handler, Wendy C. "Succession in Family Firms: A Mutual Role Adjustment Between Entrepreneur and Next-Generation Family Members." *Entrepreneurship Theory and Practice* 15 (1990): 37–51.

Handler, Wendy C., and Kathy E. Kram. "Succession in Family Firms: The Problem of Resistance." *Family Business Review* 1 (1988): 361–81.

Harris, Dawn, Jon I. Martinez, and John L. Ward. "Is Strategy Different for the Family Owned Business?" *Family Business Review* 7 (1994): 159–74.

Haynes, George W., Rosemary Walker, Barbara R. Rowe, and Gong-Soog Hong. "The Intermingling of Business and Family Finances in Family-Owned Businesses." *Family Business Review* 12 (1999): 225–39.

Hoy, Frank. "The Complicating Factor of Life Cycles in Corporate Venturing." *Entrepreneurship Theory and Practice* 30 (2006): 831–36.

Huang, Yi-Chun, Hung-Bin Ding, and M. Ming-Rea Kao. "Salient Stakeholder Voices: Family Business and Green Innovation Adoption." *Journal of Management & Organization* 15 (2009): 309–26.

Hubler, Thomas. "Ten Most Prevalent Obstacles to Family-Business Succession Planning." *Family Business Review* 12 (1999): 117–21.

Jaffe, Dennis. "Six Dimensions of Wealth: Leave the Fullest Value of Your Wealth to Your Heirs." *Journal of Financial Planning*, April (2003): 80–87.

Jaffe, Denis T., and Fredda Herz Brown. "From Entitlement to Stewardship: How a Prosperous Family Can Prepare the Next Generation." *The Journal of Wealth Management* Spring (2009): 1–18.

Jehn, Karen A. "A Qualitative Analysis of Conflict Types and Dimensions in Organizational Groups." *Administrative Science Quarterly* 42 (1997): 530–57.

Kaye, Kenneth, and Sara Hamilton. "Roles of Trust in Consulting to Financial Families." *Family Business Review* 17 (2004): 151–63.

Kellermanns, Kimberley A., and Franz Willi Eddleston. "Feuding Families: When Conflict Does a Family Firm Good." *Entrepreneurship Theory and Practice* 29 (2004): 209–28.

Kristie, Leah. "America's Oldest Family Businesses." *Family Business*, Summer (2008): 53–62.

Lansberg, Ivan. "Narcissism: The Hidden Cost of Success." *Family Business*, Summer (2000).

Lansberg, Ivan. "The Succession Conspiracy." *Family Business Review* 1 (1988): 119–43.

Leach, John. "Cognitive Paralysis in an Emergency: The Role of the Supervisory Attentional System." *Aviation, Space, and Environmental Medicine* 76 (2005): 134–36.

Leach, John. "Why People 'Freeze' in an Emergency: Temporal and Cognitive Constraints on Survival Responses." *Aviation, Space, and Environmental Medicine*, 75 (2004): 539–42.

Leach, John, and Louise Ansell. "Impaired Attentional Processing in a Field Survival Environment." *Applied Cognitive Psychology* 22 (2008): 643–52.

Leach, John, and Rebecca Griffith. "Restrictions in Working Memory Capacity During Parachuting: A Possible Cause of 'No Pull' Fatalities." *Applied Cognitive Psychology* 22 (2008): 147–57.

Leidecker, Joel K., and Albert V. Bruno. "Identifying and Using Critical Success Factors." *Long Range Planning* 17 (1984): 23–32.

Lovallo, Dan, and Daniel Kahneman. "Delusions of Success: How Optimism Undermines Executives' Decisions." *Harvard Business Review*, July (2003) 56–63.

Lubit, Roy. "The Long-Term Organizational Impact of Destructively Narcissistic Managers." *Academy of Management Executive* 16 (2002): 127–38.

Maccoby, Michael. "Narcissistic Leaders: The Incredible Pros, the Inevitable Cons." *Harvard Business Review*, January–February (2000): 1–11.

Mazzola, Pietro, Gaia Marchisio, and Joe Astrachan. "Strategic Planning in the Family Business: A Powerful Developmental Tool for the Next Generation." *Family Business Review* 21 (2008): 239–58.

Mento, Anthony, Raymond Jones, and Walter Dirndorfer. "A Change Management Process: Grounded in Both Theory and Practice." *Journal of Change Management* 3 (2002): 45–59.

Miller, Danny, Lloyd Steier, and Isabelle LeBreton-Miller. "Lost in Time: Intergenerational Succession, Change, and Failure in Family Business." *Journal in Business Venturing* 18 (2003): 513–31.

Molly, Vincent, Eddy Laveren, and Marc Deloof. "Family Business Succession and Its Impact on Financial Structure and Performance." *Family Business Review* 23 (2010): 131–47.

Moore, Jack, and Thomas Juenemann. "Good Governance Is Essential for a Family and its Business." *Family Business*, Summer (2008): 63–66.

Morris, Michael H., Roy O. Williams, Jeffrey A. Allen, and Ramon A. Avila. "Correlates of Success in Family Business Transitions." *Journal in Business Venturing* 12 (1997): 385–401.

Naldi, Lucia, Mattias Nordqvist, Karin Sjöberg, and Johan Wicklund. "Entrepreneurial Orientation, Risk Taking, and Performance in Family Firms." *Family Business Review* 20 (2007): 33–47.

Nelton, Sharon. "Fathers and Sons: No Easy Business." *Nation's Business*. 1989. http://findarticles.com/p/articles/mi_m1154/is_n2_v77/ai_7002138/.

Pearce, Julian A., and Fred David. "Corporate Mission Statements: The Bottom Line." *Academy of Management Executive* 1 (1987): 109–16.

Pearl, Jayne A. "Giving Back." *Family Business*, Summer (2007): 69–72.

Petrides, K. V., and Adrian Furnham. "On the Dimensional Structure of Emotional Intelligence." *Personality and Individual Differences* 29 (2000): 313–20.

Poza, Ernesto. "Managerial Practices That Support Interpreneurship and Continued Growth." *Family Business Review* 1 (1988): 339–59.

Rappoport Alan. "Co-narcissism: How We Accommodate to Narcissistic Parents." *The Therapist* (2005): 1–8.

Reichers, Arnon E., John P. Wanous, and James T. Austin. "Understanding and Managing Cynicism About Organizational Change." *Academy of Management Executive* 11 (1997): 48–59.

Reid, R., Barbara Dunn, Stanley Cromie, and J. Adams. "Family Orientation in Family Firms: A Model and Some Empirical Evidence." *Journal of Small Business and Enterprise Development* 6 (1999): 55–66.

Rosete, David, and Joseph Ciarrochi. "Emotional Intelligence and Its Relationship to Workplace Performance Outcomes in Leadership Effectiveness." *Leadership & Organizational Development Journal* 26 (2005): 388–99.

Rousseau, D., S. Sitkin, R. Burt, and C. Camerer. "Not So Different After All: A Cross-Discipline View of Trust." *Academy of Management Review* 23 (1998): 405–21.

Rue, Leslie W., and Nabil A. Ibrahim. "The Status of Planning in Smaller Family-Owned Business." *Family Business Review* 9 (1996): 29–43.

Salovey, Peter, and John Mayer. "Emotional Intelligence." *Imagination, Cognition, and Personality* 9 (1990): 185–211.

Salvato, Carlo. "Predictors of Entrepreneurship in Family Firms." *Journal of Private Equity* 27 (2004): 68–76.

Schwenk, Charles R., and Charles B. Shrade. "Effects of Formal Strategic Planning on Financial Performance in Small Firms: A Meta-analysis." *Entrepreneurial Theory and Practice*, Spring (1993): 53–64.

Shanker, Melissa C., and Joseph H. Astrachan. "Myths and Realities: Family Businesses' Contribution to the U.S. Economy—A Framework for Assessing Family Business Statistics." *Family Business Review*, 9 (1996): 107–23.

Sharma, Pramodita, James J. Chrisman, and Jess H. Chua. "Succession Planning as Planned Behavior: Some Empirical Results." *Family Business Review* 16 (2003): 1–16.

Sharma, Pramodita, and A. Srinivas Rao. "Successor Attributes in Indian and Canadian Family Firms: A Comparative Study." *Family Business Review* 13 (2000): 313–30.

Smith, Baker A. "Red Flags Warn of Family Business Failure." *Proceedings of the Family Firm Institute Conference*, Atlanta, GA, 1990.

Sonfield, Matthew C., and Ronald N. Lussier. "First-, Second-, and Third-Generation Family Firms: A Comparison." *Family Business Review* 17 (2004): 189–202.

Sonnenfeld, Jeffrey A., and Padraic L. Spence. "The Parting Patriarch of a Family Firm." *Family Business Review* 2 (1989): 355–75.

Sorenson, Ritch L. "The Contribution of Leadership Style and Practices to Family and Business Success." *Family Business Review* 13 (2000): 183–200.

Sundaramurthy, Chamu. "Sustaining Trust Within Family Businesses." *Family Business Review* 21 (2008): 89–102.

Tagiuri, Renato, and John A. Davis. "Bivalent Attributes of the Family Firm." *Family Business Review* 9 (1996): 199–208.

Thomas, Jill. "Attitudes and Expectations of Shareholders: The Case of the Multi-generation Family Business." *Journal of Management & Organization* 15 (2009) 346–62.

Upton, N., E. J. Teal, and J. T. Felan, "Strategic and Business Planning Practices of Fast Growing Family Firms." *Journal of Small Business Management* 39 (2001): 60–72.

U.S. Bureau of Labor Statistics. "Business Employment Dynamics." First Quarter 2010: 1–17. http://bls.gov/news.release/archives/cewbd_11182010.pdf

U.S. Department of Agriculture (USDA). "Structure and Finances of U.S. Farms: Family Farm Report." USDA Economic Research Service, July 2010. http://ers.usda.gov/publications/eib66/

Vallejo, Manuel Carlos. "Analytical Model of Leadership in Family Firms Under Transformational Theoretical Approach: An Exploratory Study." *Family Business Review* 22 (2009): 136–50.

Vallejo, Manuel Carlos. "Is the Culture of Family Firms Really Different?" *Journal of Business Ethics* 81 (2008): 261–79.

Van der Heyden, Ludo, Christine Blondel, and Randal S. Carlock. "Fair Process: Striving for Justice in Family Business." *Family Business Review* 18 (2005): 1–21.

Venter, E., C. Boshoff, and G. Maas. "The Influence of Successor-Related Factors on the Succession Process in Small and Medium-Sized Family Businesses." *Family Business Review* 18 (2005): 283–303.

Vilaseca, Alvaro. "The Shareholder Role in the Family Business: Conflict of Interests and Objectives Between Nonemployed Shareholders and Top Management Team." *Family Business Review* 15 (2002): 299–320.

Ward, John L. "The Special Role of Strategic Planning in Family Business." *Family Business Review* 1 (1988): 105–17.

Zahra, Shaker A. "Entrepreneurial Risk Taking in Family Firms." *Family Business Review* 18 (2005): 23–40.

Index

About the Authors

PRISCILLA M. CALE, MBA, is consultant, advisor, communications professional, educator, and lecturer with experience in academic and corporate environments. Her work involves advising on issues related to family business governance, strategic growth, succession, entrepreneurship, innovation, globalization, and managing communications strategies.

DAVID C. TATE, PhD, is a licensed clinical psychologist, an Assistant Clinical Professor at Yale University School of Medicine, and a Principal at Tate Consulting Group. His areas of expertise include succession planning, group facilitation, executive coaching, and promoting healthy organizational development.